Favorite Paintings from The Minneapolis Institute of Arts

Favorite Paintings from

The Minneapolis

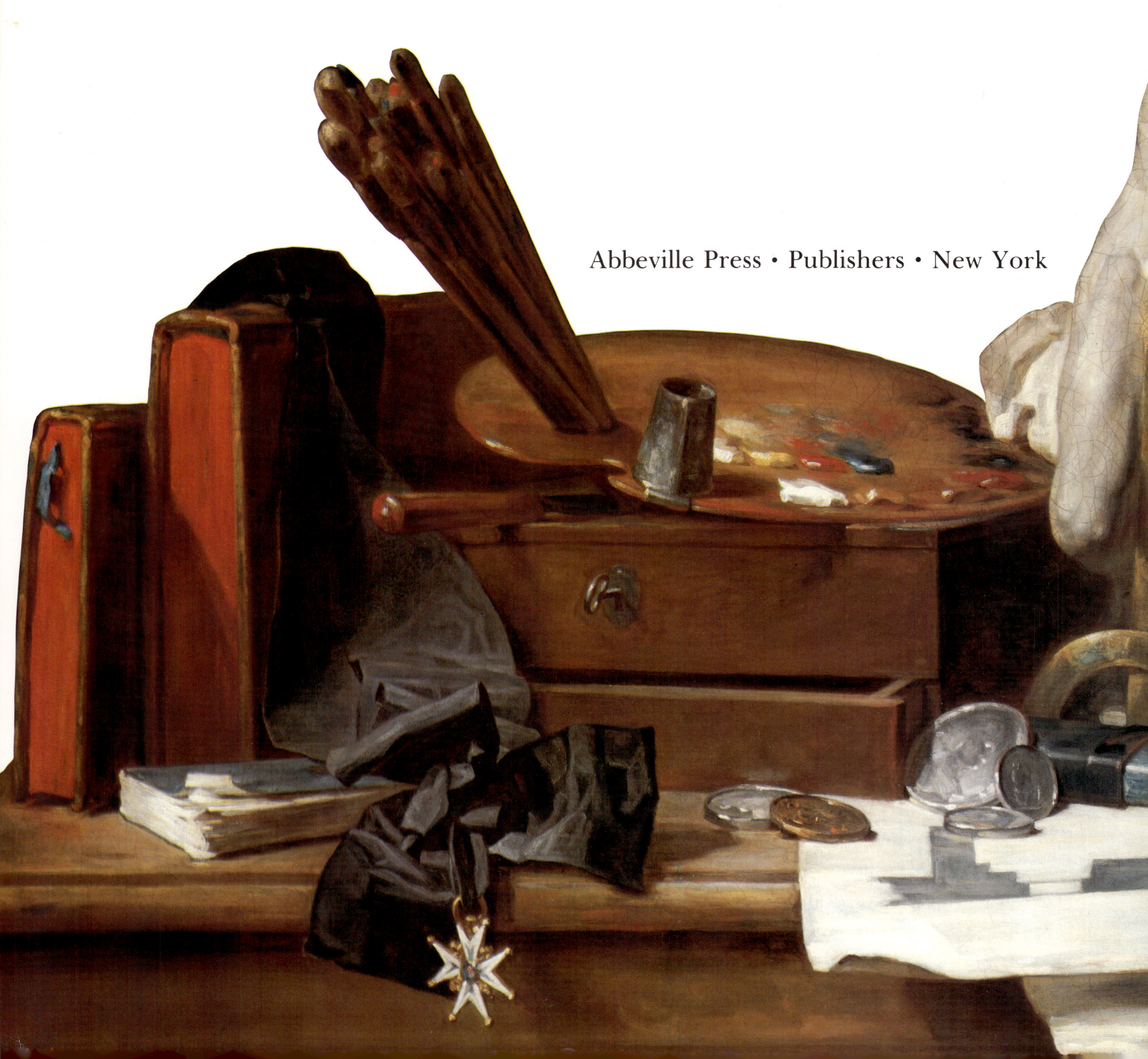

Abbeville Press • Publishers • New York

Institute of Arts

By SAMUEL SACHS II, *Director*

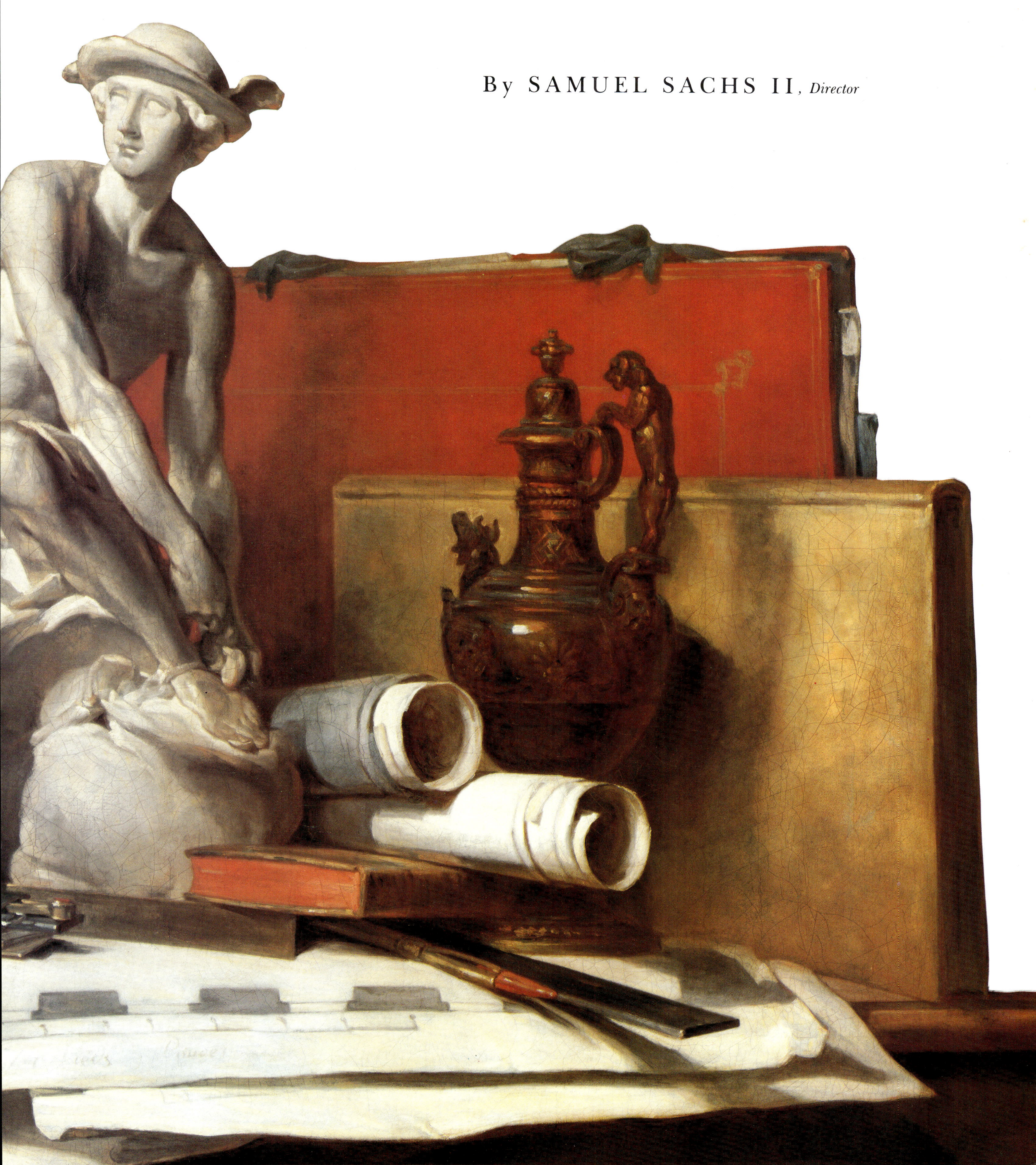

ON THE FRONT COVER

St. Paul's from the Thames (1906-07) by André Derain

ON THE TITLE PAGE

The Attributes of the Arts (detail) (1766) by Jean-Baptiste-Siméon Chardin
Full picture on page 9.

ON THE BACK COVER

The Springtime of Life (1871) by Jean-Baptiste-Camille Corot

Commentaries on these works will be found on page 104.

Library of Congress catalog card number: 80-70412

ISBN: 0-89659-224-3 (cloth)
0-89659-189-1 (paper)

Contents

Contents

Introduction

By SAMUEL SACHS II

Director, The Minneapolis Institute of Arts

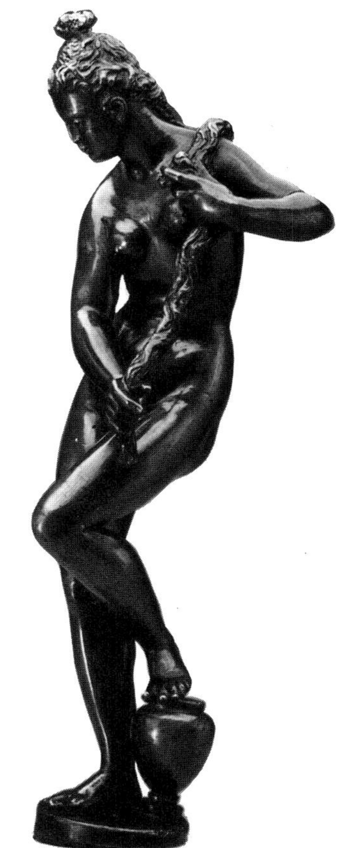

ABOVE: Giovanni Bologna (Italian, 16th c.)
La Fiorenza
Bronze with marble base, H. 14½″

BELOW: Kitagawa Utamaro (Japanese, 1754–1806)
The Waitress Okita (*c.* 1793)
Color woodcut, 14¾ x 9¾″

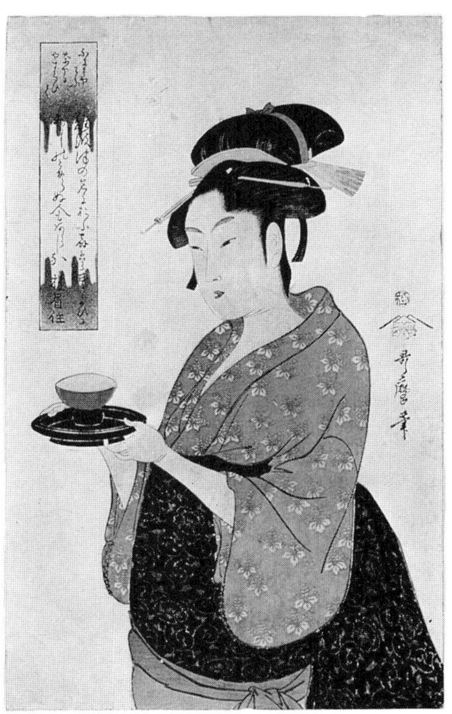

John Walker, former director of the National Gallery of Art, once stated that there are two art museums of international standing in the United States: The Metropolitan Museum of Art in New York City and the National Gallery in Washington, D.C. Then come the great regional museums in Boston, Philadelphia, Cleveland, and Chicago. "And after that," he said, "comes Minneapolis."

This is a statement that can and should, no doubt, be challenged. But a final consensus would certainly place us among the top ten museums in the United States. Since Minneapolis is only the thirty-fourth largest city in America, the disparity in rank calls for at least a passing comment. So, too, does the observation often made (and not only by our own people) that the M.I.A. is the finest museum between Chicago and Tokyo. While much of the intervening territory is occupied by ocean, and consequently too damp to sustain culture, the region in question comprises nearly half the world's surface area. The M.I.A. may be a regional museum, but its region is not an inconsiderable one.

There is no single reason for this. The success of a museum depends on a great many factors, and some, like climate and geography, are beyond human control. It has been stated that a rich cultural atmosphere is essential here so as to sustain life on the edge of the tundra. It could also be argued that historically the generous support for the Institute has been the envy of the nation because accidents of geography have made Minneapolis the home-office city for many corporations. A healthy mixture of self-interest and civic pride insists on a high quality of life here in order to attract and retain the executives the city's many businesses require. Corporate support for the Instiute has been extremely generous, and a list of donors would include many of the most respected names in American industry.

Individual support has also been strong. For over a hundred years, Minneapolis has been the home of a group of wealthy, cultured people, many of them collectors as well as patrons of art. At the turn of the century, they were described as follows: "Such extraordinary tranquility and high-mindedness seemed to flow about them. They were all so public-spirited, gentle, intellectually searching, serious, polite and noble." It is surely no mere accident of geography that so many of these old-fashioned qualities are still to be found in present generations of Minnesotans.

Community support is perhaps the main reason for the Institute's success. But curatorial policy, adhered to with varying degrees of tenacity throughout the years, has also had its effect. The paintings reproduced in this book are more than just examples of the works of master artists. In instance after

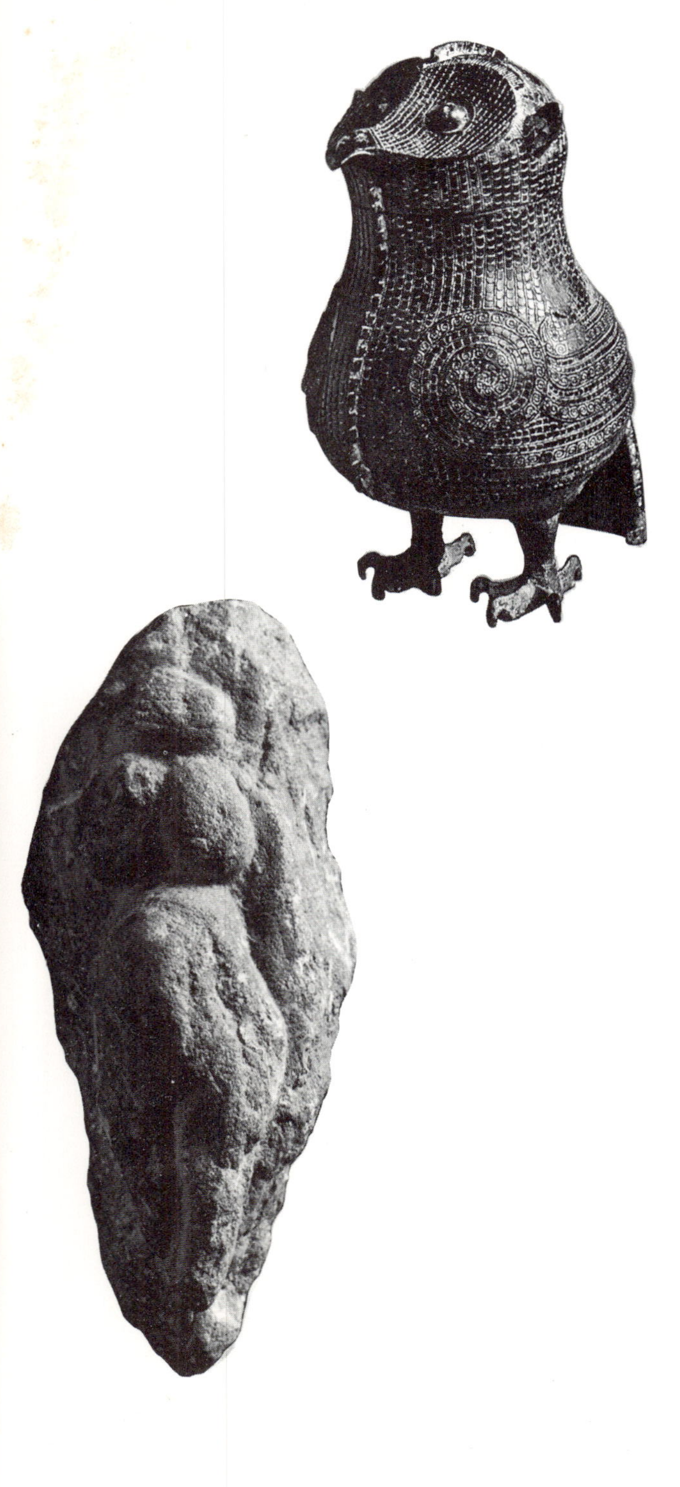

AT TOP: (China, Yin or early Chou Dynasty)
Wine vessel in the shape of an owl
Bronze, H. 12½", W. 8¼"

ABOVE: (France, *c.* 20,000 B.C.)
Paleolithic Venus
H. 5¼", W. 2¼"

BELOW: Giovanni Battista Piranesi (Italian, 1720–1778)
Table (*c.* 1768)
Gilt wood and marble, H. 35½", W. 59", Diam. 29½"

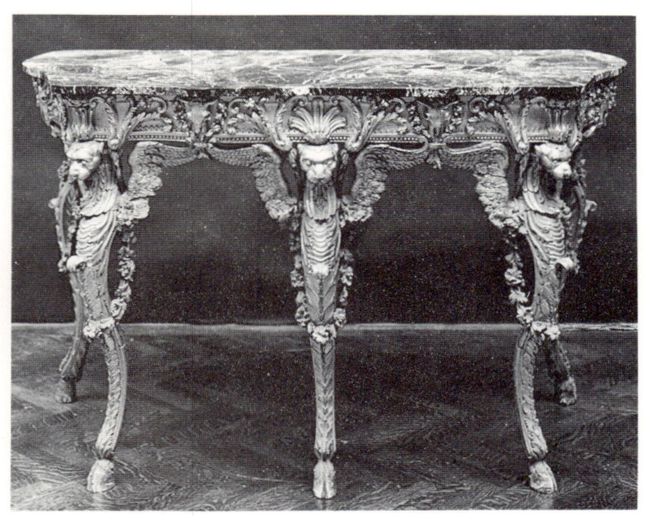

instance, they are masterworks. For many years now, it has been Institute policy to select from available works those that both extend the scope of the permanent collection and represent the very best examples of the work of an individual artist or school.

While other museums may specialize in a particular genre, region, or period, the M.I.A.'s collection spans a period of more than 25,000 years and covers all the major cultures of the world. As this book is confined to the painting collection (and only a portion of that), it is appropriate here at least to mention some of the other highlights.

The collection of Chinese bronzes is world famous. Formed in the main by Alfred Pillsbury, this group of works from the Han and Chou dynasties would be impossible to collect today—at any price. Foresight, impeccable taste, and the help of a great dealer made it possible. The Chinese jade collections in Minneapolis, too, are among the finest in the world. Given by the Pillsbury and Searle families, they form, together with loans from the T. B. Walker Foundation, a group matched perhaps only in mainland China.

Again within the Asian world, the collections of Japanese prints given by Richard P. Gale and an anonymous St. Paul friend place the Minneapolis Institute among the centers for the study of these cultures.

Among the treasures of Western culture are the collections of prints formed around the group originally given by Herschel V. Jones. It spans the period from the earliest woodblock and dotted metal prints to the present day and includes 40,000 items in all.

English and American silver is another of the museum's holdings, and here, too, a single family has been identified with many of the major objects—the James F. Bells. Two of the most significant objects are the Paul Revere Tea Service (the only complete one known to exist) and the Duke of Sutherland's Paul de Lamerie Wine Cistern.

In furniture and sculpture, the museum boasts great strengths. A well-known example of the former is the table by Piranese, one of two extant specimens. In 1980 the M.I.A. acquired a hitherto unrecorded figure by Giovanni Bologna—an important addition to our large sculpture collection.

Annually, the collections contrive to grow both through acquisitions and continued, generous gifts. Each year we add approximately one thousand items to our holdings, which have become an important repository of the cultural heritage of mankind.

It has often been said that what the Institute's collection lacks in depth it more than makes up for in breadth and quality. This book can do little more than hint at the scope and richness of the treasures of Minneapolis, but at the very least, it will allow you to judge the truth of that statement for yourself. I hope it will also bring you a great deal of pleasure.

Favorite Paintings from The Minneapolis Institute of Arts

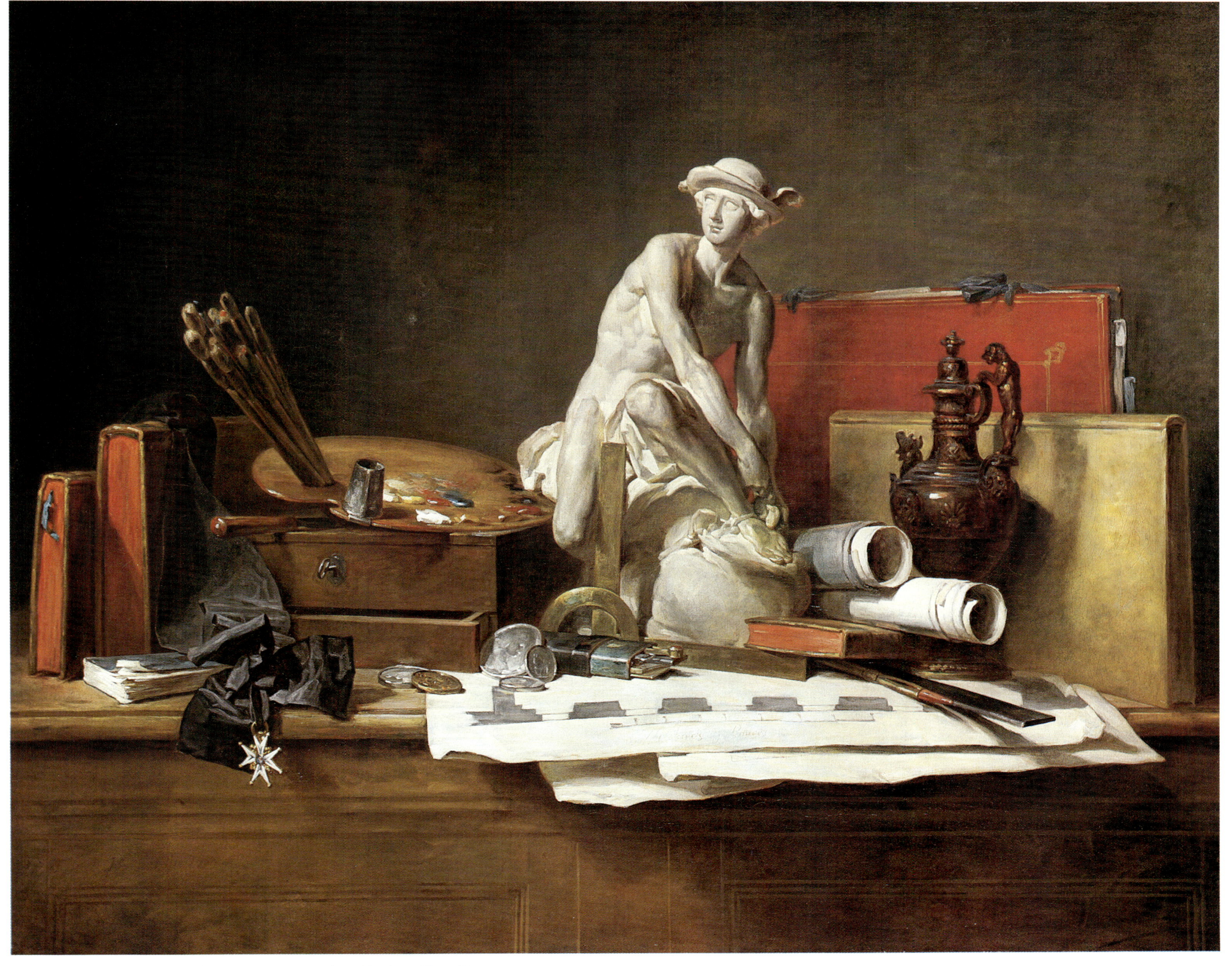

The Attributes of the Arts (1766) by Jean-Baptiste-Siméon Chardin (COMMENTARY ON PAGE 104)

Bernardo Daddi

ITALIAN (Active ca. 1312–1348)

Triptych: The Madonna and Child (1339)

This small devotional altar was made to be portable; the side panels fold inward to protect the central scene. Bernardo Daddi was a close follower of Giotto, the artist whose work first fully expressed an interest in the natural world rather than in heavenly realms—a change of viewpoint that ushered in the Renaissance. Daddi's debt to Giotto is evident in his depiction of human emotion and his secure setting of figures in real space.

As with almost all paintings of this period, the work shows scenes from the life of Christ. Here we see St. Francis receiving the stigmata, the Madonna enthroned, and the Crucifixion. At the peak of the left wing is the angel Gabriel, at the right the Virgin Annunciate signifies the spiritual birth of Christ.

With the fluidity and ease of oil paint yet undiscovered, this tempera triptych retains a brilliancy of color and subtlety of modeling that attest extraordinary technical skill. Deep spatial rendition is still beyond the grasp of the fourteenth-century artist, but the lavish use of gold gives a luster and depth to this work that more than compensates for its lack of perspective.

Tempera on poplar panels 23½ x 10" (60 x 25 cm) center
18½ x 4¾" (47 x 12 cm) left
18½ x 5" (47 x 13 cm) right

The Ethel Morrison Van Derlip Fund, 1934

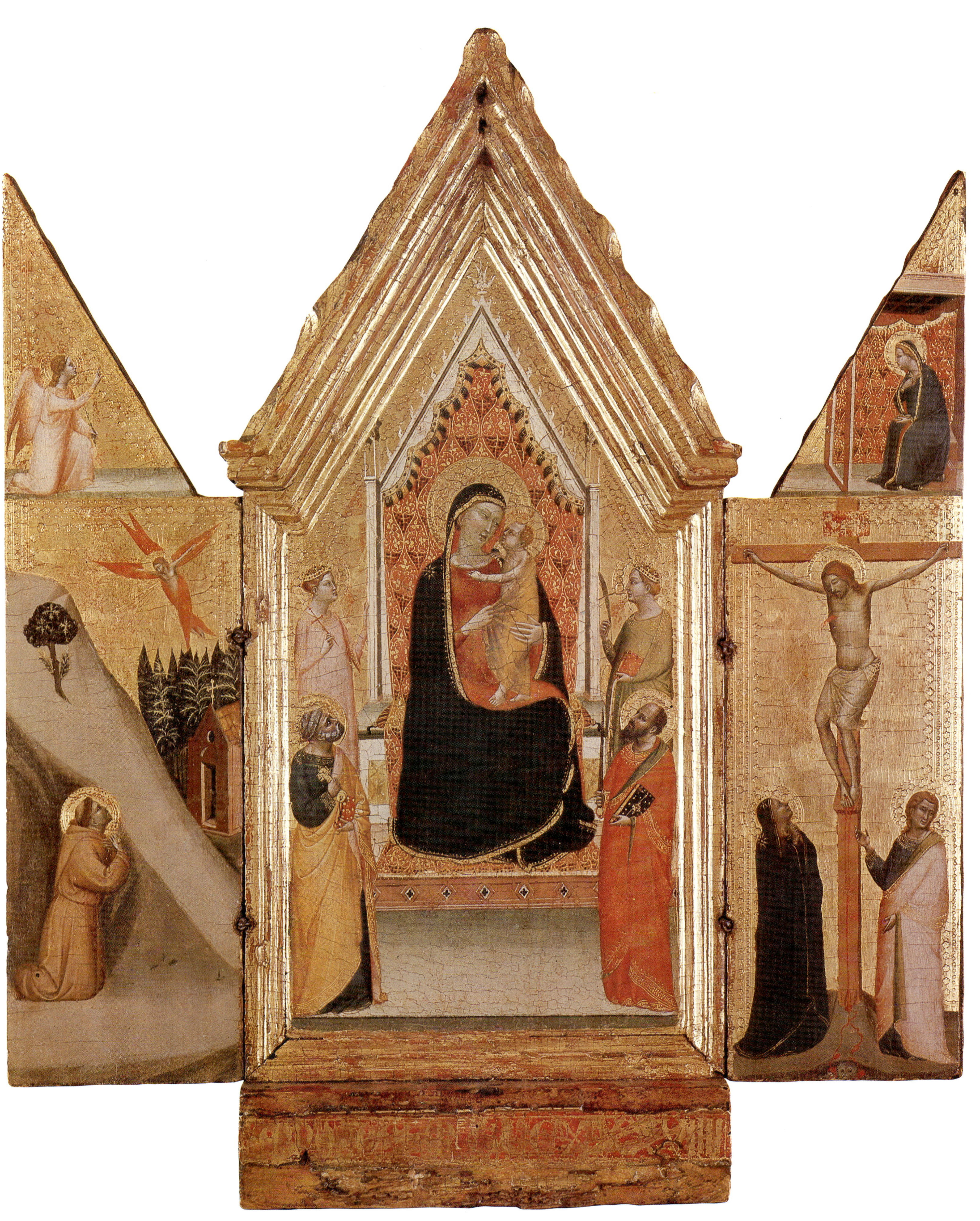

Mariotto di Nardo

ITALIAN (Active 1394–1431)

The Coronation of the Virgin (1408)

This large panel once formed part of a far larger altar piece, now dismembered. Other parts of the original work are to be found in the J. Paul Getty Museum and the Grand Rapids Art Museum. Christ here crowns his mother as the Queen of Heaven in a real and perceptibly deep space. In this early renaissance work, spirituality is already clothed in corporeal mass; the weight of the bodies can be sensed on the cushions on which they sit; the angels in front and the altar screen behind provide a spatial framework in which their presence is defined.

The angels offer not only a chorus of music for this celestial scene but also a symphony of dazzling pastel colors in celebration of this sacred moment.

Tempera on panel 61¾ x 31" (157 x 79 cm) with frame
The Putnam Dana McMillan Fund, 1965

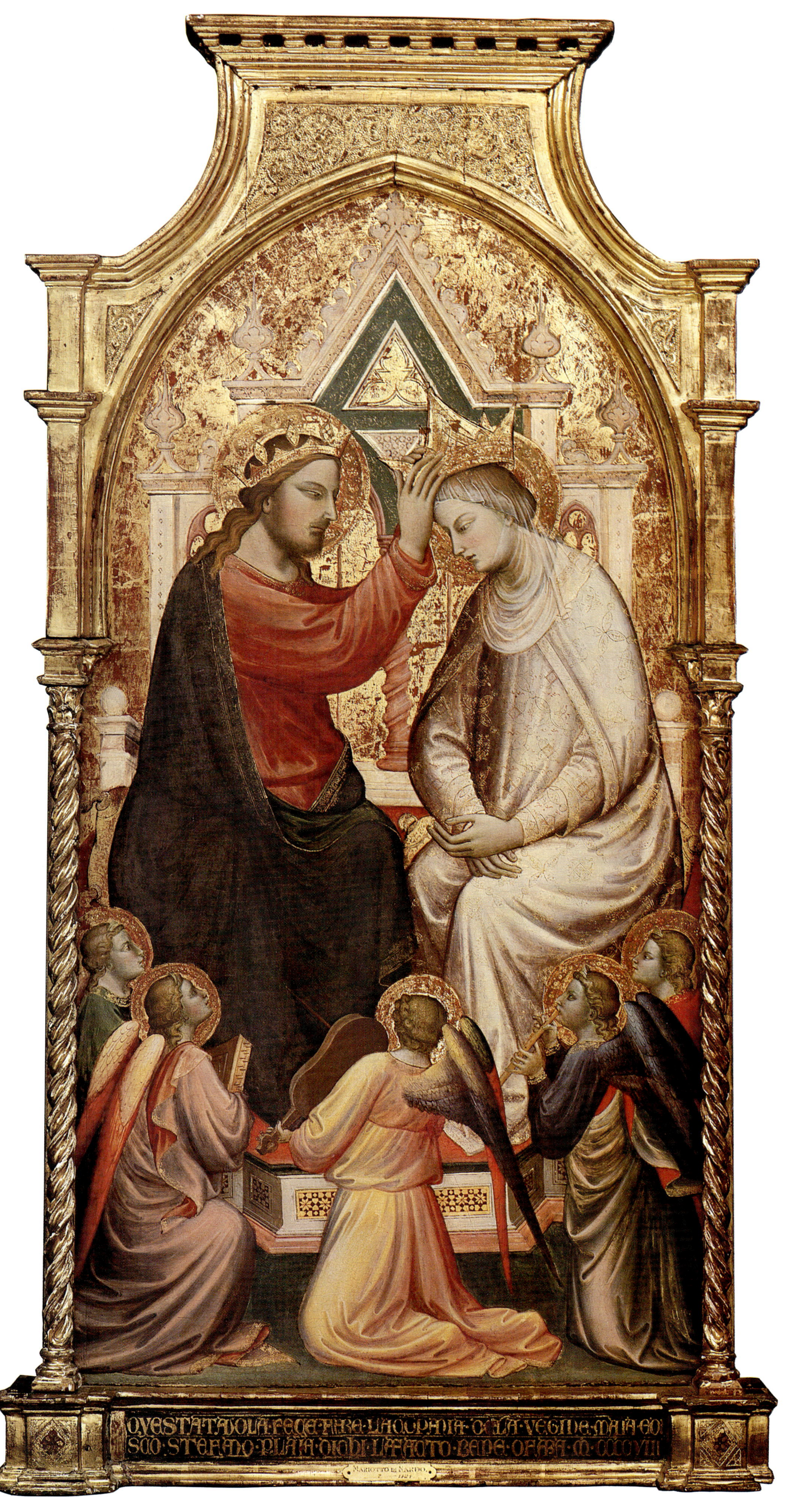
MARIOTTO DI NARDO

Nicola di Maestro Antonio d'Ancona

ITALIAN (Fifteenth century)

Madonna and Child Enthroned (ca. 1475)

Here, toward the end of the fifteenth century, a "lesser" master has depicted an elegant and aloof Madonna enthroned in all her glory. The angels, traditionally dominant, are relegated to the uppermost region of the throne and become merely onlookers. The Virgin's halo, rich with gilding, proclaims, "Hail Mary full of grace," while the child–man Christ appears to anticipate His passion.

The greatly elongated hands of the Madonna anticipate the later mannerist style and lead the eye downward not only to her sumptuous robe but to the remarkable still life detailed at the base of the throne. Each of the items in it has its own iconographic significance: the fly, for example, represents evil. Perhaps most fascinating is the crack in the throne itself; it appears to relate to the triumph of faith over earthly instability. It is likely that the panel itself was commissioned in gratitude for their salvation by the people of the village of Ancona after it was struck by an earthquake in 1474.

Tempera on panel 55¾ x 19" (142 x 48 cm)
The John R. Van Derlip Fund, 1975

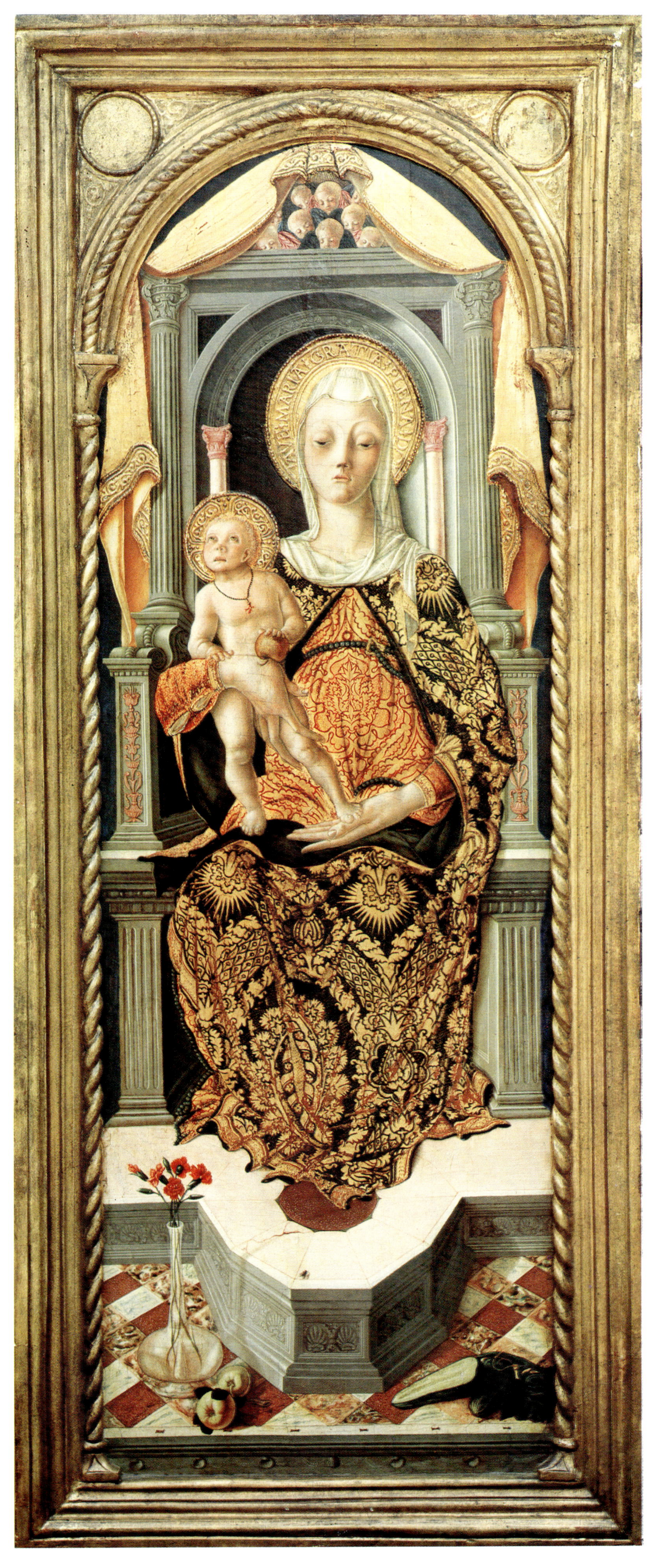
AVE MARIA GRATIA PLENA D

Master of the Saint Lucy Legend

FLEMISH (Active 1470–1490)

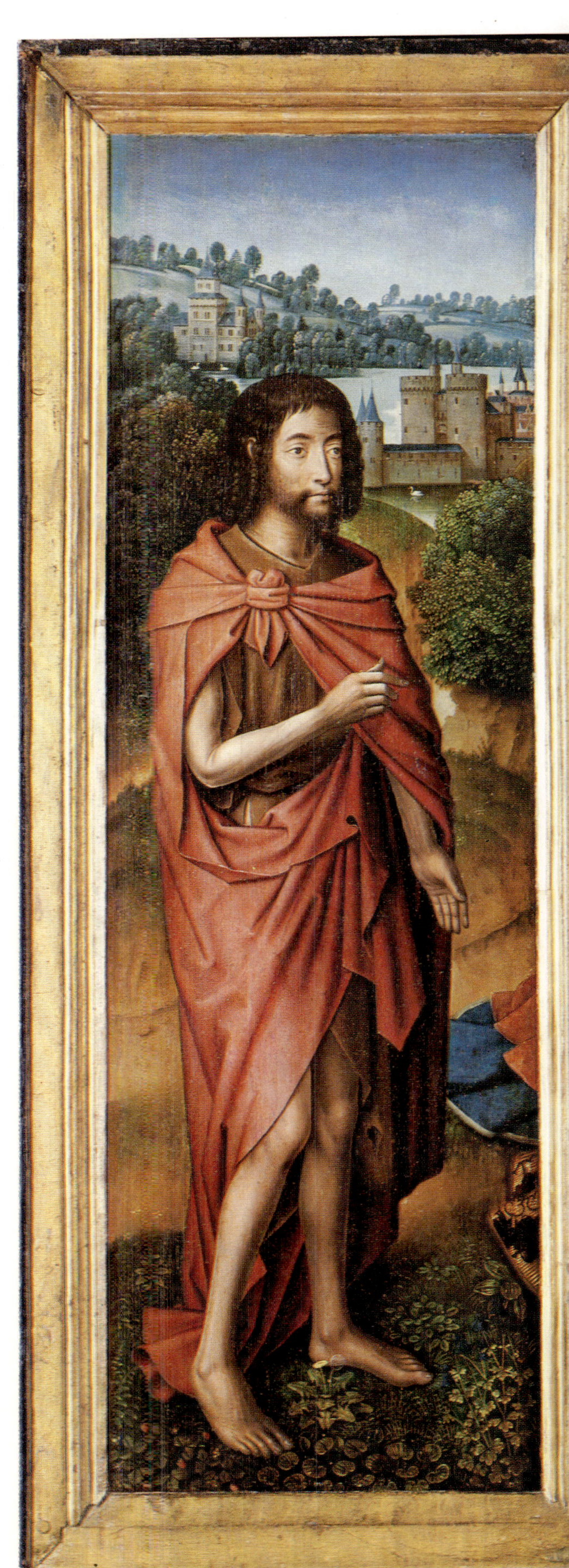

Triptych: Pietà and Panels of Saint John and Saint Catherine

The name of the artist of these panels has been lost to us; he is identified only by means of his most famous paintings, a series of works depicting the life of Saint Lucy. Here the Virgin, attended by the saints John and Catherine, mourns the death of Christ. His body has been removed from the cross, and the wounds of His passion are clearly evident. The sorrow of this moment is shown in a somewhat naive but nonetheless touching manner.

To the left of the central panel is Joseph of Arimathea, the Jewish councilman who paid for Christ's tomb. The richness of his robes clearly indicates his status and wealth. The couple at the right are probably the donors of the painting who wanted to be shown mourning the death of Christ as an act of piety.

We know that the Master of the Saint Lucy legend was active in Bruges in the fifteenth century. Behind the central scene is a literal rendition of the city as it appeared at the time. Bruges was still an active seaport in those days, before its harbors became silted up in the seventeenth century.

Tempera on panel 35 x 11" (89 x 28 cm) side panels
35 x 26¼ (89 x 67 cm) center
Bequest of John R. Van Derlip, 1935

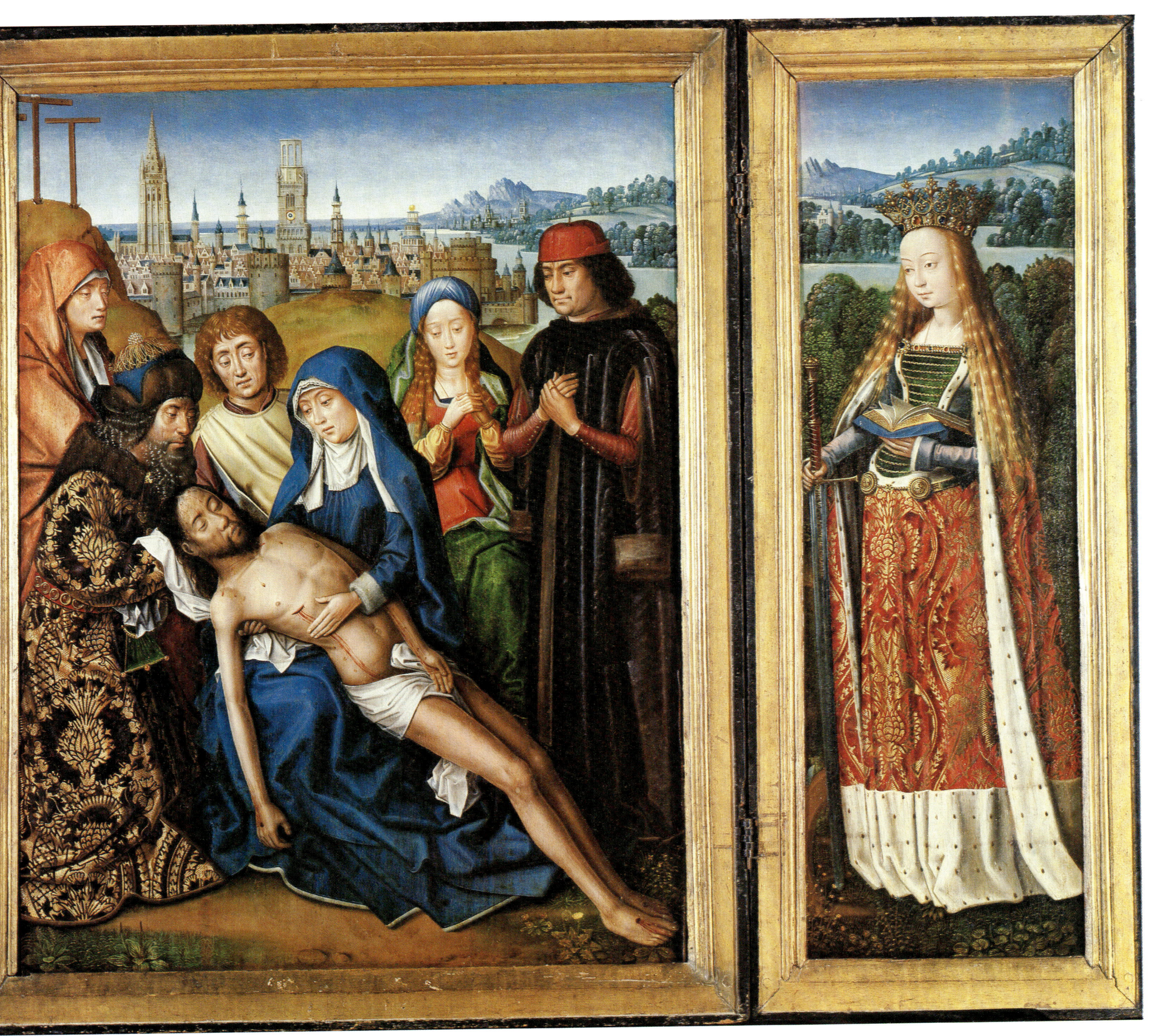

ATTRIBUTED TO

Correggio (Antonio Allegri)

ITALIAN (1494–1534)

Portrait of a Renaissance Cardinal as Saint Jerome

Originally attributed to Lorenzo Costa, more recently to Correggio, this panel is a powerful evocation of emerging humanist interests in sixteenth-century Italy. The work is unsigned and undated, but careful analysis and close comparison with known paintings of Correggio suggest that this, too, may be by his hand.

Authorship notwithstanding, we have before us a real man in real space; a painting whose spirituality is firmly rooted in the temporal world. The brilliant red robes of this young cardinal set off a face at once strong and gentle, pensive yet full of character. The books, and the pen in his hand, attest to the importance of learning among the clergy who formed the intelligentsia of the age.

The influence of the oil-painting technique, developed and perfected in northern Europe, had by now reached Italy. So, too, had the northern interest in landscape and deep space. St. Jerome and his lion present the cardinal's patron saint as an extension of the cardinal's world; they also allow the artist to extend his physical space from the immediate to the world beyond.

Oil and tempera on wood panel 32¼ x 30" (82 x 75 cm),
The John R. Van Derlip and William Hood Dunwoody Funds, 1970

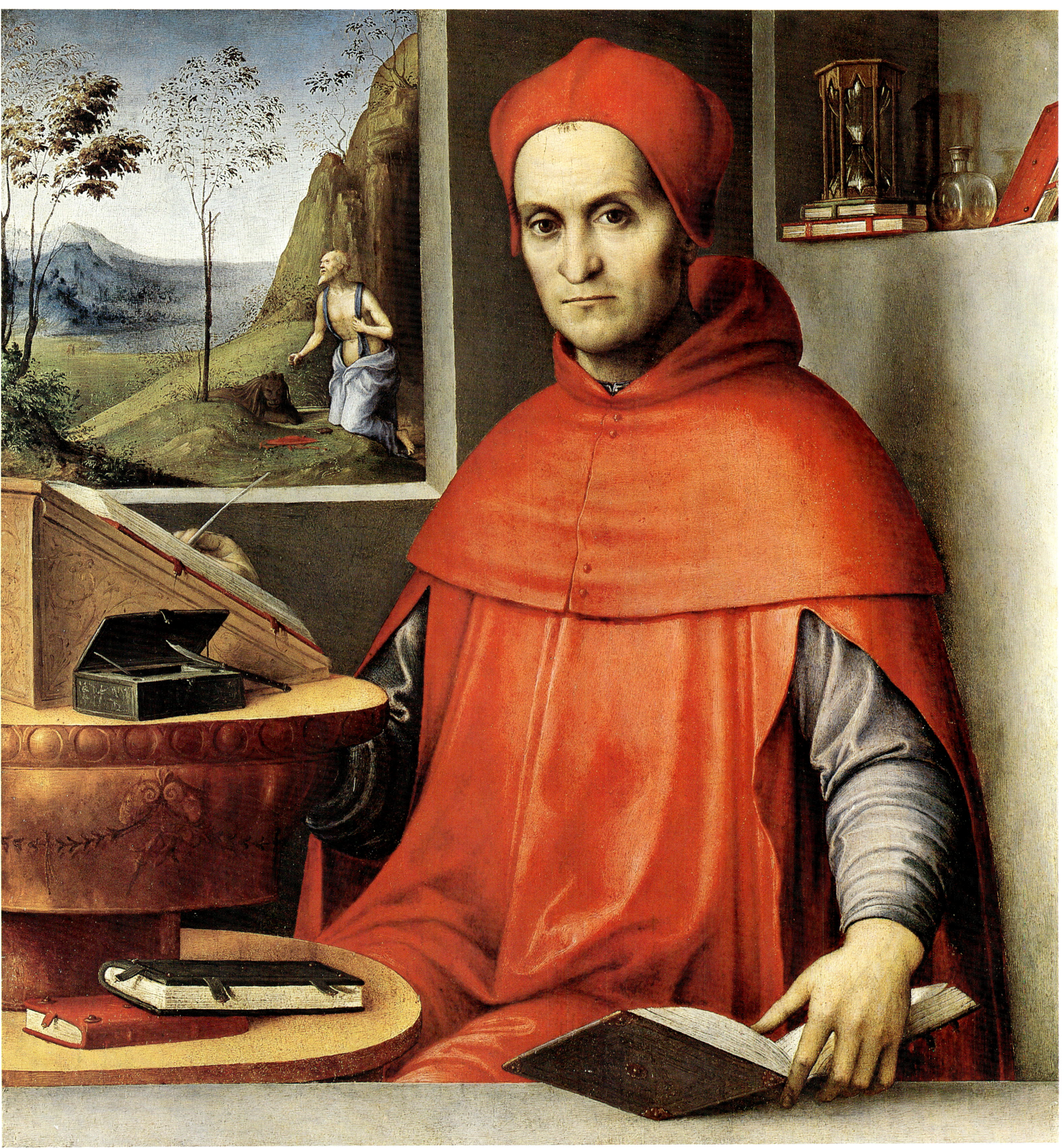

Jean Clouet the Younger

FRENCH (1475–1541)

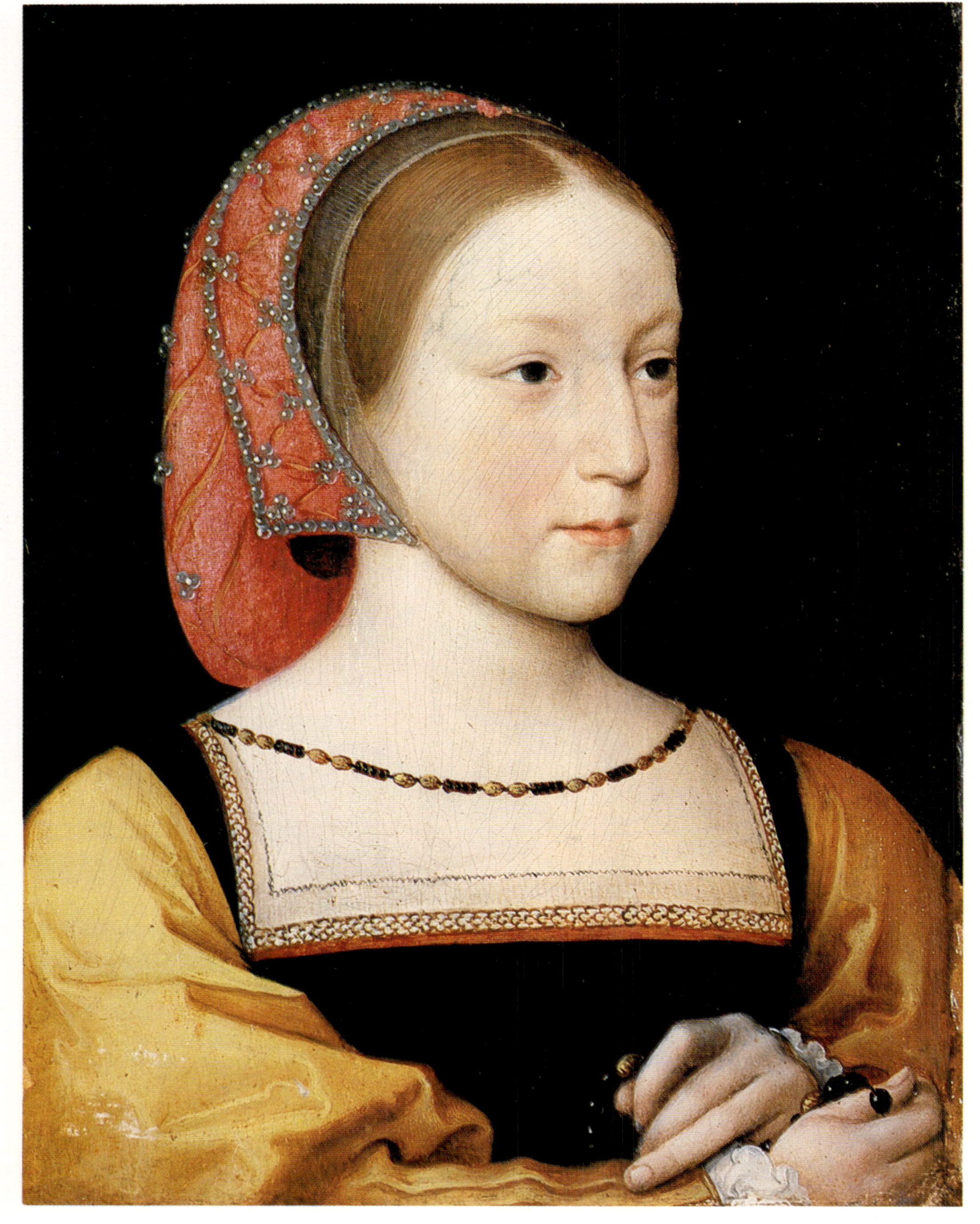

SHOWN ACTUAL SIZE

Princess Charlotte of France (ca. 1522)

Clouet was portraitist to the court of Francis I of France and has preserved for us many remarkable images of the nobility of his time. None is more charming, touching, or elegant than this small picture of the king's daughter, Princess Charlotte.

She was born in 1516 and here, aged about six, sits demurely for her portrait with her pearl-festooned hairdress, her delightfully simple necklace, and her rosary. The slightly impish look on her face takes on tragic overtones when we recall that she was killed at the age of eight by her father's rivals and successors. Clouet's mastery of the oil technique has given us, however, a perfect "memento mori," and his flawless brushstrokes provide a unique insight into the childhood of a sixteenth-century princess.

Oil on panel 7 x 5½" (18 x 14 cm)

Bequest of John R. Van Derlip in memory of Ethel Morrison Van Derlip, 1935

DETAIL ▷

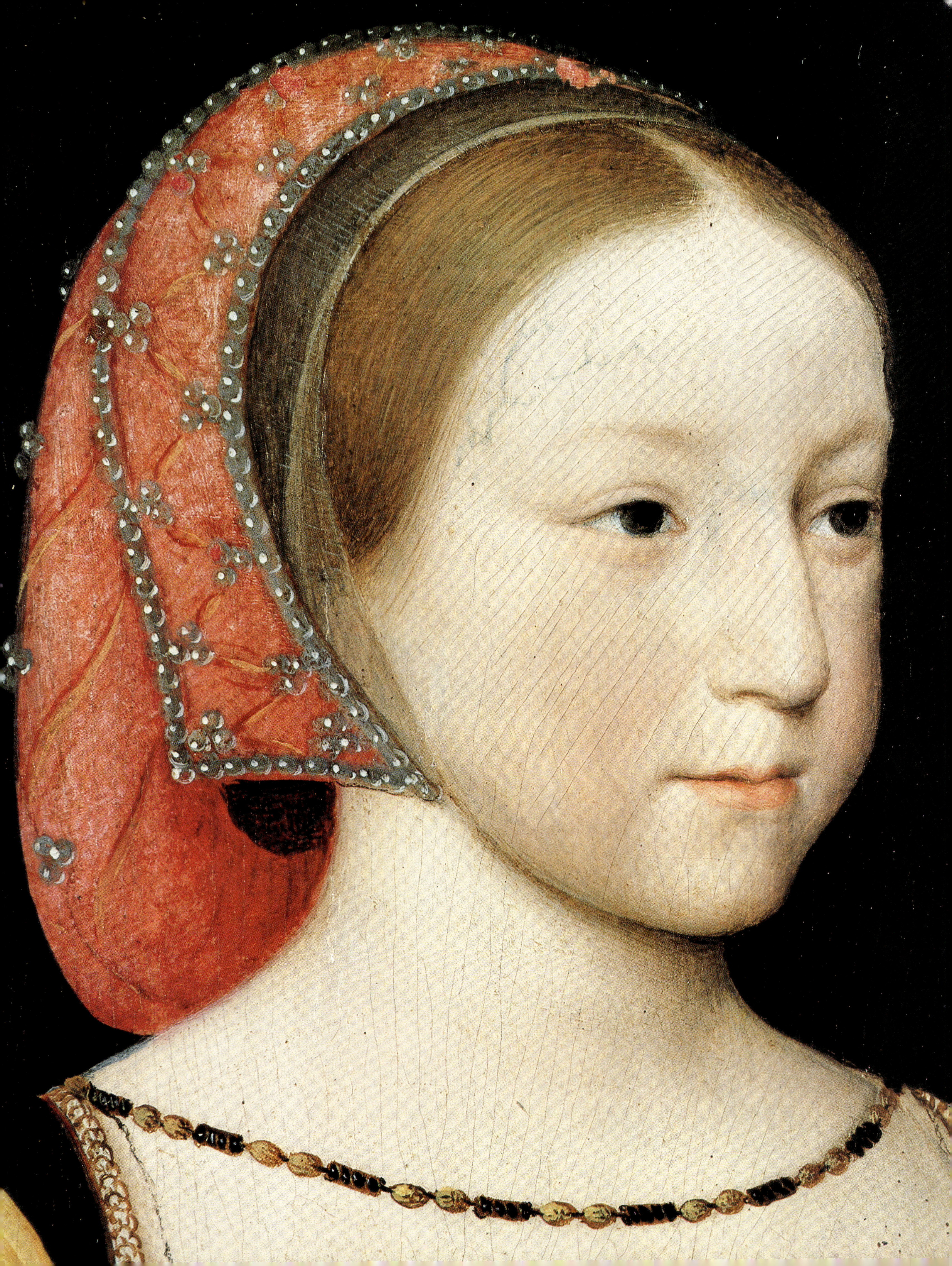

El Greco (Domenikos Theotokopoulos)

SPANISH, BORN GREEK (1541–1615)

Christ Driving the Money Changers from the Temple (ca. 1575)

In the text of Matthew 21:12 we read the story of Christ driving the money changers and dove sellers from the temple. It is a powerful theme, and one which El Greco depicted many times. Here Christ, resplendent in red and blue, is caught in a moment of sorrowing anger—a contradiction mirrored by the doves, which quietly watch this scene of writhing violence.

Born in Crete, El Greco painted this picture in Italy before settling in Spain. His pride in his origins is evident from his signature beneath Christ's feet, written in Greek characters. However, his debt to Italy is acknowledged in the group of four portraits at the right, which depict Titian, Michelangelo, El Greco's friend Julio Clovio, and Raphael. The influence of the Venetians is evident in the use of color; also evident is a foreshadowing of the agitation, the contortion, and the flickering, ethereal light that typified the artist's later works.

Oil on fabric 46 x 59" (117 x 150 cm)
The William Hood Dunwoody Fund, 1924

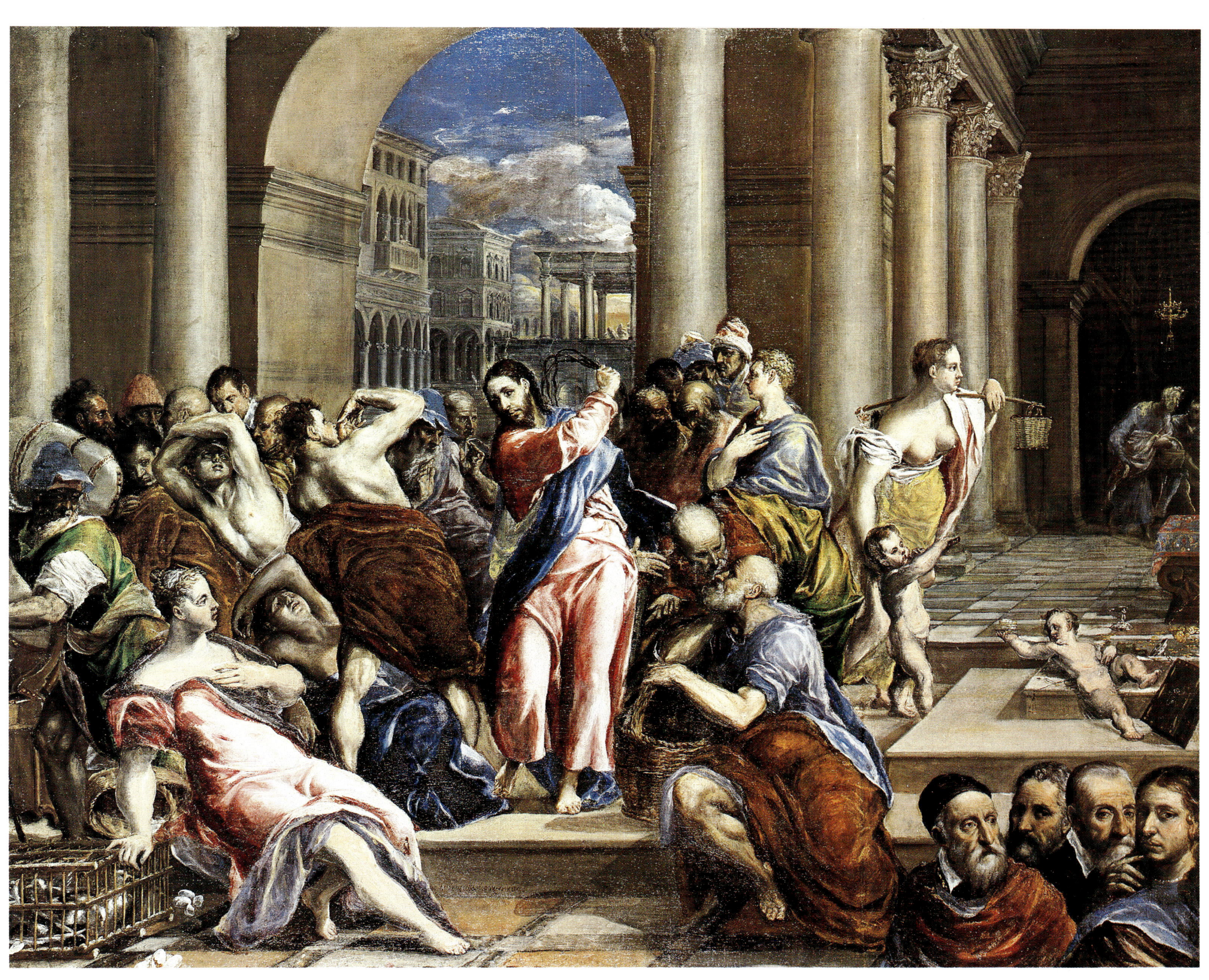

Sir Anthony Van Dyck

FLEMISH (1599–1641)

The Betrayal of Christ (ca. 1622)

From the New Testament, Mark 14 and John 18, we learn the details surrounding the betrayal and arrest of Christ as he walked with his disciples in the garden of Gethsemane. *And Judas also, which betrayed him, knew the place: for Jesus ofttimes resorted thither with his disciples. Judas then, having received a band of men and officers from the chief priests and Pharisees, cometh thither with lanterns and torches and weapons.*

The young Van Dyck charged this event with drama and energy. The mass of soldiers roll like a wave over the rocklike figure of Christ, who stands meekly submissive yet indomitable. In the flickering torchlight we catch the robes of Judas, yellow in the traditional color of treachery. To the left, *Simon Peter having a sword drew it, and smote the high priest's servant, and cut off his right ear.* And the power of the disciple's anger literally forces the man out of the picture.

This is a preparatory study for a larger work, now in the Prado in Madrid. Less "finished" than the final version, this painting benefits greatly from the freedom and spontaneity Van Dyck allowed himself in its creation.

Oil on linen 55 x 44½" (140 x 113 cm)
The William Hood Dunwoody, Ethel Morrison Van Derlip and John R. Van Derlip Funds, 1957

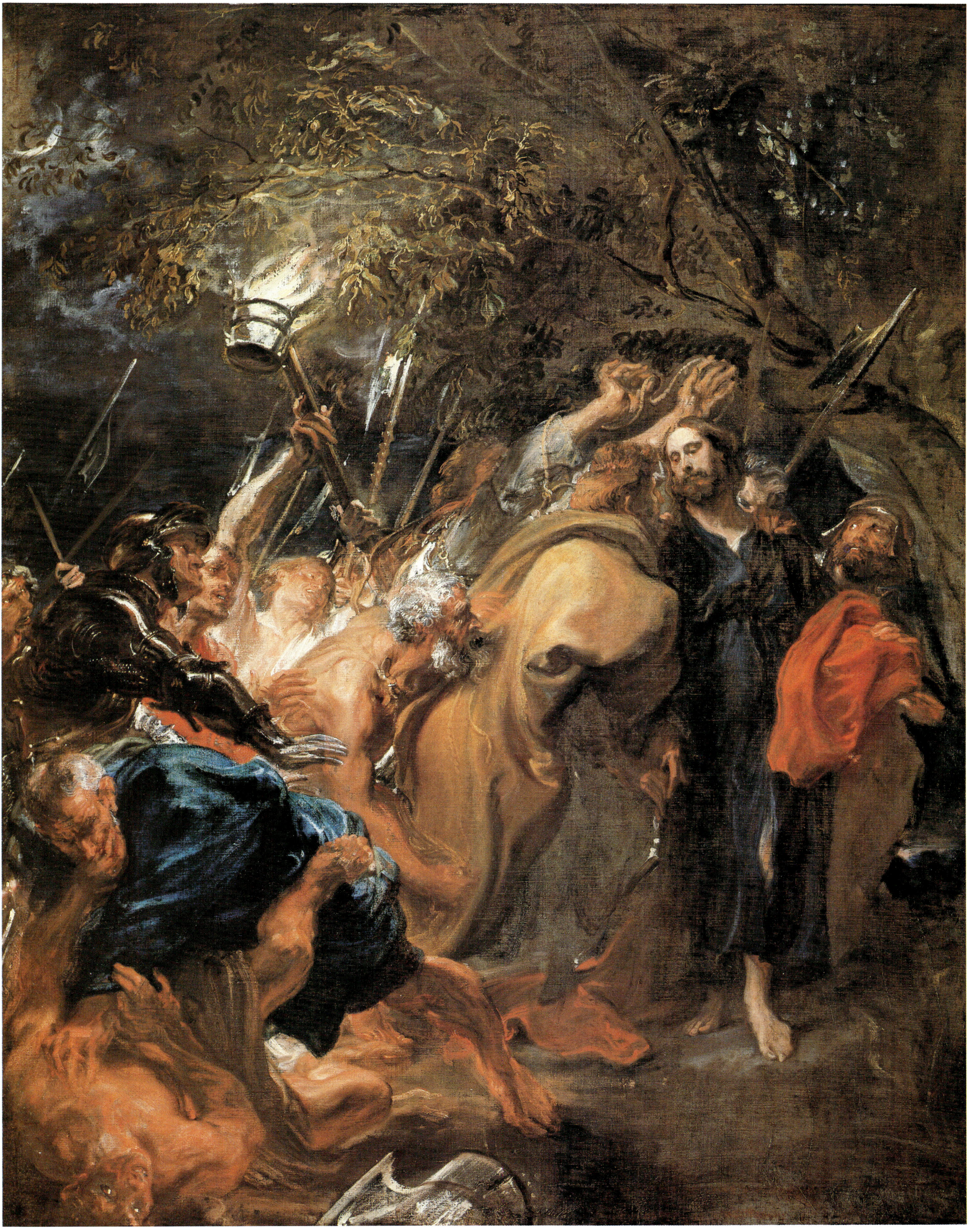

Nicolas Poussin

FRENCH (1593/4–1665)

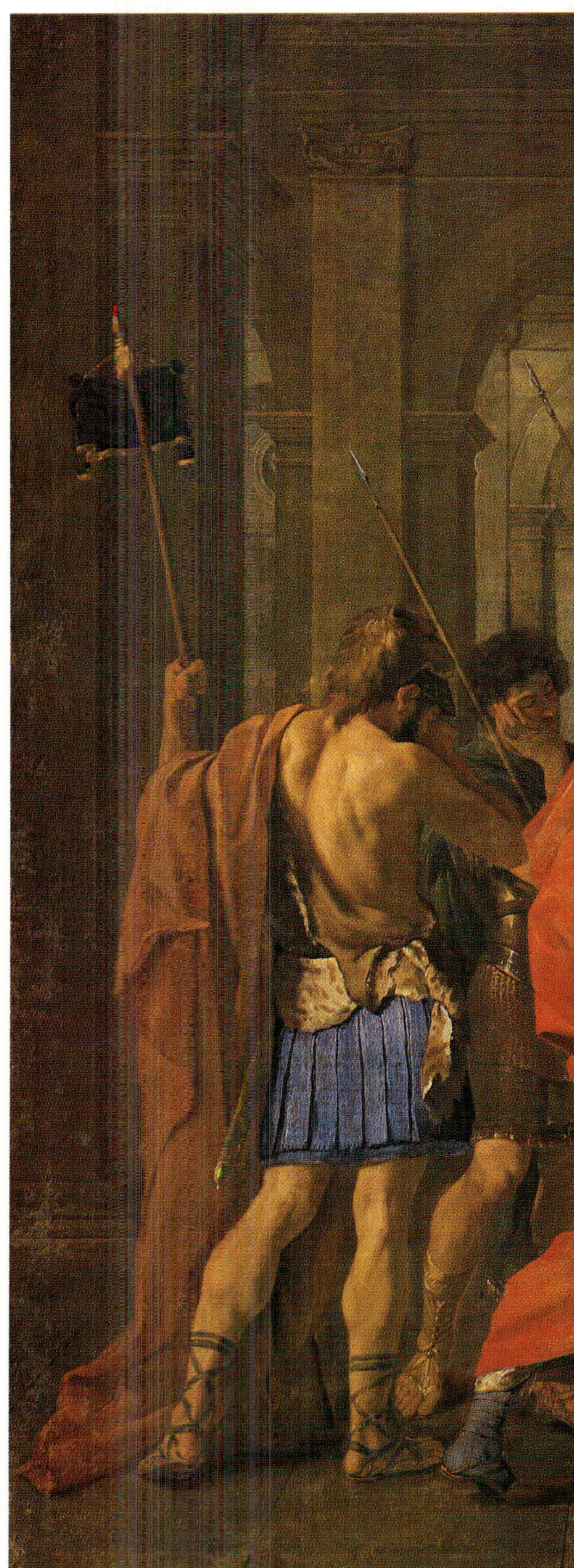

The Death of Germanicus (1627)

Poussin is revered in France as one of the nation's greatest artists, even though he spent most of his working life in Rome. From the eighteenth century onwards it became almost mandatory for French artists in Rome to make a pilgrimage to view Poussin's works, and this painting in particular.

The work has had immense influence. Napoleon, on viewing it, wished all French painting were in a similar style. It was a statement that understandably spurred the French neoclassical movement.

The Roman governor Germanicus was poisoned by his uncle and rival, the emperor Tiberius. Here, he lies on his deathbed, swearing his loyal followers to revenge. The static, friezelike composition recalls Roman triumphal decorations, and the figure of Germanicus is brilliantly singled out in silhouette against his white pillow. Touches of vivid color accentuate the interplay between verticals and horizontals, and the monumental architecture provides a grandly sombre setting for the tragedy.

This, one of the largest of Poussin's works, was painted for Cardinal Francesco Barberini. It was the artist's first major commission.

Oil on linen 58¼ x 77½" (148 x 197 cm)
The William Hood Dunwoody Fund, 1956

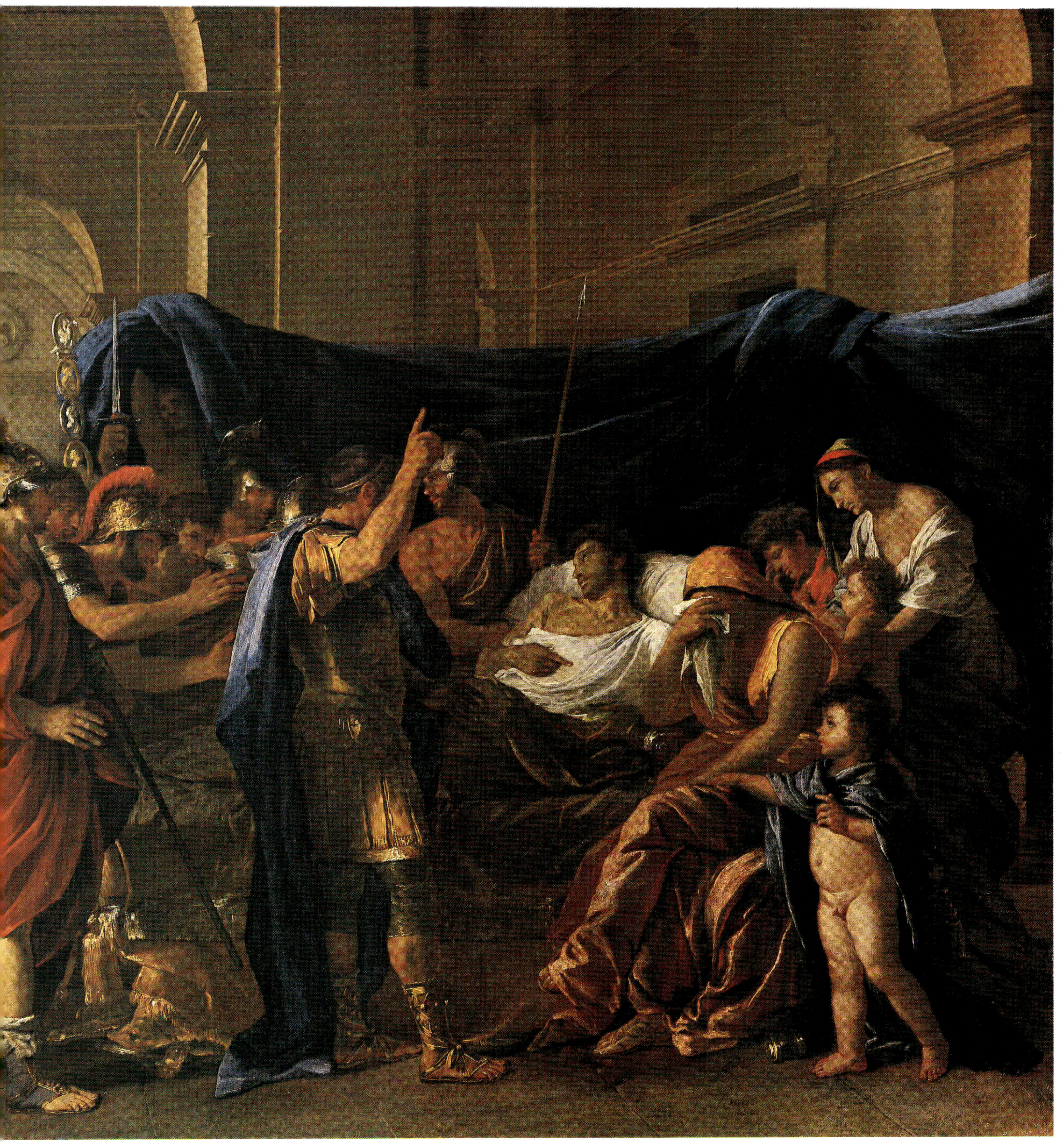

Pieter Claesz

DUTCH (1597/98–1661)

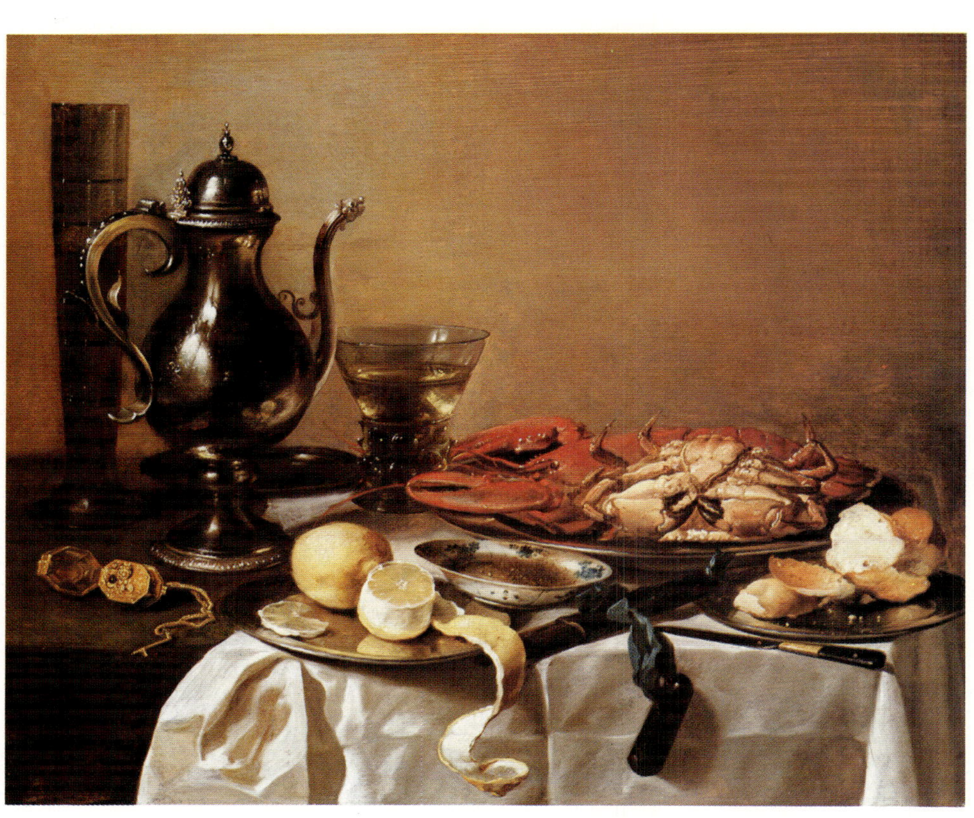

Still Life (1643)

The rising middle class in seventeenth-century Holland produced a group of burghers who developed specialized tastes in art and bought paintings according to those tastes. Aside from portrait, landscape, and seascape painters, artists who produced still lifes were among the most popular, and among them Pieter Claesz was one of the most highly respected.

His gift for rendering a myriad of different textures in paint, his warm, mellow light, and his subtle yet masterly composition made him one of the outstanding artists of his day. This work goes far beyond mere photographic realism; it is as if the textures and surfaces of the objects themselves were present in the painting—the fluidity of the wine, the brittle transparency of the glass, the soft sheen of the metals and the smooth hardness of the lobster and crab shells all contrast with the softness of the bread, the lemon rind, and the rumpled cloth.

It is quite an audacious trick of balance to leave the upper right-hand half of the painting completely blank, divided from the rest of the composition by a sharp diagonal. So, too, is the lemon rind dangling out of the picture and the plate precariously hanging over the table edge. But it is this kind of dynamic stability that made Claesz's still lifes so popular.

Oil on panel 29½ x 35" (75 x 89 cm)

The Eldridge C. Cooke Fund, 1945

DETAIL ▷

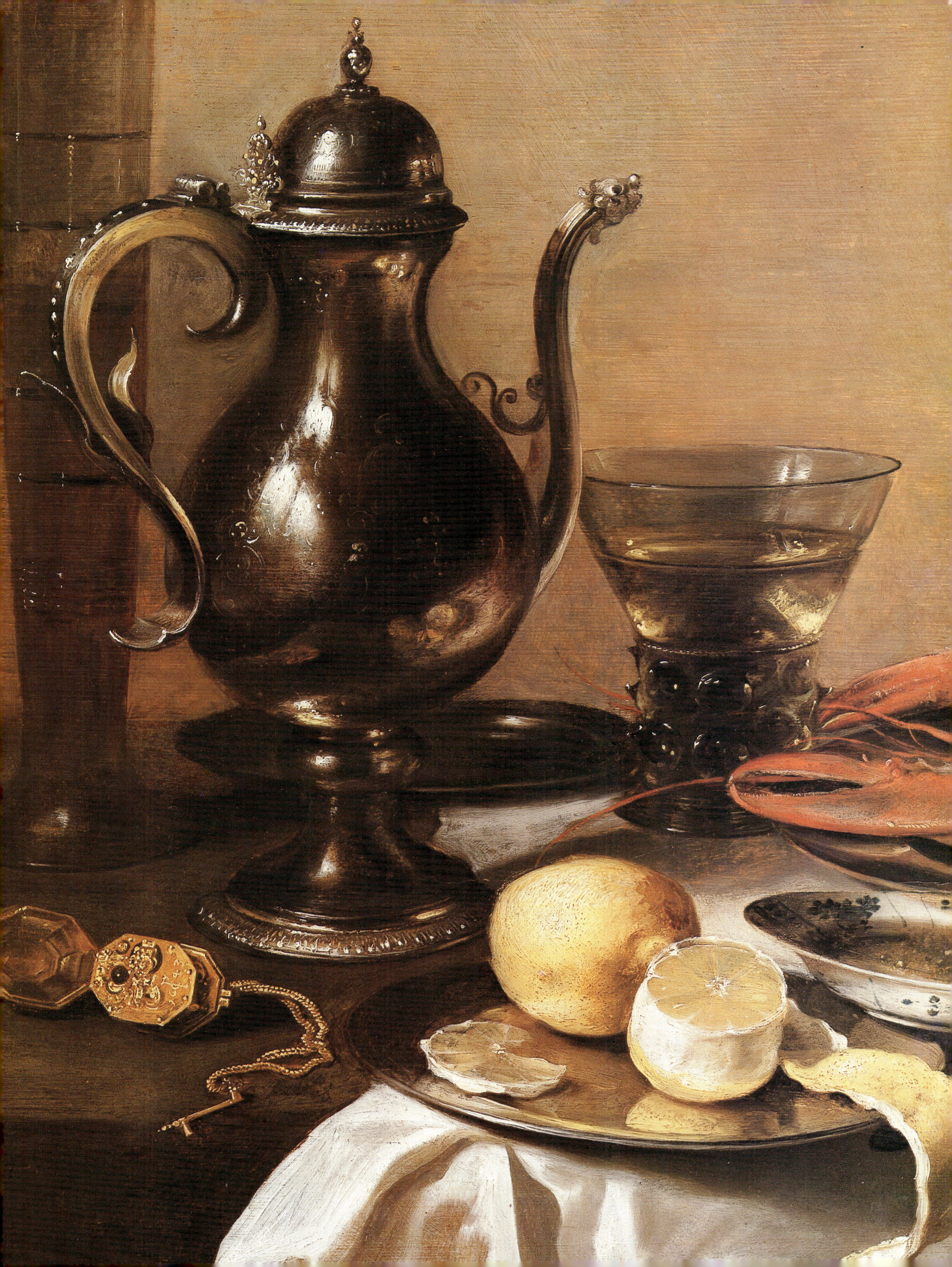

Guercino (Giovanni Francesco Barbieri)

ITALIAN (1591–1666)

Herminia and the Shepherds (1649)

As the Bible had been the source of inspiration for earlier artists, the baroque period saw the subjects of paintings increasingly drawn from secular literature. Here, the source is a poem by the sixteenth-century Italian poet Tasso, titled *Jerusalem Delivered*. In the seventh canto one reads:

She rose: and gently, guided by her ear
Came where an old man on a rising ground
In the fresh shade, his white flocks feeding near,
Twin baskets wove, and listened to the sound,
Thrilled by three blooming boys, who sate
disporting round.
They at the shining of her silver arms
Were seized at once with wonder and despair;
But sweet Herminia soothed their vain alarms;
Discovering her dove's eyes, and golden hair . . .

Guercino has not only followed the literal sense of the text with great accuracy, but he has also injected into the painting the rhythm of the lines. It is staged as if on the set of an opera, strongly lit from the wings, and it presents a sense of drama and expansiveness appropriate to both period and subject.

Oil on fabric 93½ x 111" (237 x 282 cm)
The William Hood Dunwoody Fund, 1962

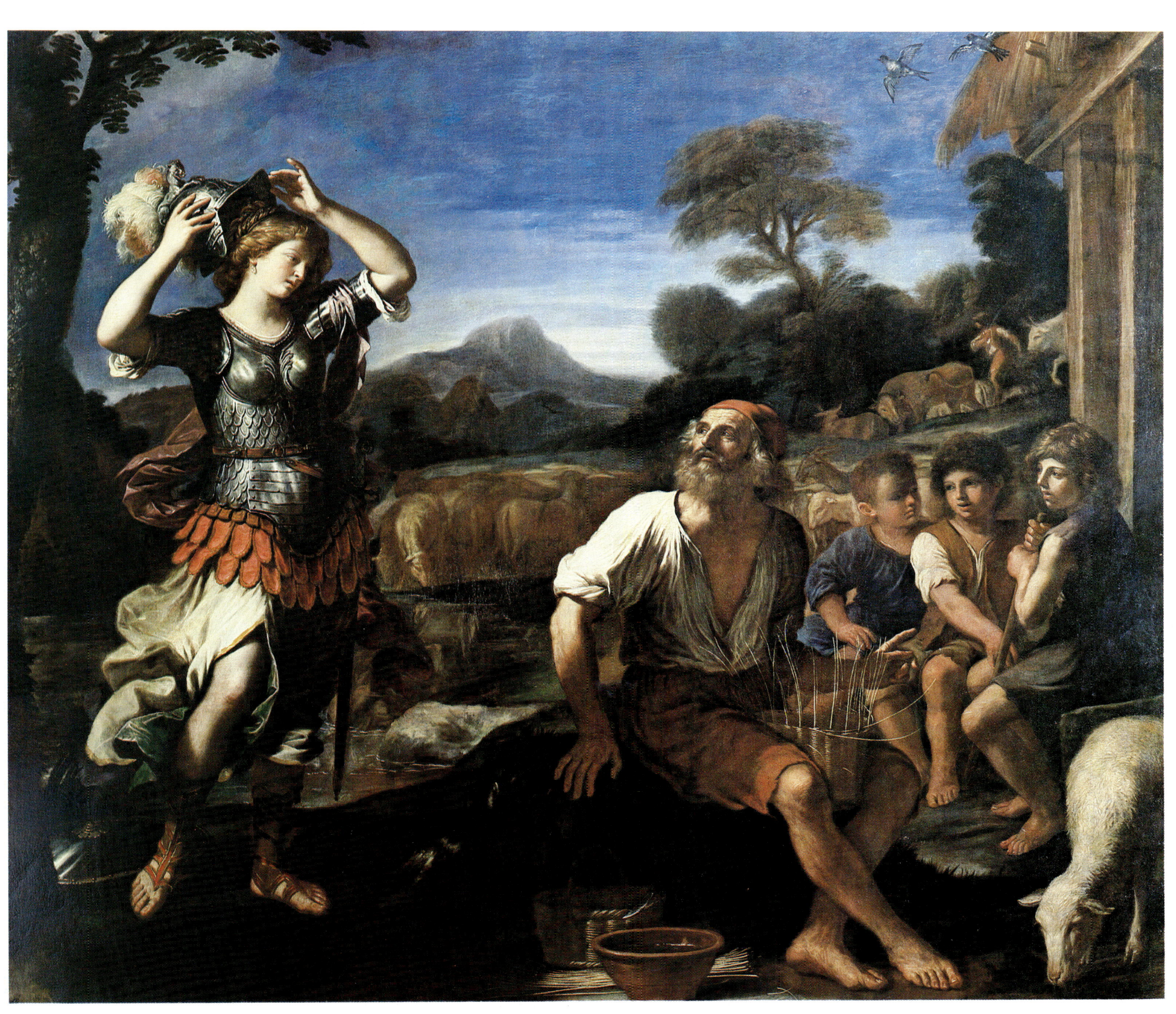

Giovanni Benedetto Castiglione

ITALIAN (ca. 1611–1665)

The Immaculate Conception with Saints Francis and Anthony of Padua (1649–50)

We are spectators here at a scene that is intended to both dazzle and overwhelm. The life-size saints and the Virgin Mary are overpowering in the reality of their presence. The Virgin hovers on her crescent moon, attended by adoring angels, in a blaze of light and color. The saints, rooted to the ground, are clad in monks' robes yet seem to represent all humanity. At the left is Saint Francis revealing the stigmata, with a skull nearby. The white lily near Saint Anthony is an allusion to the Virgin's purity.

Castiglione studied with Van Dyck in his native Genoa, worked in Rome, Florence, Naples, and Venice, and died in Mantua. This altar painting was commissioned while the artist was living in Rome. Traditionally, a work like this merely illustrated a scene from church liturgy. Here, however, Castiglione has gone far beyond illustration; the work itself has become a hymn of praise.

Oil on fabric 12'0½ x 7'3" (3.67 x 2.21 m)
The Putnam Dana McMillan Fund, 1966

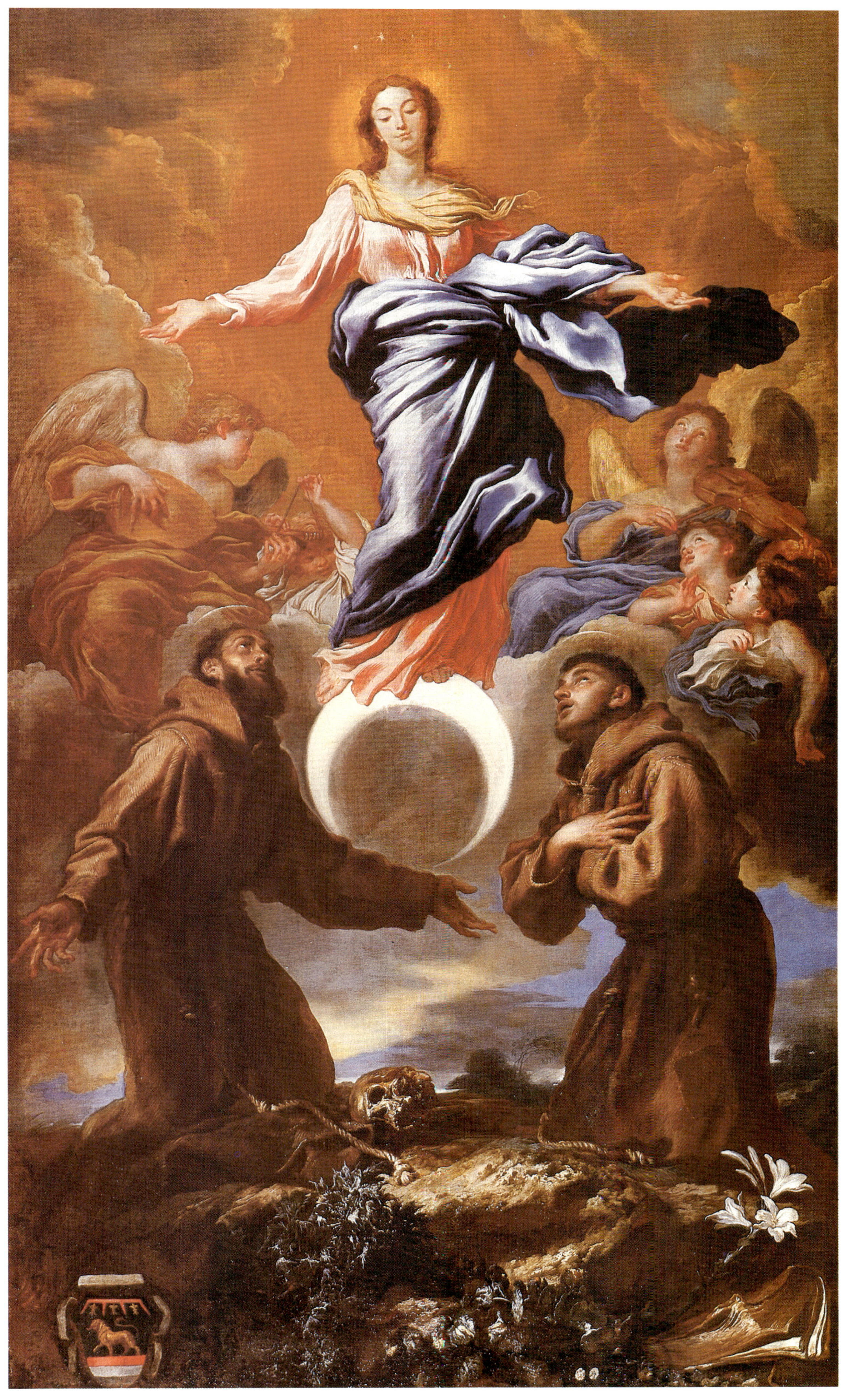

Rembrandt van Rijn

DUTCH (1606–1669)

Lucretia (1666)

According to legend, Lucretia, niece of the ancient Roman king Tarquin the Proud, was raped by her husband's friend, the king's son, Sextus. The next morning, Lucretia sent for her husband and her father and swore them to revenge. Then, to restore the family honor, she killed herself.

This is almost certainly the finest Rembrandt in America. It speaks eloquently, not only to the tragedy of an unjust fate, but to the tragedy of Rembrandt's own life and how he, himself, must have identified with Lucretia. Rembrandt's own wife was dead. So was his son. He had lost his standing in the community and his reputation as an artist. He was only three years from death. All the misery of Rembrandt's later years is caught in this painting, reflected in the pathetic eyes of Lucretia. This is her last moment. Blood flows from her wound and stains her gown. Falling, she catches a curtain rope before sinking to the ground.

Oil on fabric 43½ x 37" (110 x 94 cm)
The William Hood Dunwoody Fund, 1934

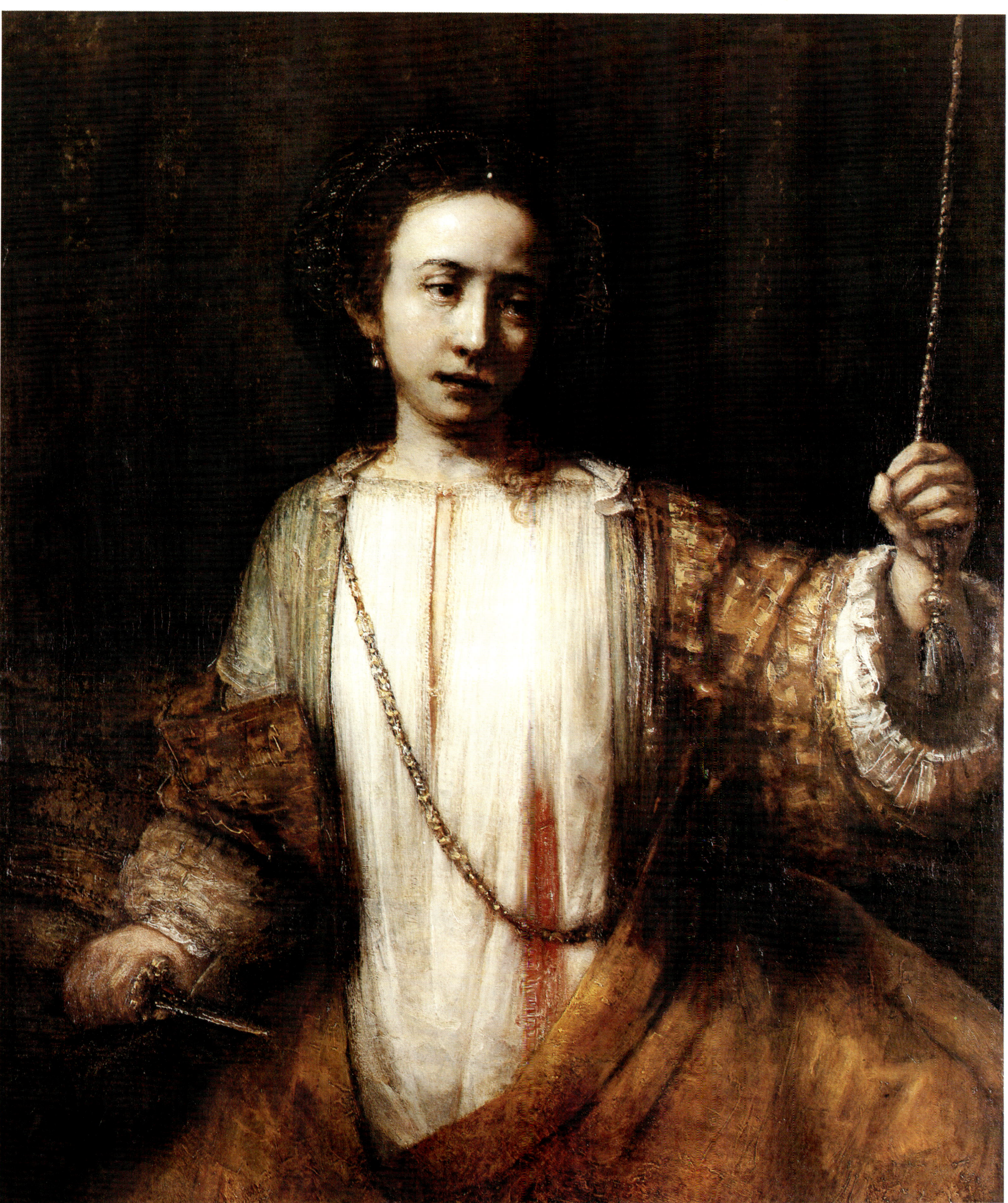

Meindert Hobbema

DUTCH (1638–1709)

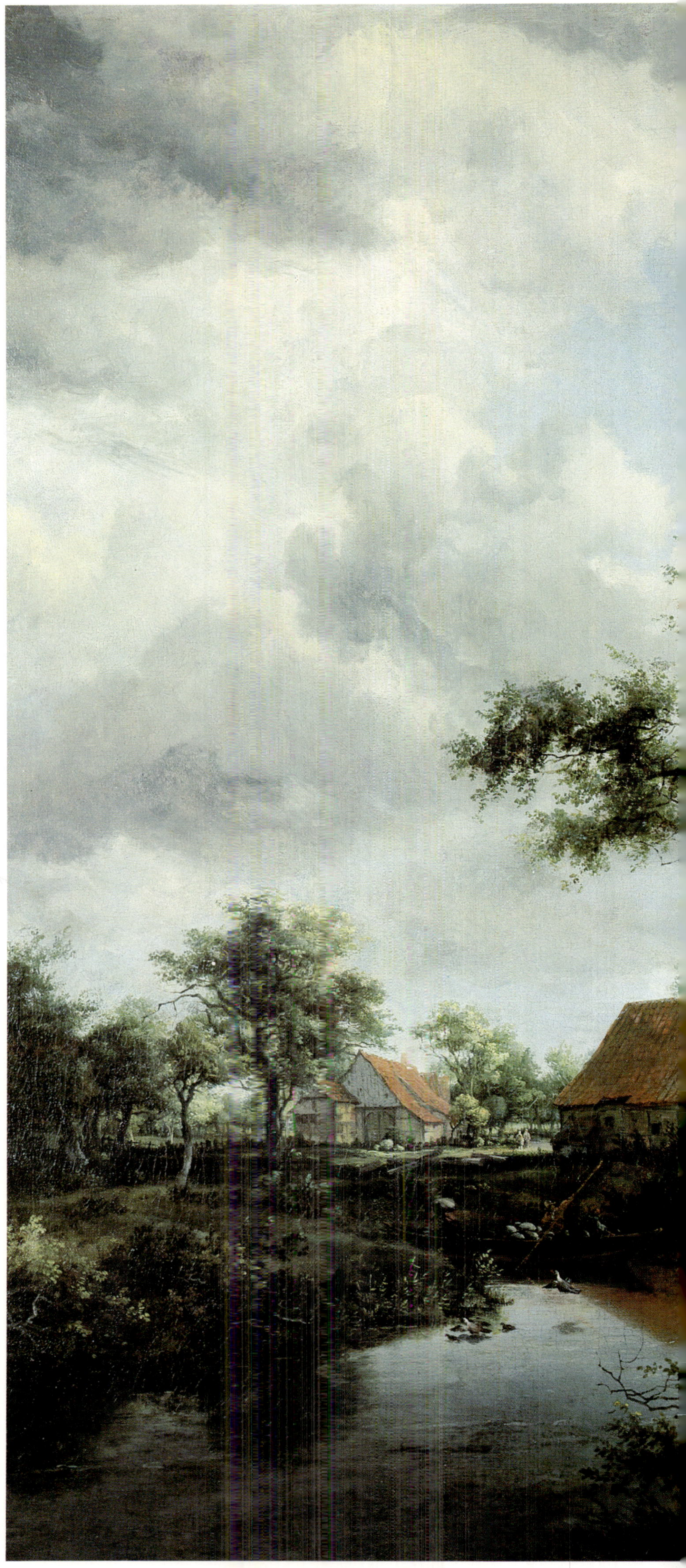

Wooded Landscape with Watermill

This large and handsome painting represents a superb example of collaboration between two artists. It is likely that Hobbema painted the entire landscape but left the figures to the hand of another painter. Even in the seventeenth century specialization was a well-established tradition, and Hobbema recognized his limitations when it came to the human form. His gifts for landscape, however, are quite evident in this work.

Unlike other artists who reveled in the angry side of nature, Hobbema preferred her more placid face. His colors are lush and soft; the old watermill quietly goes about its business, and only a few unlucky ducks are threatened with any harm at all. If we avert our eyes from the scarlet-coated hunter we may retreat into the woods, into a world where stillness and peace reign supreme.

This is the golden age of Dutch art. A thirty-year war had finally won Holland her independence from Spain, and her merchant navy now dominated the seas, reaping large profits from her colonies. Her wealthy (and largely non-Catholic) burghers wanted art to decorate the walls of their homes rather than their churches, and the art of Hobbema was in justifiably high demand.

Oil on fabric 40¼ x 53" (102 x 135 cm)
The William Hood Dunwoody Fund, 1941

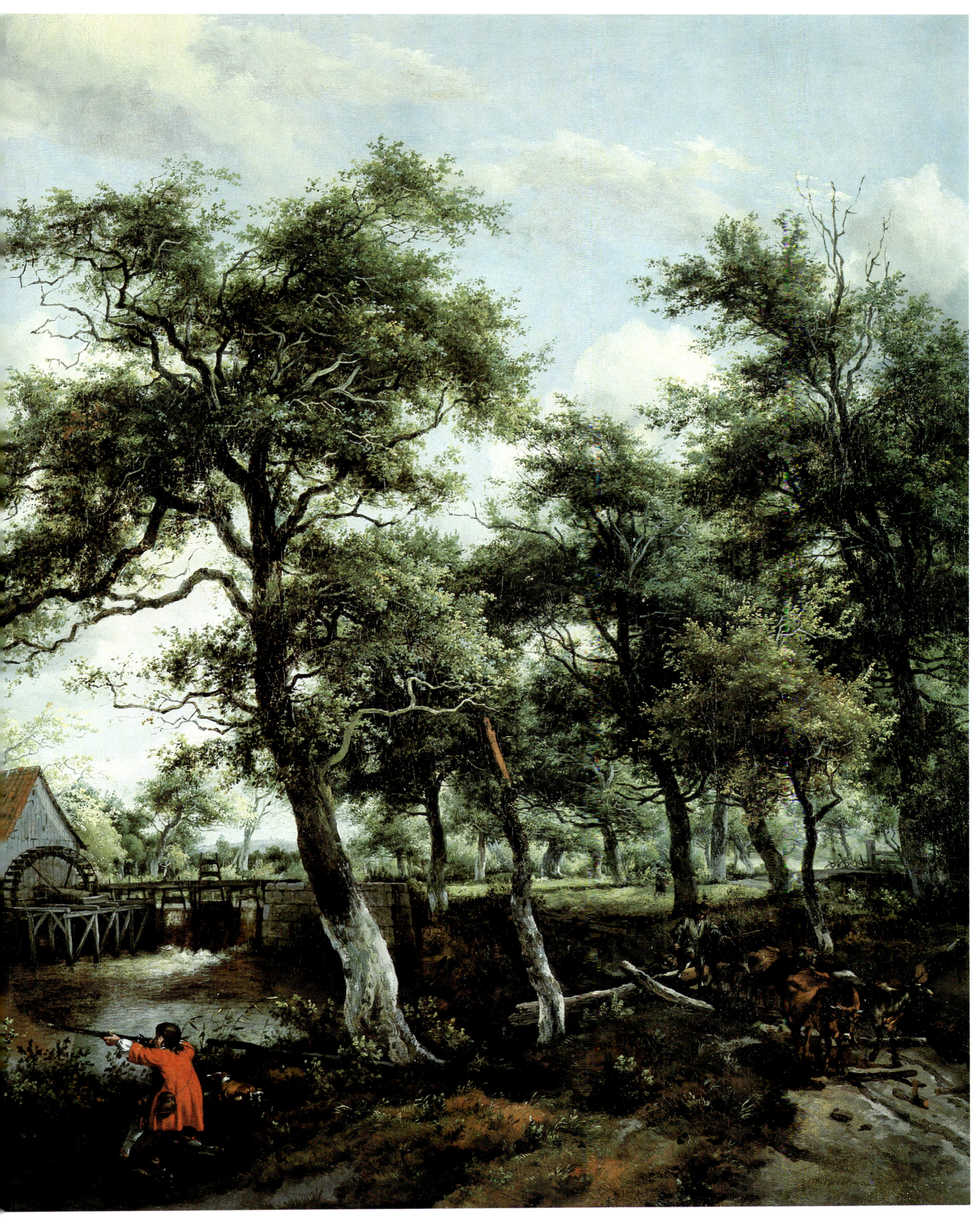

Nicolas de Largillière

FRENCH (1656–1746)

Portrait of the Marquise of Castelnau and Her Son Leonor (ca. 1700)

The reasons for Largillière's popularity as a portraitist are perhaps nowhere more clearly evident than in this painting. His clientele were the elite of the age, and he rendered them with a presence and magnificence appropriate to their standing in society. The intensity of coloration, the aristocratic bearing of the subjects, the elegance and opulence of their clothes are the baroque style at its peak.

Born in Paris, Largillière studied in Antwerp where he was acclaimed as a master painter. At eighteen, he went to England as assistant to a court portraitist. After his return to Paris he was elected to the French Royal Academy and eventually became its director. He was soon recognized as a leading portrait painter and, aged twenty-nine, was summoned back to London by King James II to paint the royal family and members of the court. His style combines elegance with insight, and much of his popularity is due to his portrayal of personality as well as appearance.

Oil on canvas 54½ x 41¾" (138 x 106 cm)
The John R. Van Derlip Fund, 1977

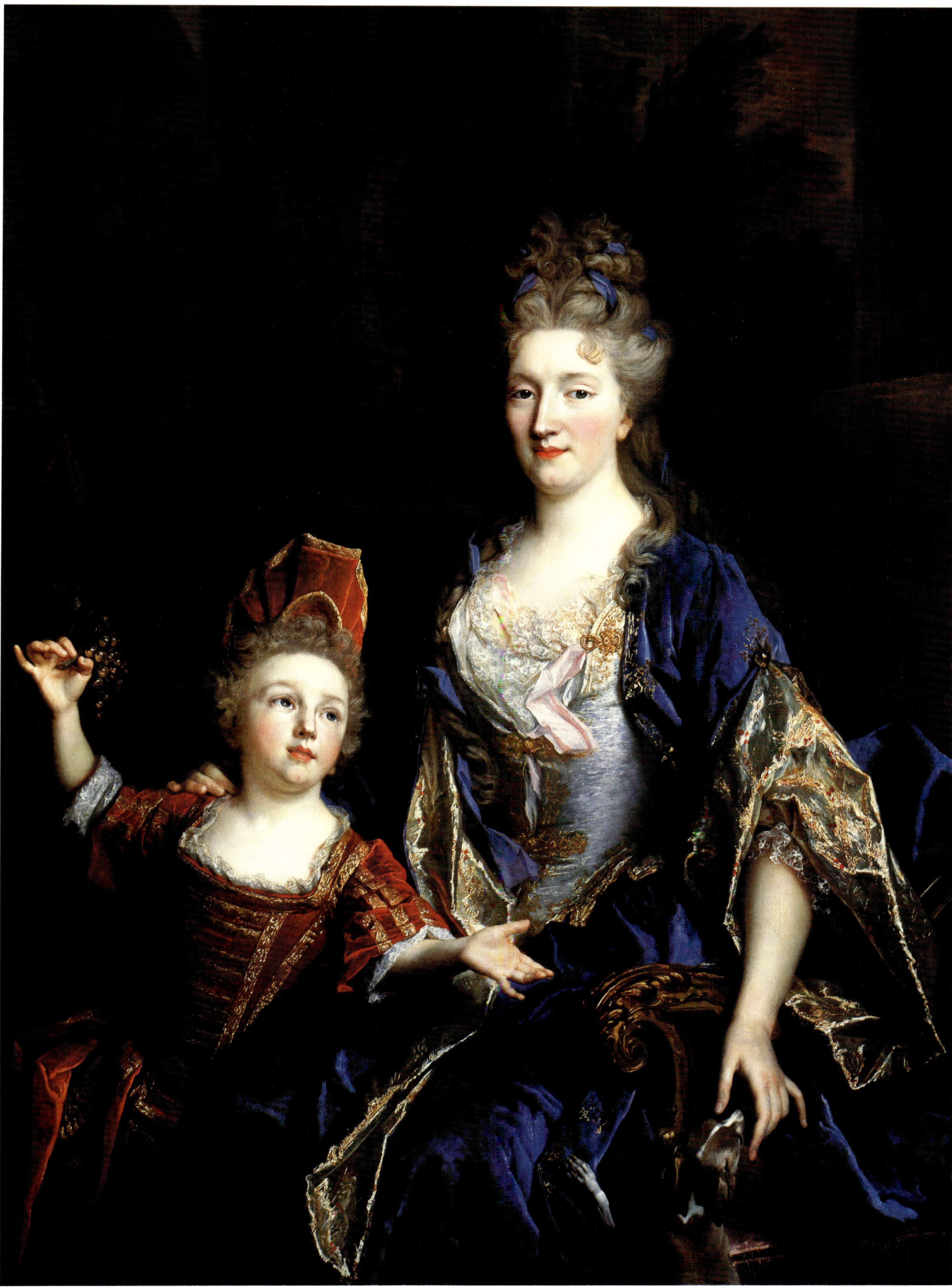

Thomas Gainsborough

ENGLISH (1727–1788)

The Fallen Tree (ca. 1743)

Thomas Gainsborough was largely self-taught and is best known for the many singularly expressive portraits he painted during the greater part of his life. However, he started, and ended, his career as a landscapist; it was an interest that led him to include glimpses of the English countryside in the background of many of his portraits. His vision of the landscape was extraordinary and is rarely better seen than in this early work.

The painting was done near his home in Sudbury, Suffolk, and shows his considerable debt to the Dutch artists of the seventeenth century. The receding planes of this deep space are threaded together by a winding path leading to a distant steeple. But the Dutch influence ends there. The low horizon of Dutch land- and seascapes is higher here, and their richer colors are muted compared to Gainsborough's largely pastel palette.

Oil on linen 40 x 36" (102 x 91 cm)
The John R. Van Derlip Fund, 1953

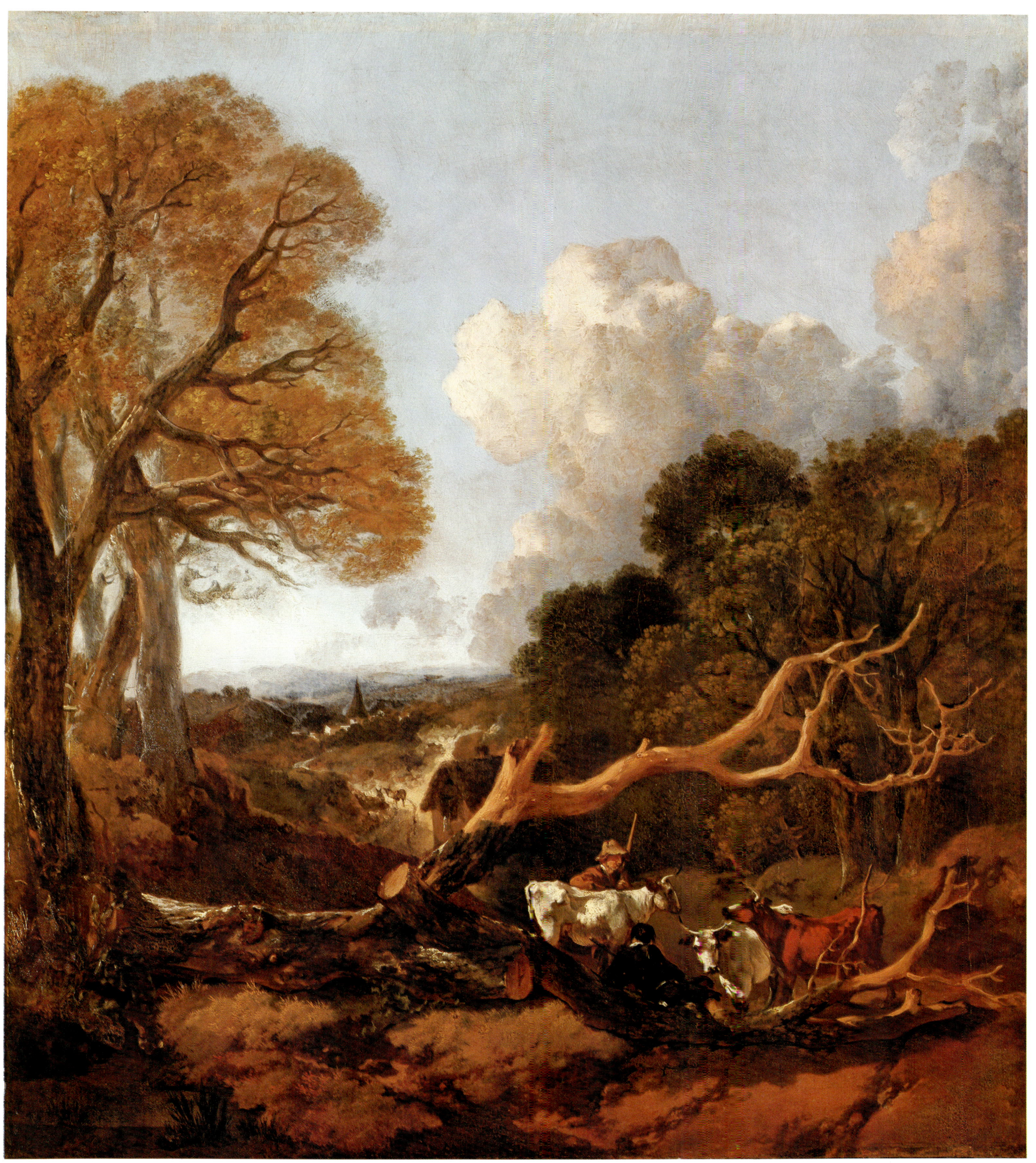

Pompeo Girolamo Batoni

ITALIAN (1708–1787)

Pope Benedict XIV Presenting in 1756 the Encyclical Ex Omnibus *to the Duke de Choiseul* (1757)

In the seventeenth and eighteenth centuries, the Catholic Church and the parliament of France disagreed about the interpretation of St. Augustine's teachings on the questions of free will and predeterminism, with opposing views held by the Jesuits and the Jansenists. At a time when matters of faith were taken much more seriously than they are today, this division brought France to the brink of civil war and threatened a rift between the papacy and the Gallic church. Under the papal bull *Uni Genitus*, Jansenists were condemned as heretics and were excommunicated.

Two of the greatest negotiators of the day met to solve the problem. Pope Benedict XIV was a man of moderation and sound sense—in Horace Walpole's words, ". . . a prince without favorites, a pope without nephews." The Duke de Choiseul acted as roving ambassador for Louis XV of France, serving in so many capacities and traveling so widely he became known as "the coachman of Europe." On October 16, 1756, Pope Benedict gave Choiseul a letter to deliver to the French bishops. It readmitted to the Church all Jansenists except those whose resistance to the bull had been "public and notorious." This compromise saved France from civil war.

Batoni, one of the greatest portraitists of his time, has depicted this historical event symbolically. The pope is seated on the throne of St. Peter and is flanked by Religion and Faith. St. Peter with his keys, and St. Paul with his sword, protectors of Rome, watch over the scene, the Holy Ghost between them. At the left, two *putti* hold the Sanctuary and the Triple Tiara. In the background is a view of St. Peter's Basilica. The style is clearly baroque, in all its magnificence, but the formal composition, the idealization of the subject matter and its solemn, powerful presentation herald in this work the beginnings of the neoclassical movement in French painting.

Oil on linen 50¾ x 70½" (129 x 179 cm)
The William Hood Dunwoody Fund, 1961

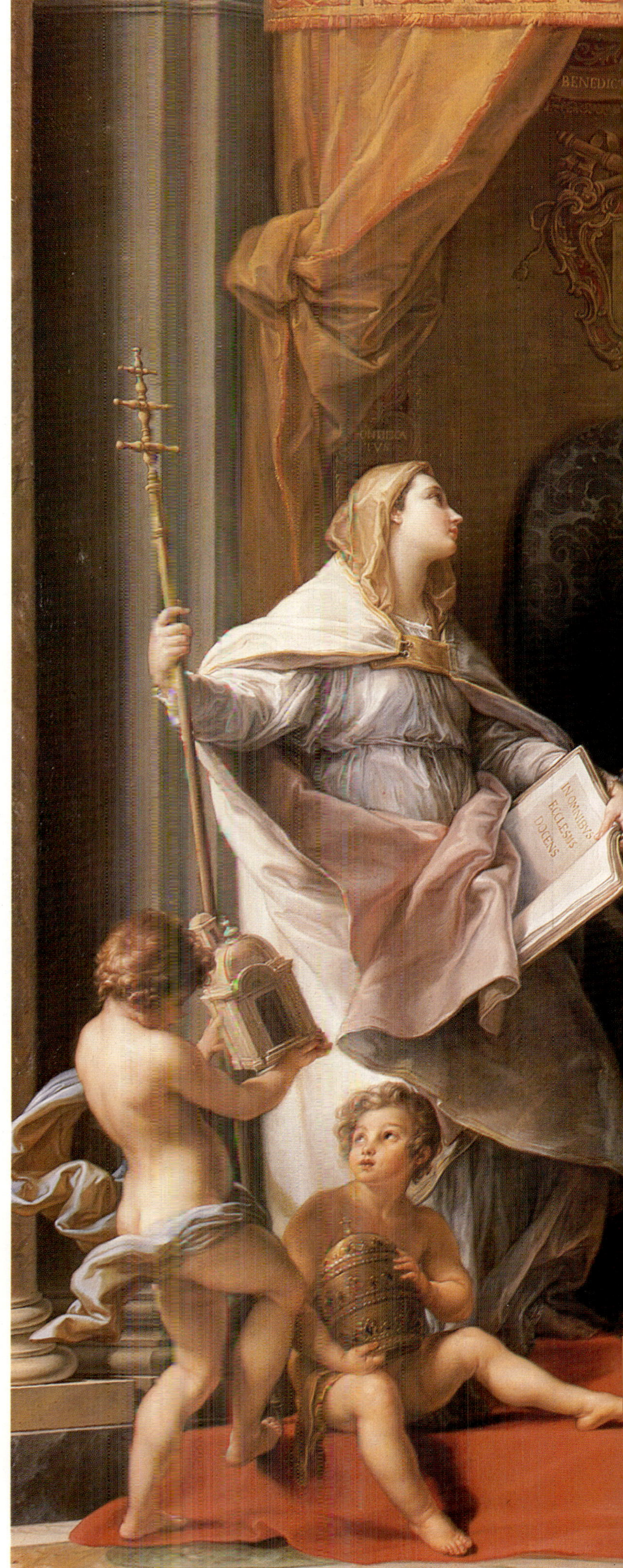

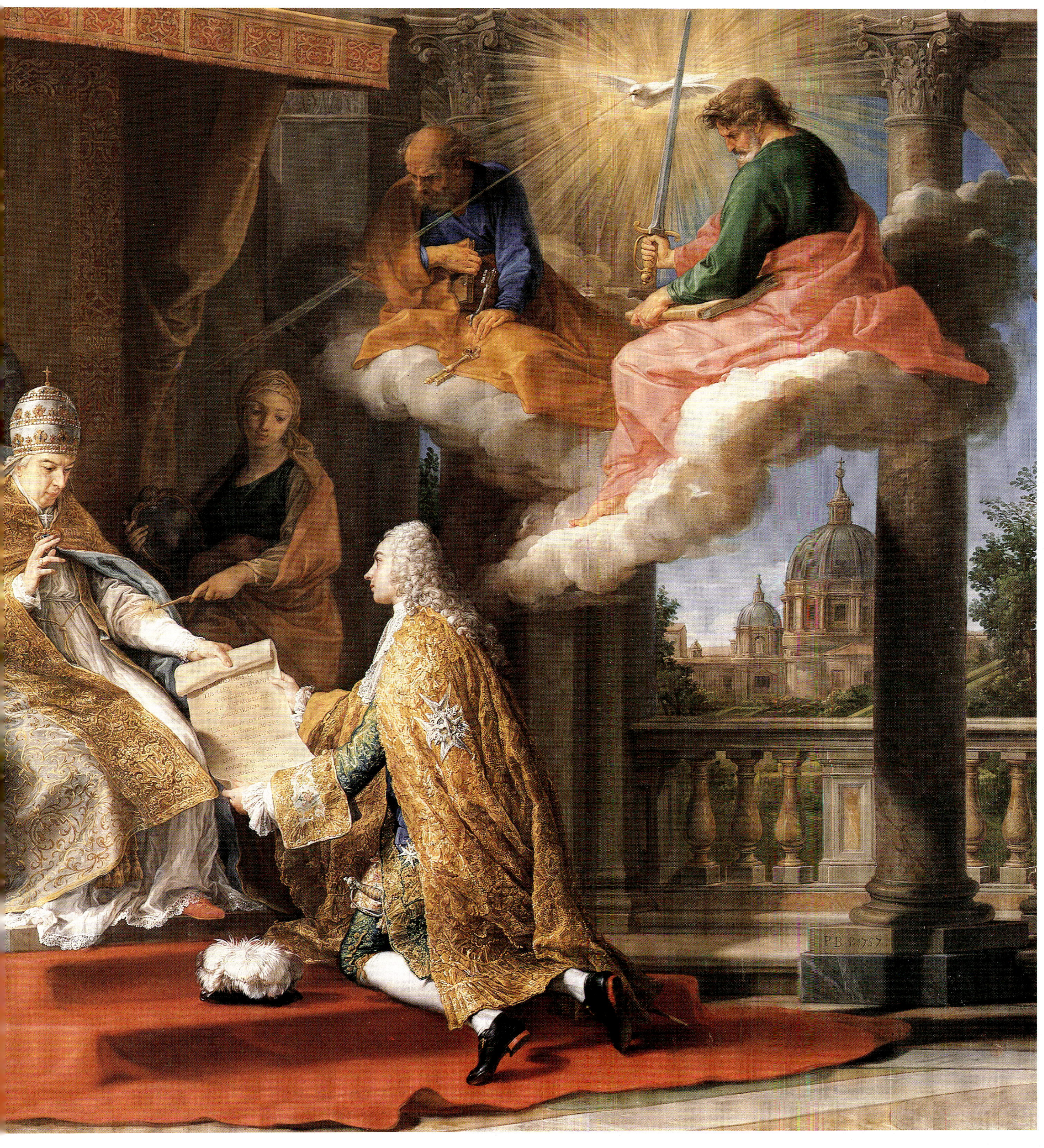
ANNO
XVII
P.B.P.1757.

Pierre-Paul Prud'hon

FRENCH (1758–1823)

The Union of Love and Friendship (ca. 1793)

Prud'hon's life coincided almost exactly with the great age of French neoclassicism, and he himself was one of its most able exponents. Reacting against rococo frivolity, the neoclassicists sought to regain the noble simplicity and quiet grandeur of the art of ancient Greece and Rome. Art, they felt, should portray the ideal, not just physically but morally, ethically, and spiritually as well. Prud'hon excelled at combining intellectual concept with classical composition. Here, the union of Love and Friendship is symbolized by the winged Eros and his mortal love, Psyche. In the background, a little cupid or *amoretto* plays with Eros' quiver of arrows while Eros himself holds another of his attributes, the burning torch that signifies love.

The torch contrasts dramatically with the icy, sculptural coldness of the young boy's flesh, its marblelike quality suggesting the immortality of sculpture, and echoes the warmer tones of the girl's body, mortal but glowing with life. In fact, it has been suggested that this work is also an allegory representing Painting and Sculpture.

Prud'hon studied and worked in Rome until he was nearly thirty, and the influences of the great Italian romantic visionaries such as Correggio and Leonardo are evident in this, his first major commission after his return to Paris.

Oil on fabric 57½ x 44½" (146 x 113 cm)

The William Hood Dunwoody and John R. Van Derlip Funds, 1964

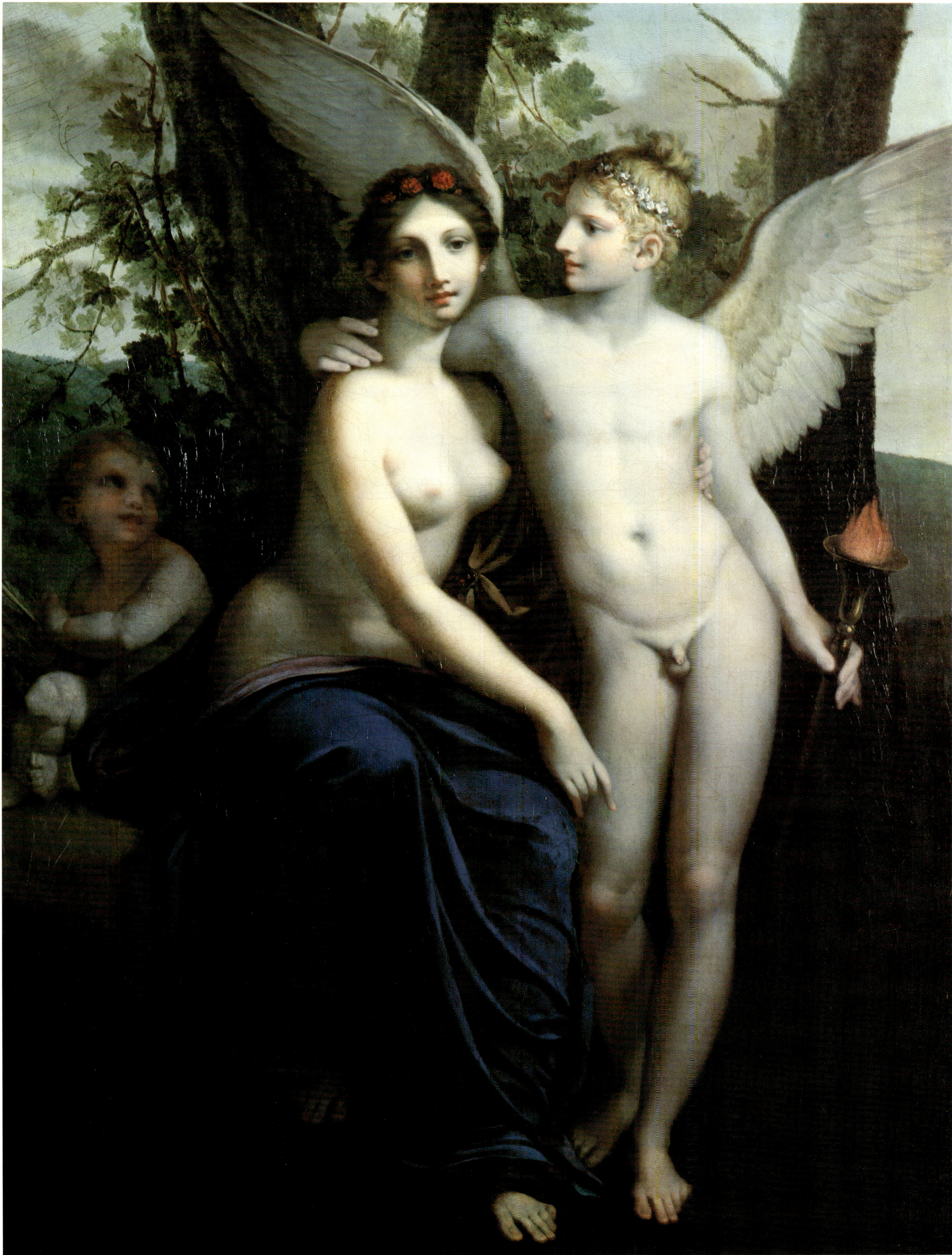

Anne-Louis Girodet de Roucy Trioson

FRENCH (1767–1824)

Portrait of Mlle Lange as Danaë (1799)

At first glance, this is a charming if somewhat mannered portrait of a lady. It is only on closer examination that one realizes that it is also a subtle and devastating act of revenge.

Danaë was one of the many ladies pursued by Zeus; she fell victim to his charms when he appeared in the guise of a shower of gold. Mlle Lange was a well-known Parisian actress and, for a while, Girodet's mistress. However, a certain banker appeared on the scene, presumably ready to shower her with gold, and La Lange apparently chose to devote her life to comfort rather than to art.

In this portrait of his erstwhile love, Girodet's bitterness is fully unleashed. Allusions to her fickle, avaricious, and self-centered nature abound. The mirror she holds in her right hand is cracked. Peacock feathers, symbols of empty pride, not only adorn her Medusa-like hair but are also being stuffed by an enthusiastic cherub into the tail of a turkey, the symbol of cuckoldry. By her side, the dove of fidelity lies wounded by the shower of gold; near her feet, the actor's mask is blinkered by a gold coin.

Girodet was evidently not a man to be jilted lightly. When this painting was completed he entered it in the Salon of 1799 for all the world to see. Mlle Lange had to institute a public law suit to have it removed from view.

Oil on canvas 25½ x 21¼" (65 x 54 cm)

The William Hood Dunwoody Fund, 1969

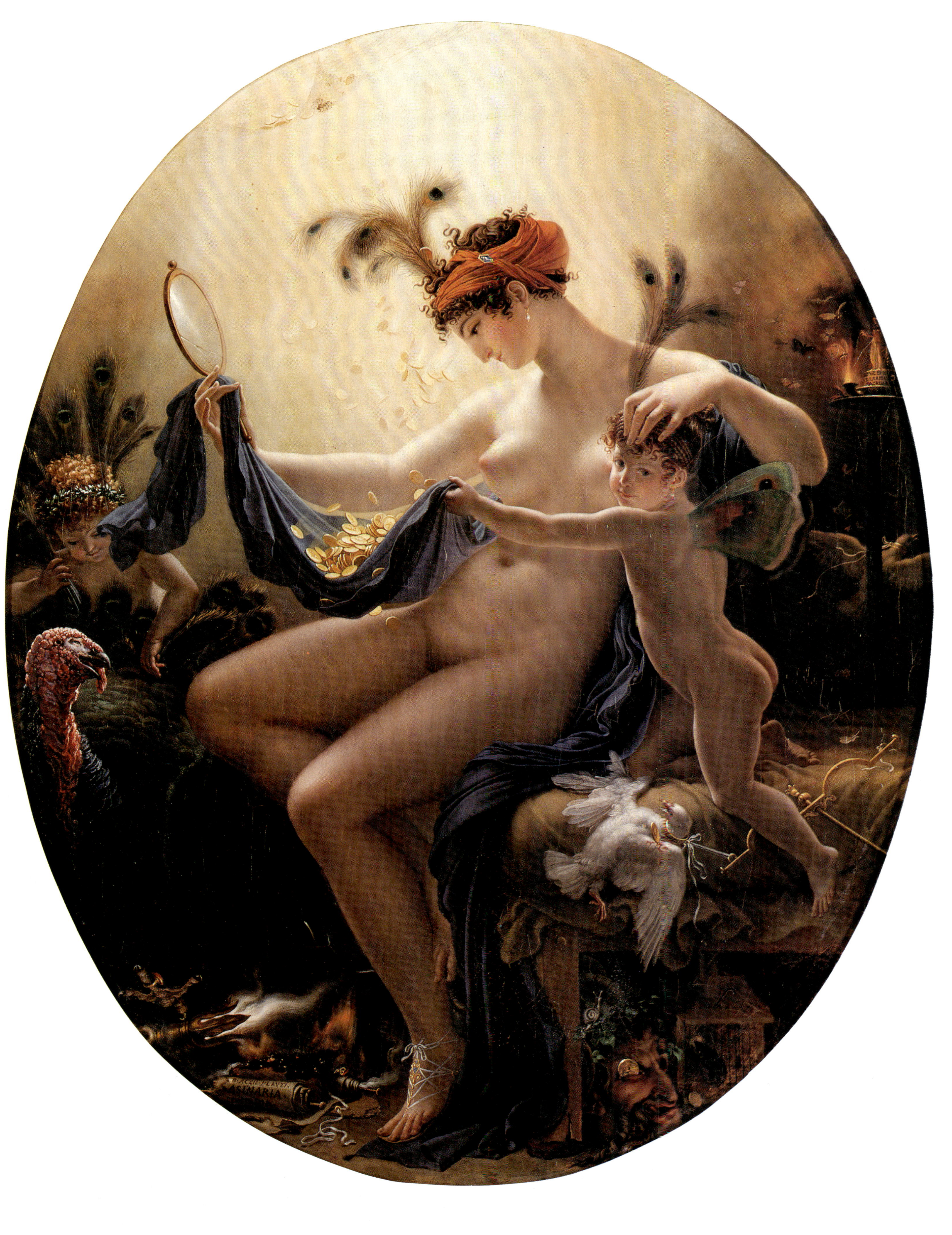
ACCII PLAVTI
ASINARIA

Francisco José de Goya y Lucientes

SPANISH (1746–1828)

Self-Portrait with Doctor Arrieta (1820)

Goya, the first of the modern artists, fell dangerously ill in 1819. In the course of his sickness he was to suffer the loss of his hearing. Nevertheless, on recovery, he felt a great debt of gratitude to his doctor who had attended him throughout.

Here, Goya eulogises Dr. Arrieta. The inscription at the bottom reads: *Goya thanks his friend Arrieta for the sureness and care with which he saved his life from the serious and dangerous illness at the end of the year 1819 at the age of seventy-three. Painted in 1820.*

The painting was a gift to the doctor, shown here holding a glass of what seems to be particularly vile medicine while Goya clutches weakly at the bedclothes. The shadowy, almost hallucinatory figures in the background may be a priest, Goya's housekeeper, and Death. They presage the macabre red-and-black paintings of his later years.

Oil on canvas 45½ x 31" (116 x 79 cm)

The Ethel Morrison Van Derlip Fund, 1952

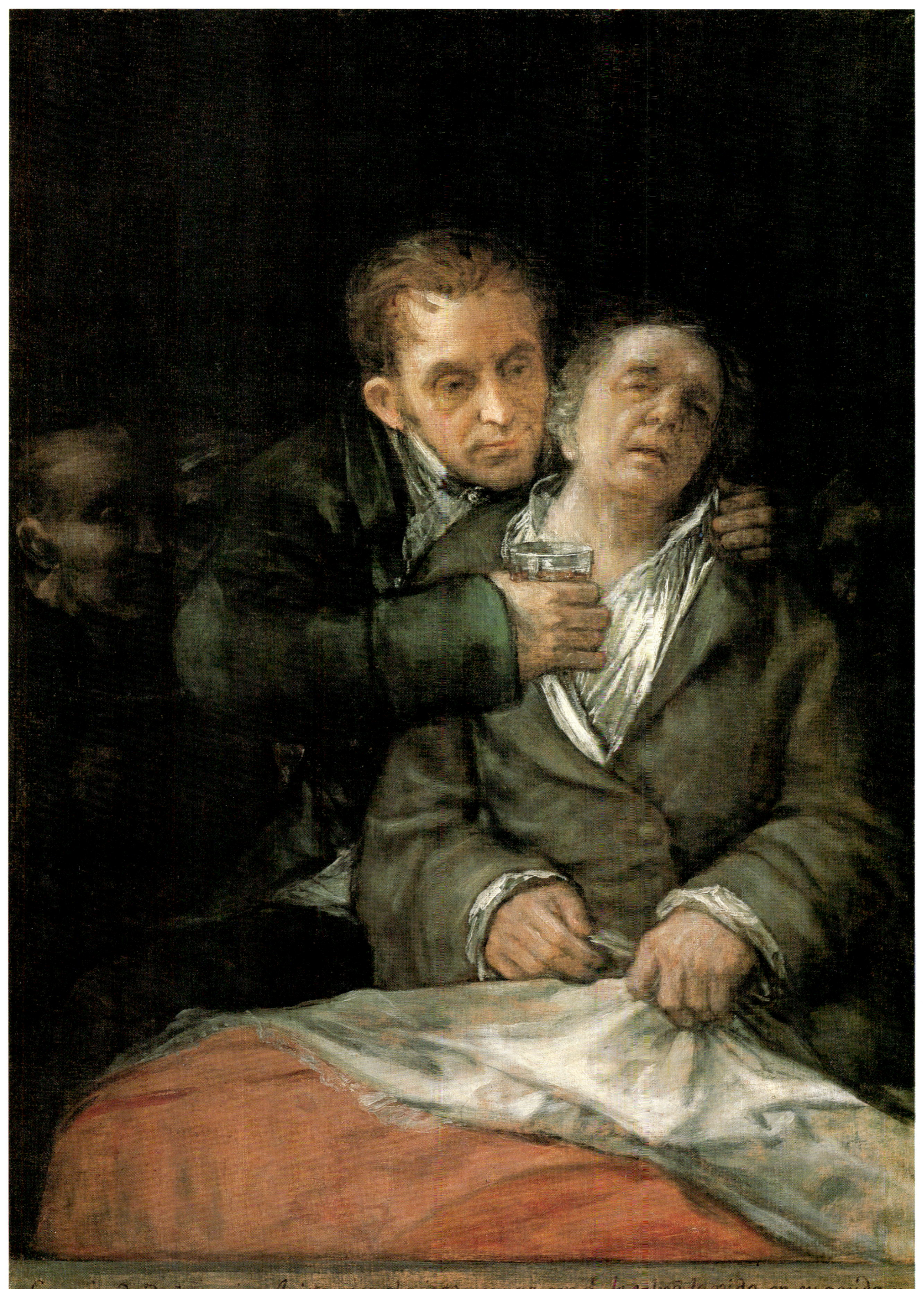
Goya agradecido, á su amigo Arrieta: por el acierto y esmero con q. le salvó la vida en su aguda y
peligrosa enfermedad, padecida á fines del año 1819. a los setenta y tres de su edad. Lo pintó en 1820.

Ferdinand-Victor Eugène Delacroix

FRENCH (1798–1863)

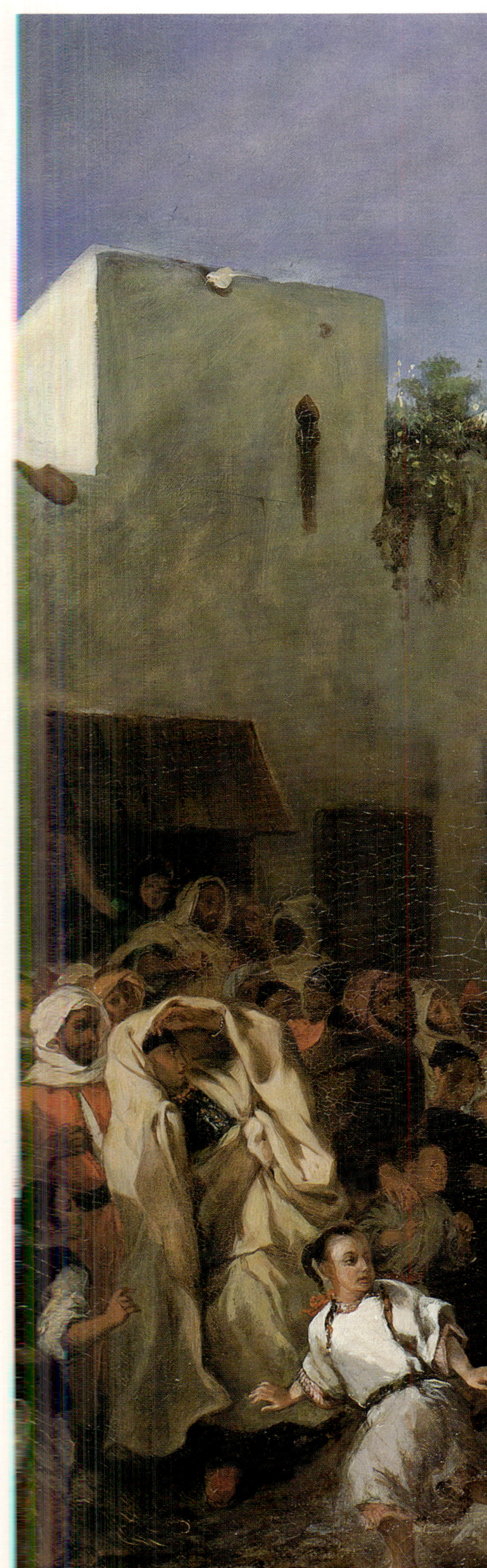

The Fanatics of Tangiers (1838)

In the period of disillusionment following the unfulfilled promises of the Revolution, French popular fancy turned readily from the mundane to the exotic. In the 1830s, travel outside Europe was still slow, difficult, and often dangerous. To the French, in those days predating jet planes and the *National Geographic*, Algiers was another world.

The so-called "Fanatics" of Tangiers were a Muslim sect who periodically aroused themselves to a hysterical religious frenzy, then swept through the city in a torrent of uncontrolled violence. It was forbidden for foreigners to witness this ceremony and Delacroix had to hide, peering through the cracks of a shuttered window, as he watched this awesome scene.

To nineteenth-century Paris, this painting was a complete revelation. Painted with all the vigor and mastery at his command, it represents one of the triumphs of Delacroix's oeuvre.

Oil on canvas 38½ x 51½" (98 x 131 cm)
Bequest of Mr. J. Jerome Hill, 1973

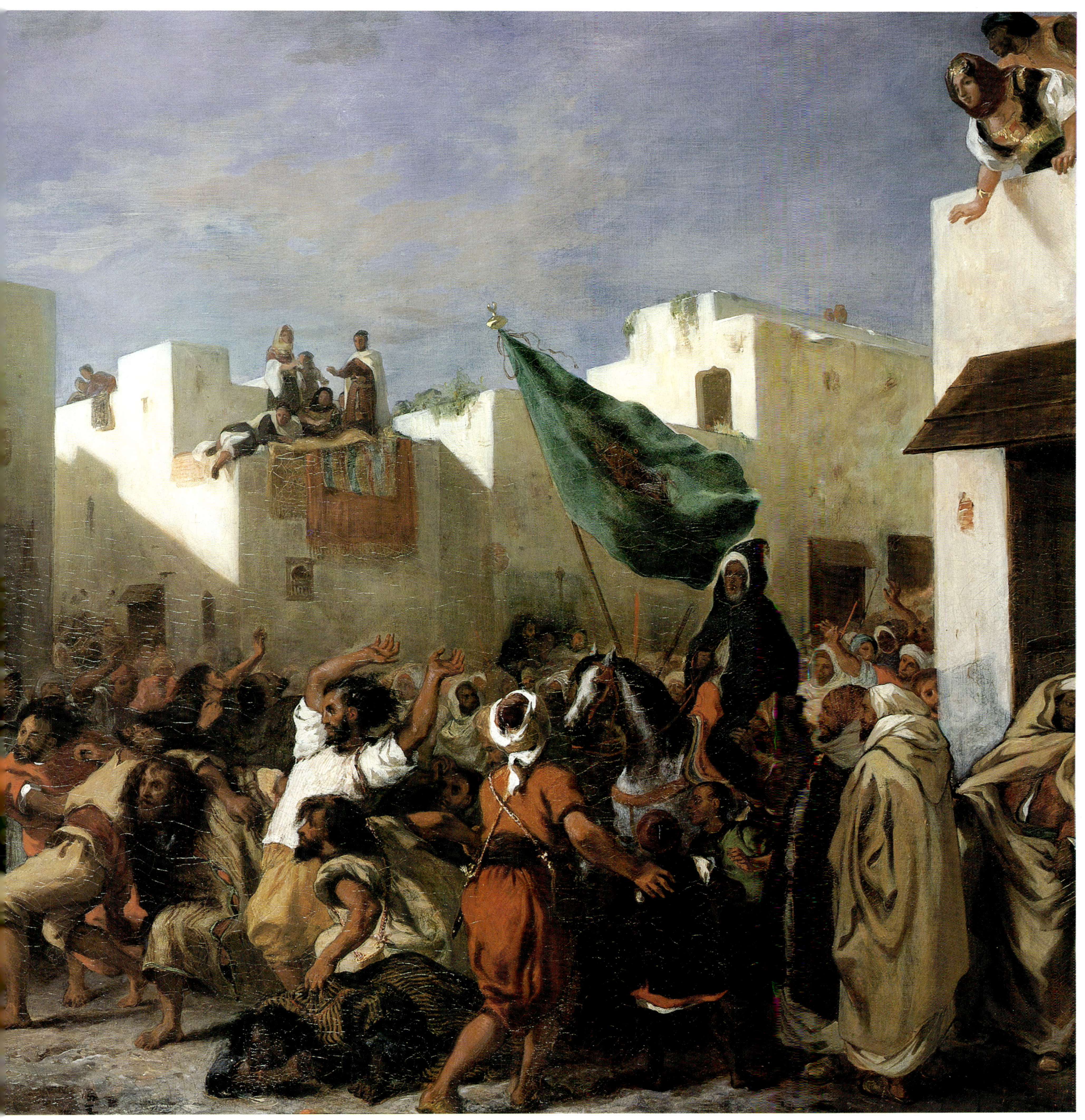

Jasper F. Cropsey

AMERICAN (1823–1900)

Catskill Mountain House (1855)

This glorious view across a desolate woodland depicts a once-famous hotel on the Hudson River. Catskill Mountain House was one of America's first holiday resorts, built at a time when the young nation was discovering the beauties of its landscapes, guided, as usual, by the eyes of its artists.

This is the Hudson River school of painting, its colors as bright and robust as the country itself, and Cropsey's exuberance is well suited to this splendid fall afternoon. For perhaps the first time, we are seeing *America*. Cropsey's contemporaries frequently painted the American scene through European eyes, regimenting the wilderness into carefully landscaped estates with hardly a twig out of place. This is the New World—a seemingly endless expanse, with a beauty entirely its own.

Oil on canvas 29 x 44" (74 x 112 cm)

Bequest of Mrs. Lillian Lawhead Rinderer in memory of her brother, William A. Lawhead; the William Hood Dunwoody Fund, 1931

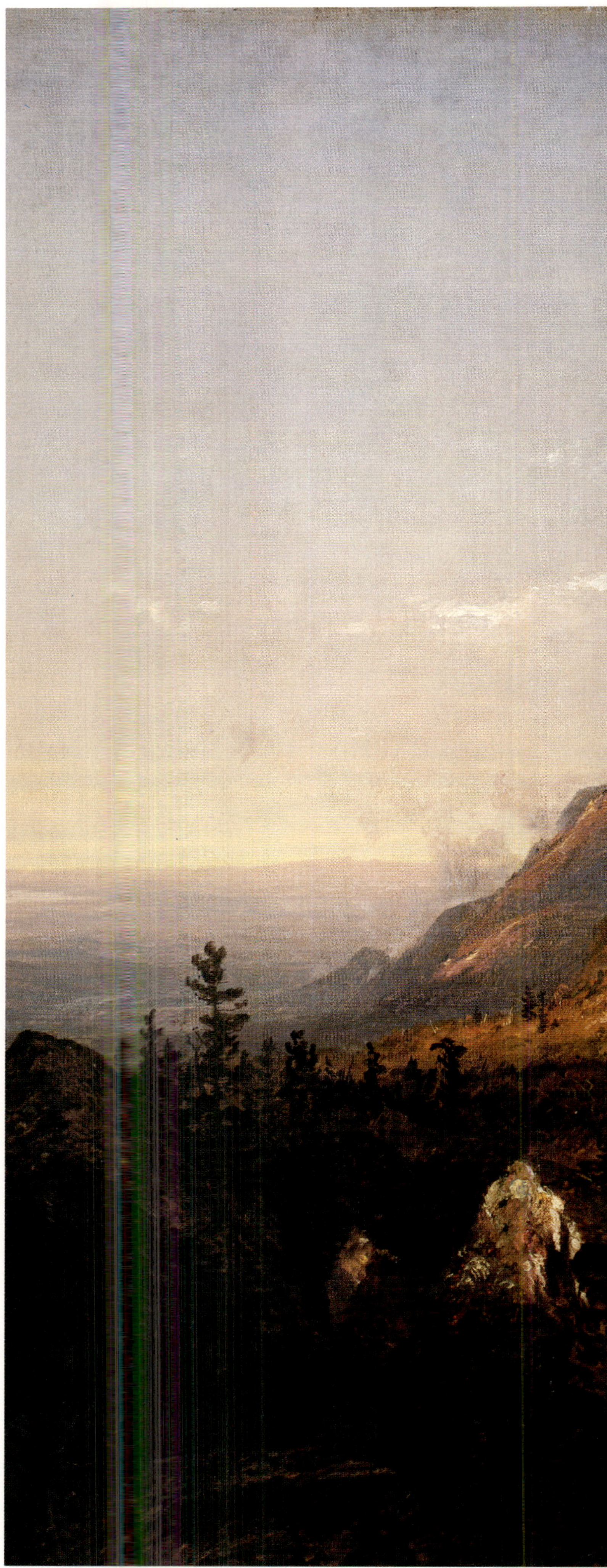

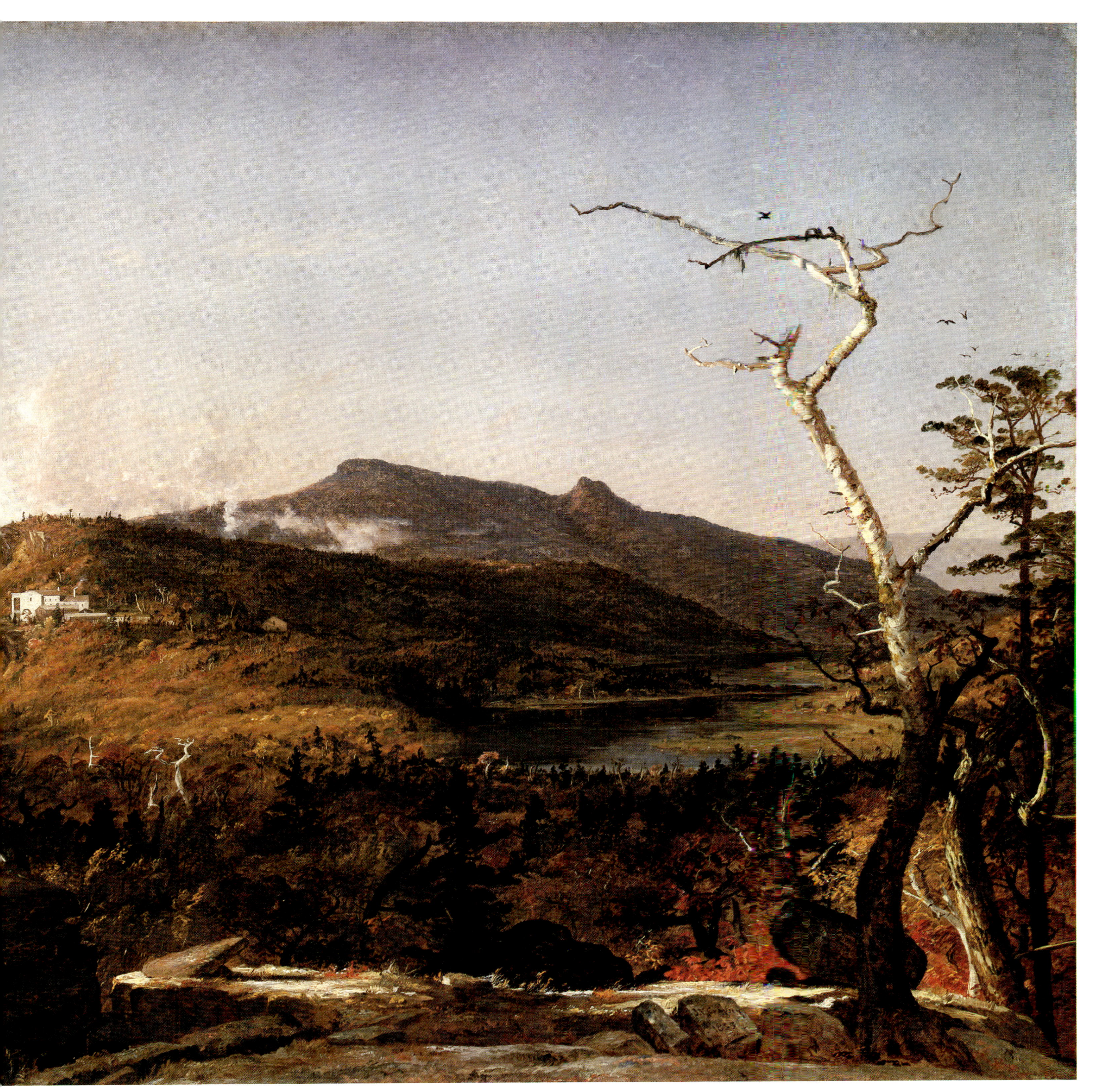

Sir John Everett Millais

ENGLISH (1829–1896)

Peace Concluded (1856)

Millais painted this picture in celebration of the end of the Crimean War. The central figures include the artist's new wife, Effie, his close friend, Colonel Malcolm Paton, and his pet wolfhound, Roswell. The joys of peace are clearly extolled in this scene of Victorian domesticity; the wounded soldier is shown returned to his home and family.

It is a miraculously detailed work, filled with small allegories—the British lion, the Russian bear, the dove of peace, the olive tree—even the London *Times*. John Ruskin, Effie's first husband and one of the foremost art critics of the day, proclaimed in a most expansive gesture that this painting should be ranked "among the world's best masterpieces."

Millais, with Hunt and Rossetti, founded the Pre-Raphaelite movement in 1848, but his interest in the movement was short-lived; eight years later we find works like this one marking a return to the much more marketable narrative style, which was to bring him wealth, a title, and ultimately, the presidency of the Royal Academy.

Oil on canvas 46¼ x 36" (117 x 91 cm)

The Putnam Dana McMillan Fund, 1969

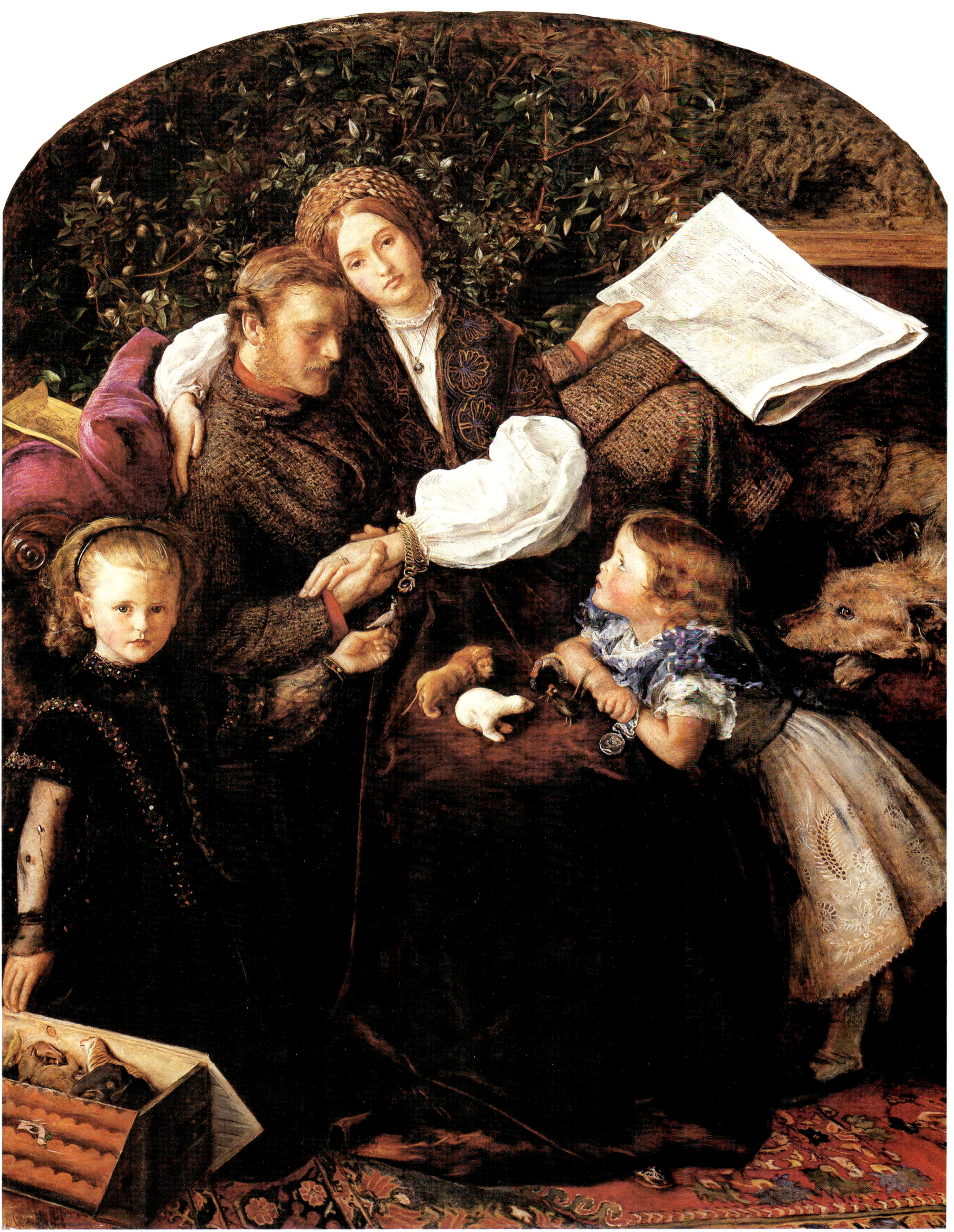

Severin Roesen

AMERICAN (?–1871)

Still Life with Fruit

America in the nineteenth century was in many ways similar to Europe in the seventeenth: There was an increasing demand for paintings that would serve the purposes of decoration as opposed to those of religion or politics, and the rise of a wealthy middle class produced a ready market for works extolling leisure, accomplishment, and natural beauty. Roesen, an immigrant from Germany where he had trained as a porcelain painter, worked in his early years in a manner reminiscent of the Dutch painters van Huysum and van Os, but later he developed a more personal style.

His work here is quite American in its austerity and comes close to that of Raphael Peale. In this carefully organized work, Roesen follows a tradition begun in the United States in the early 1800s, which equates beauty with harmony and order. He has proudly displayed his signature in the lower left corner, formed, as if by nature, from a spiraling grape tendril.

Oil on canvas 21½ x 26¼" (55 x 67 cm)

The William Hood Dunwoody Fund, 1969

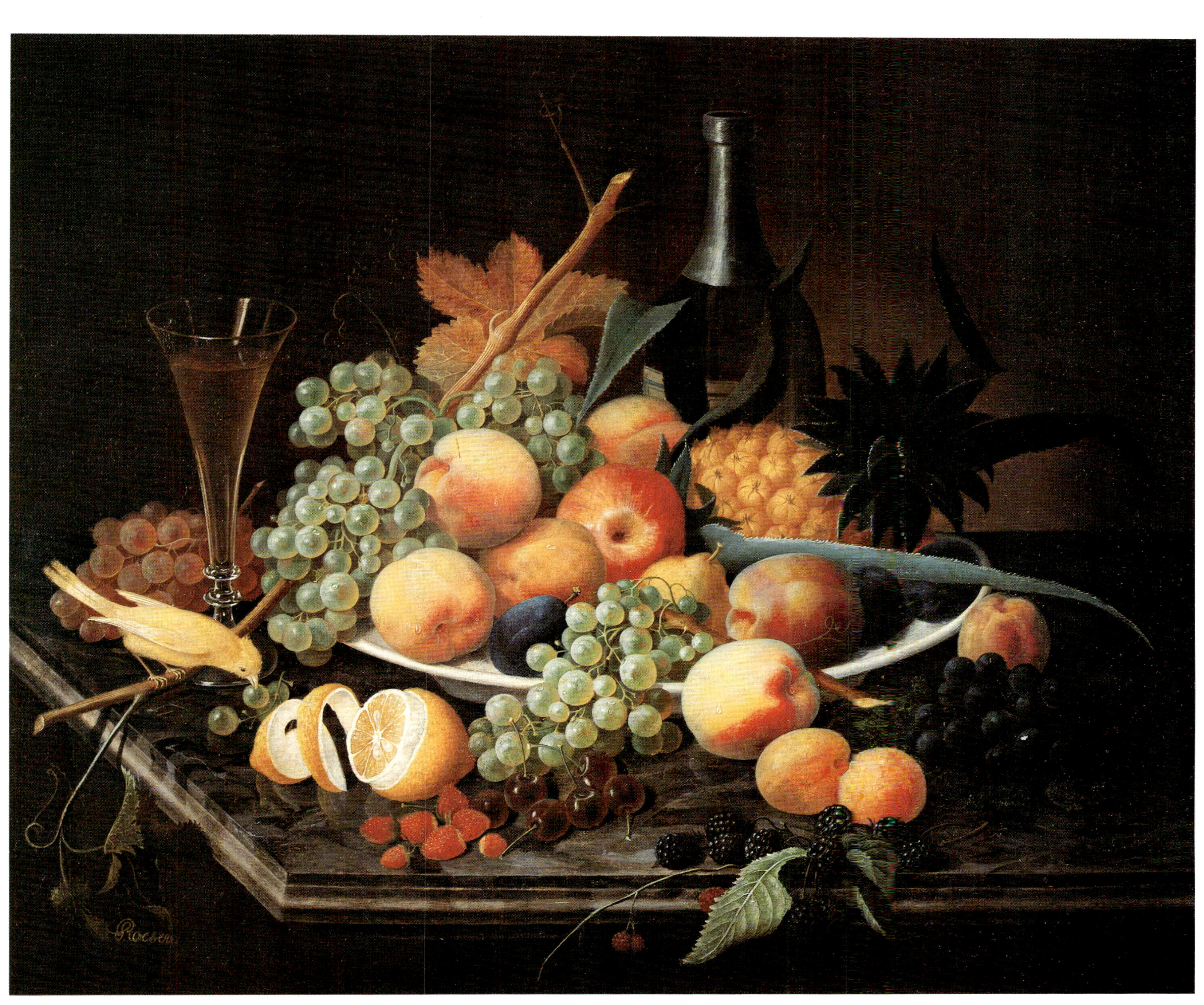
Roesen

Edouard Manet

FRENCH (1832–1883)

The Smoker (1866)

Manet's early training was with the painter Thomas Couture, but before he reached thirty he reacted strongly against the academic tradition and developed his own style, largely influenced by his studies of Spanish painting. His palette became very restricted, and his early work in this new style is characterized by stark contrasts of light and shade. *The Smoker* is typical; its dark values and neutral hues are relieved only by the small patch of blue cloth.

The subject is presented with great solidity in a very shallow space, its somberness barely lightened by the sketchily defined wisps of smoke trailing from the smoker's pipe. The strong value contrasts and the two-dimensionality of this work mark it as undeniably modern. However, Manet's evident affinity for such Spanish artists as Goya and Velásquez gives this painting an old-master quality that clearly places it at the transition between traditional and modern art.

Oil on canvas 39½ x 32 (100 x 81 cm)
Gift of Mr. and Mrs. Bruce B. Dayton, 1968

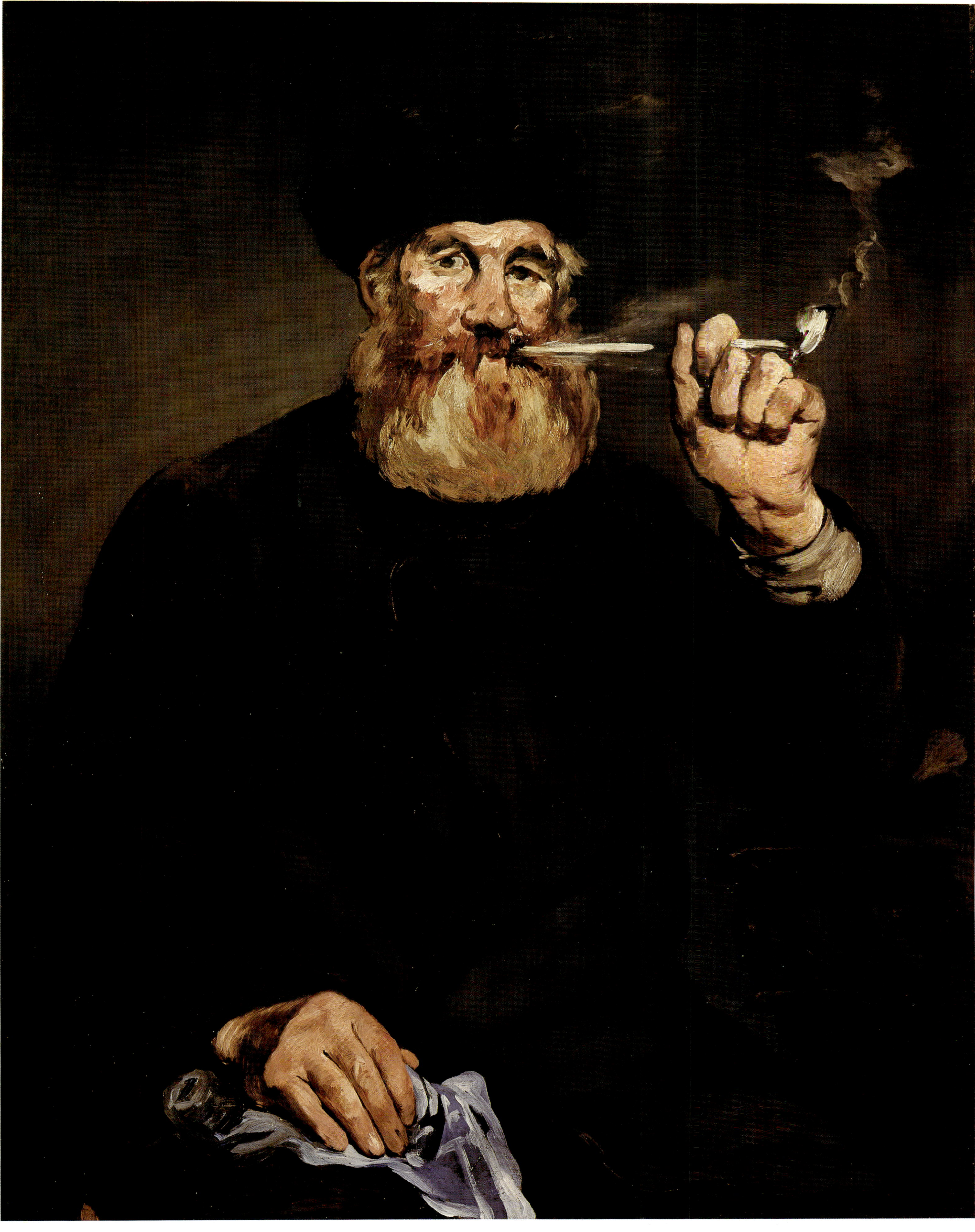

Edgar Degas

FRENCH (1834–1917)

Mlle Hortense Valpinçon (1871)

In the Institute's collection is another painting by Degas, a portrait of Paul Valpinçon, this young lady's father. The two families were very close and Degas portrayed this impish little girl while he was a guest at the Valpinçons' summer home in Orne. The capricious, off-center composition lends great intimacy to this charming portrait. The multiplicity of detail in the background and in the fabrics to the left focus attention on the simplicity of the gown and on the young girl's face.

Degas was one of the first painters to respond to the rapidly developing science of photography, and the sense of uncontrived (although carefully calculated) immediacy in this work clearly shows a photographic influence. It shows another influence, too: Degas' interest in the Japanese print, with its asymmetric composition and brilliant color patterns.

Hortense was an active child, and the story is told that Degas would give her an apple cut into pieces if she would sit still while he painted. Here, he catches her as she is about to consume the last morsel before dashing out of this intensely rewarding "snapshot." The friendship between Degas and Hortense was lifelong, and in his old age, it was Hortense who took care of him.

Oil on fabric 29¾ x 44¾" (76 x 114 cm)
The John R. Van Derlip Fund, 1948

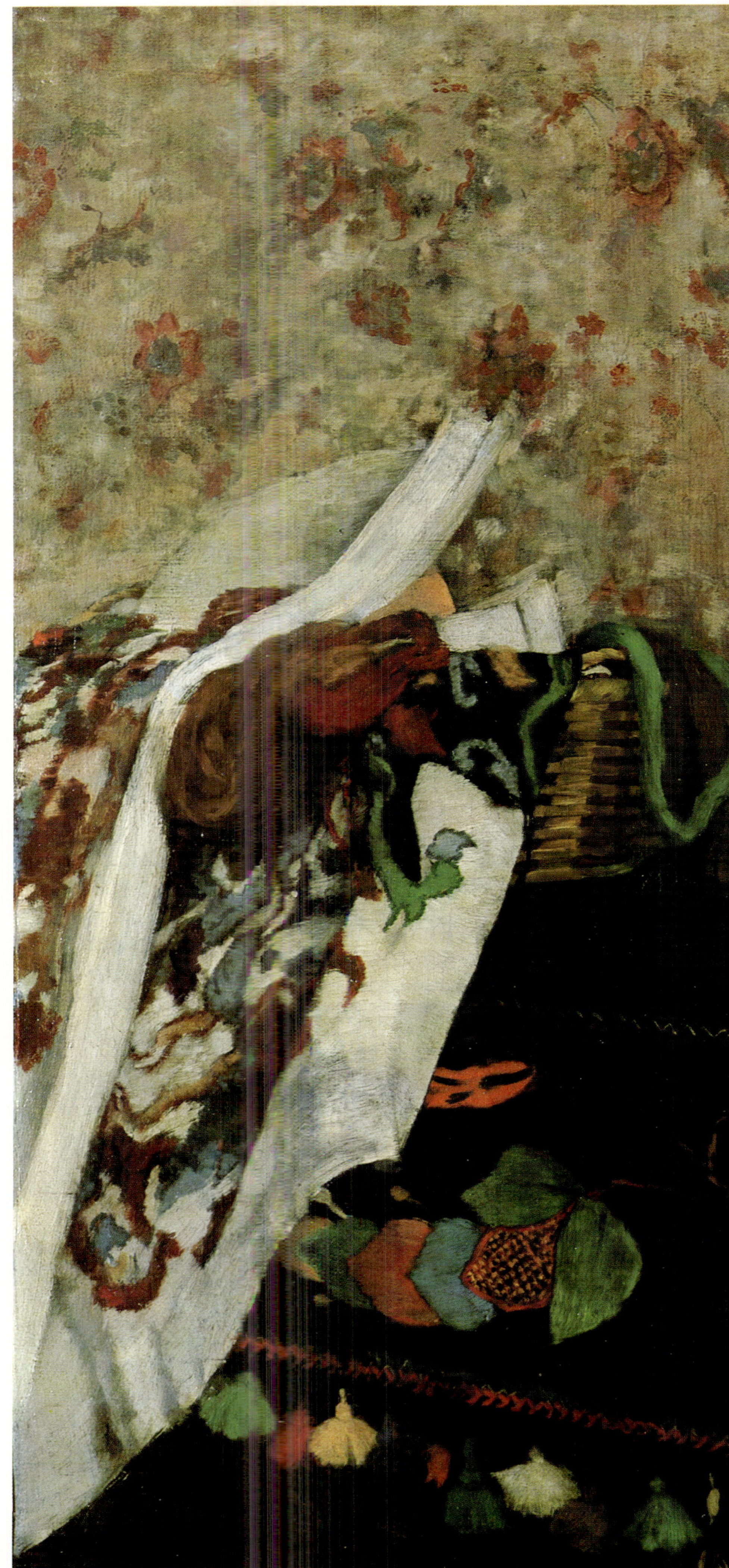

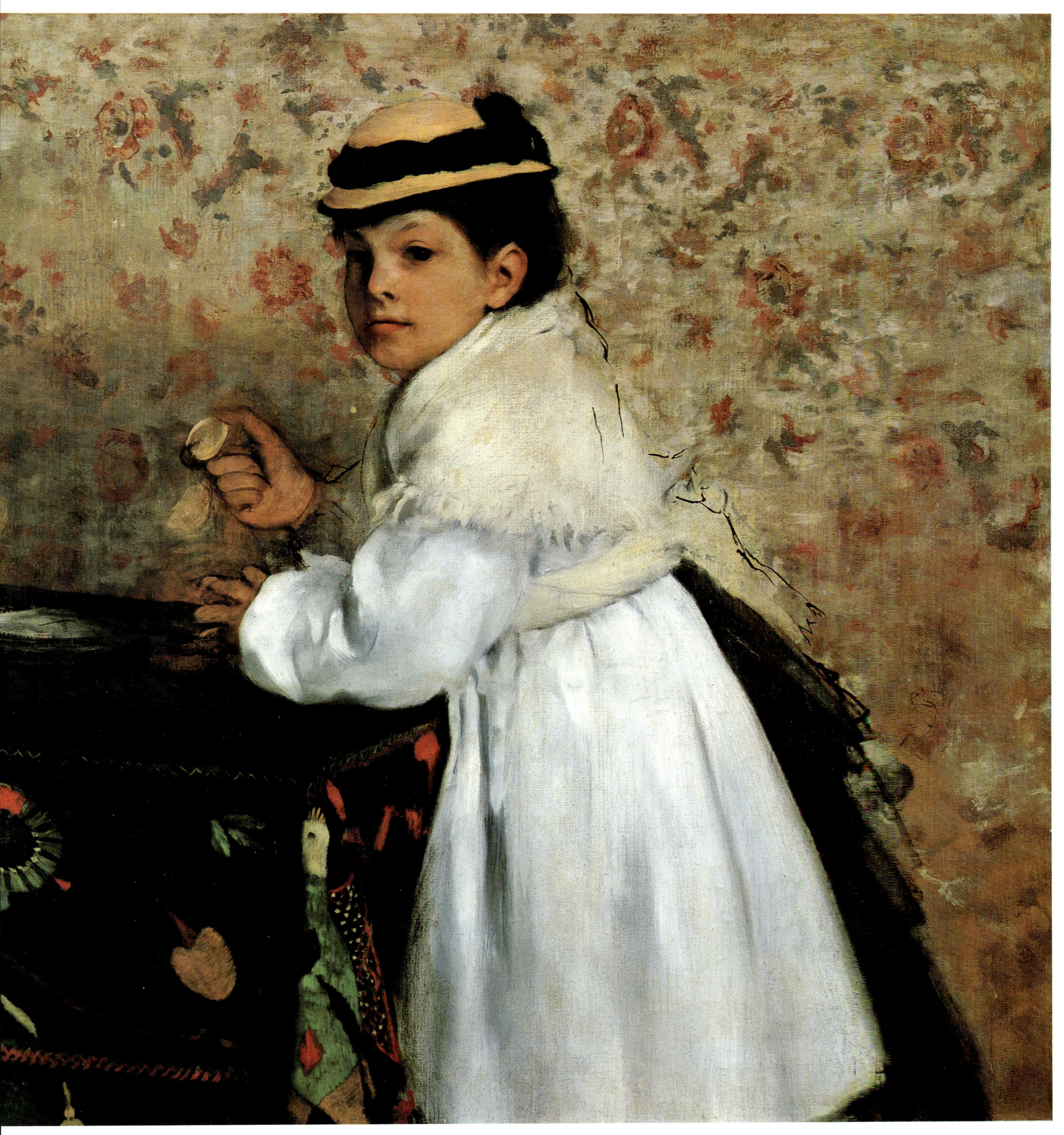

John Singer Sargent

AMERICAN (1856–1925)

Luxembourg Gardens at Twilight (1879)

John Singer Sargent was born of American parents in Italy and spent his youth traveling with his peripatetic family throughout Europe. His father was a doctor and his mother a woman of some inheritance. It was at her instigation that the family had moved to Europe, and she decided that the young Sargent should study art there. It was not until 1876 that he visited the United States for the first time. Much of the painting of his early years was done on the Continent, and he was especially fond of Paris.

This glorious and poetic vision of the Luxembourg Gardens is a tribute to the young artist's abilities as a draftsman and to his appreciation of the teachings of impressionism. It is dedicated to his friend Charles Follen McKim, also a member of the rich American expatriate society in late nineteenth-century Europe and, later, one of the partners in the architectural firm of McKim, Mead, and White, which designed The Minneapolis Institute of Arts. Better known for his society portraits, the work reveals the romantic side of Sargent's nature. The soft tones, the deep, warm space, the rising moon and the gently strolling couple all make for a wistful souvenir of one of the world's most beautiful cities.

Oil on canvas 29 x 36½" (74 x 93 cm)

Gift of the Martin B. Koon Memorial Collection, 1916

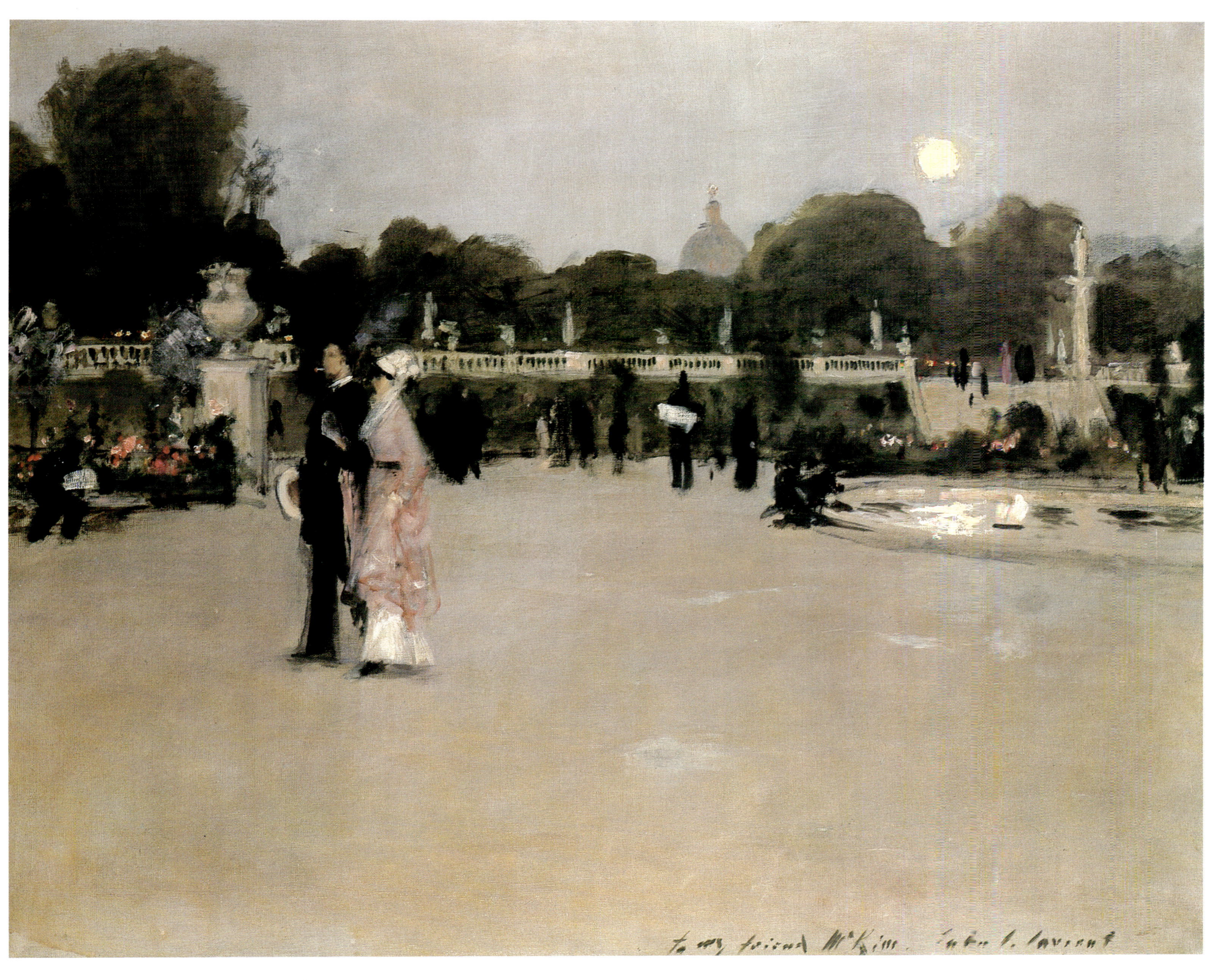

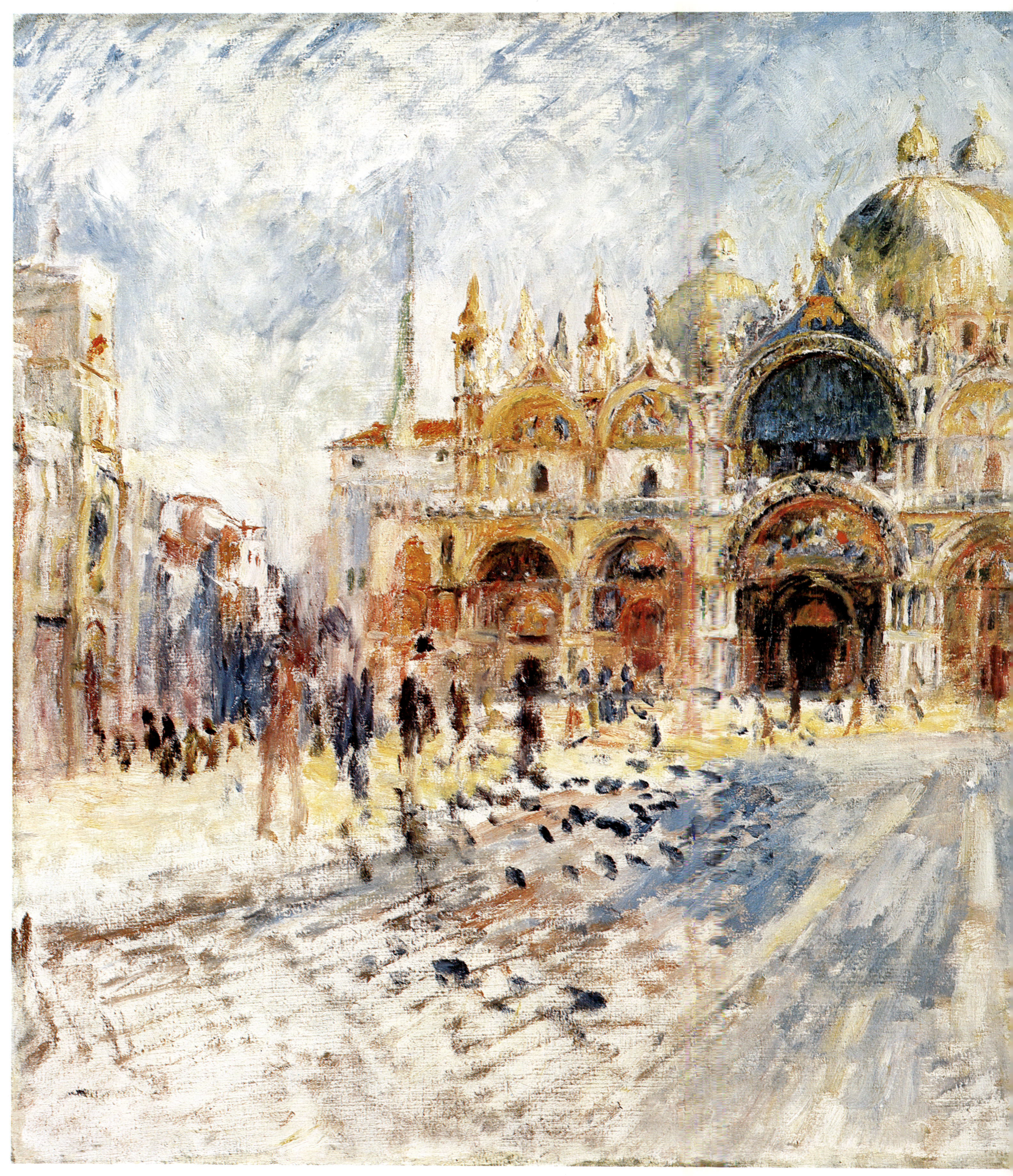

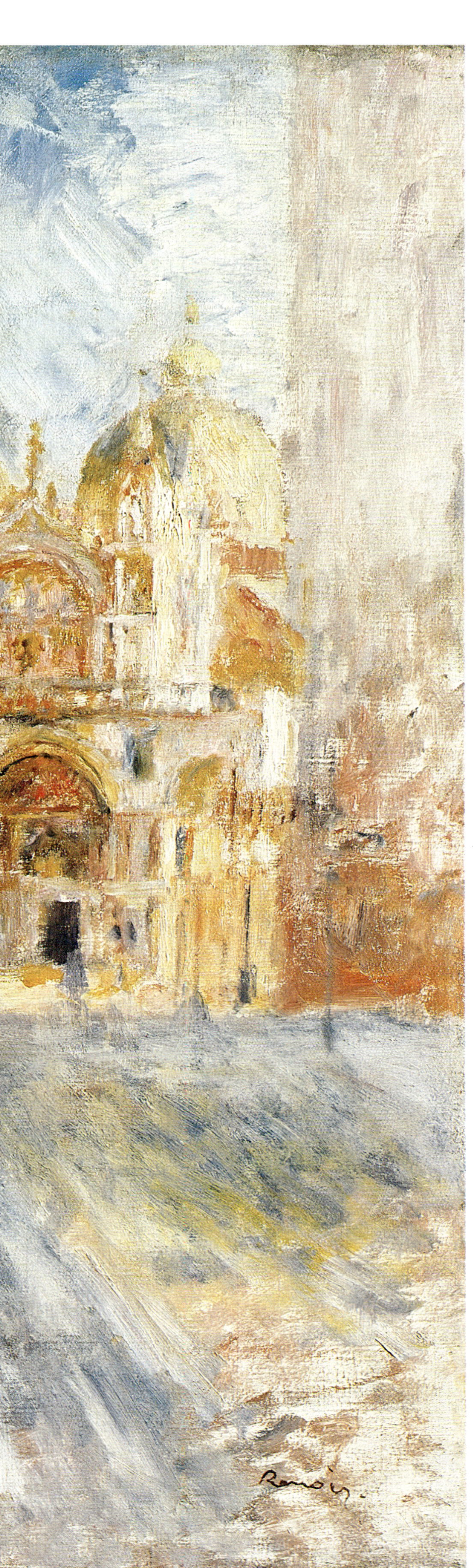

Pierre-Auguste Renoir

FRENCH (1841–1919)

San Marco, Venice (ca. 1881)

At the age of thirteen, Renoir started work as a porcelain painter for the Limoges factory. This early experience, coupled perhaps with his special fondness for the works of the rococo artists Boucher, Fragonard, and Watteau, is seen in his palette of strong colors interspersed with delicate pastel tints.

Renoir was basically a simple man who found great joy in life and responded readily to elegance, gaiety, and glitter wherever it might be found. Here, in the Byzantine glory of the cathedral of San Marco, he was in his element. His colors echo those earlier Venetians, Titian and Bellini, whose palettes captured so brilliantly the special qualities of the light of this city of water, sky, and spectacle. He had traveled to Venice to paint a portrait of Richard Wagner. The composer arrived several days late and Renoir whiled away the time with this painting. The sharp and sparkling light, and the quality of unpremeditated immediacy make this work one of the most truly impressionistic masterpieces of this master of impressionism.

Oil on linen 25 x 32" (64 x 81 cm)

The John R. Van Derlip Fund, 1951

Paul Cézanne

FRENCH (1839–1906)

Chestnut Trees at the Jas de Bouffan (ca. 1885/87)

In their eagerness to capture space, light, and atmosphere, the impressionists tended to neglect solidity and volumetric composition. It was to these traits that Cézanne wished to return in order "to make of impressionism something solid and durable like the art of the museums." He once mused that every natural form could be reduced to a cube, a cone, or a cylinder. Years later, it was this idea which provided the foundation of cubism.

Here in a landscape showing the distant Mont Sainte-Victoire, painted from the grounds of his father's home, Cézanne has created a masterpiece of stability and order from a stark and somewhat awesome winter scene. With sure hand and agile brush, he reduces a profusion of detail to its basic elements, its forms and planes clearly and carefully defined, its structure and composition almost mathematically plotted. But for all his painfully worked-out theory, there is nothing artificial or contrived in this work; Cézanne's statements have a directness and immediacy which always belie the labor of their creation.

Oil on linen 29 x 36½" (74 x 93 cm)

The William Hood Dunwoody Fund, 1949

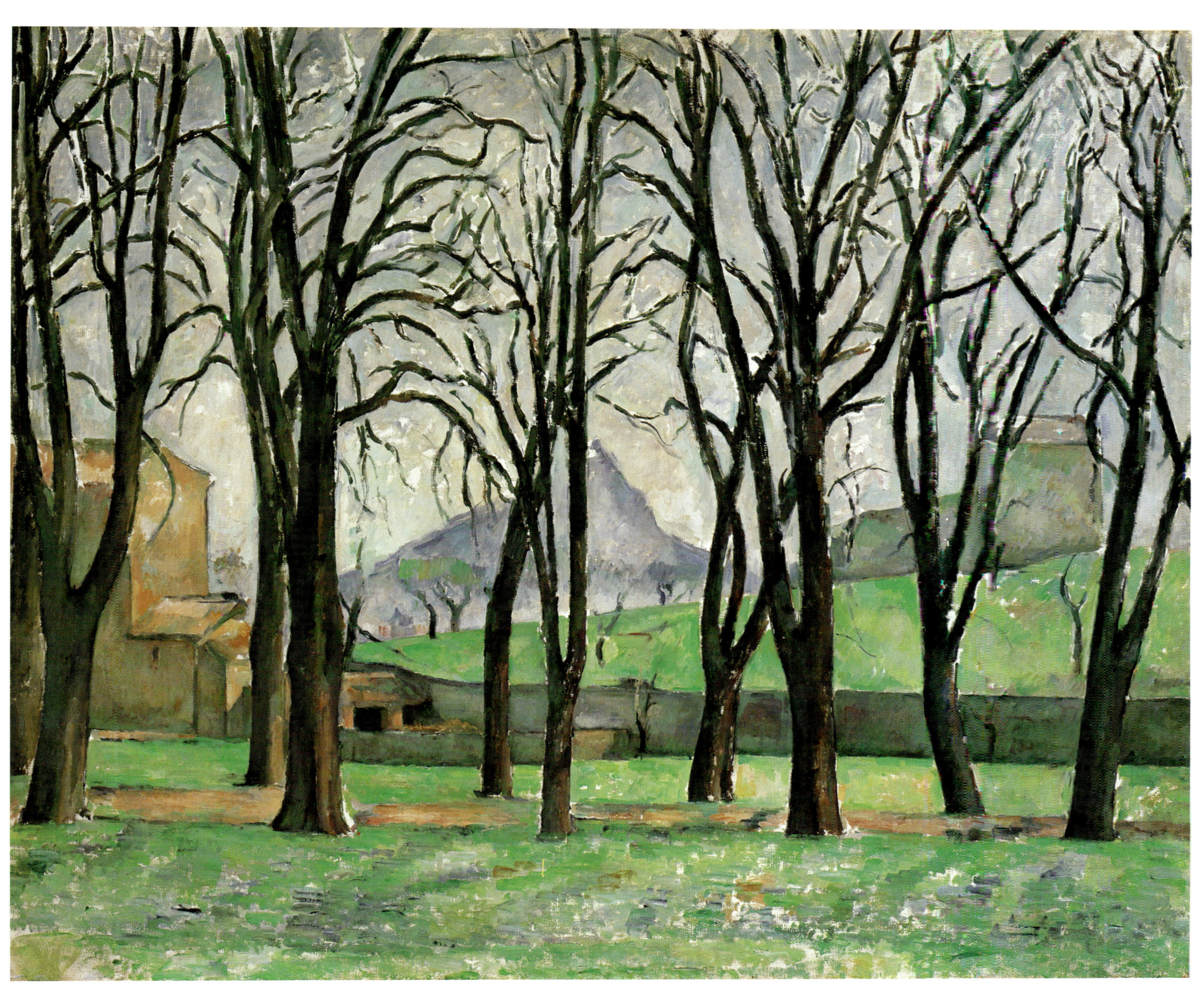

Jean-Léon Gérôme

FRENCH (1824–1904)

The Rug Merchants (1887)

Like Delacroix, Gérôme was attracted by the exoticism of North Africa and the Near East. This particular scene is an almost photographic rendition of an actual rug market in Cairo, remembered from his travels in Egypt in 1875. Even after a lapse of twelve years Gérôme's memory proved remarkably accurate; travelers report that, until recent times, the scene remained almost unchanged from that depicted here.

It is Gérôme at his best, capturing the romance, mystery, and spectacle of the East, the brilliant colors of the immense carpet cleverly accentuated by the multihued turbans of the prospective buyers. Smaller carpets, piled on the floor in the foreground, form a visual counterpoint to the cool and neutral shadows of the upper right, bringing the eye continually back to the central figures.

This is not a work that lends itself readily to classification. Its incisive draftsmanship and brilliant coloration bespeak neoclassicism; its subject matter would have been seen as pure romanticism; both are subordinated to realism—a real event portrayed in a naturalistic manner.

Oil on canvas 33 x 25½" (84 x 65 cm)
The William Hood Dunwoody Fund, 1970

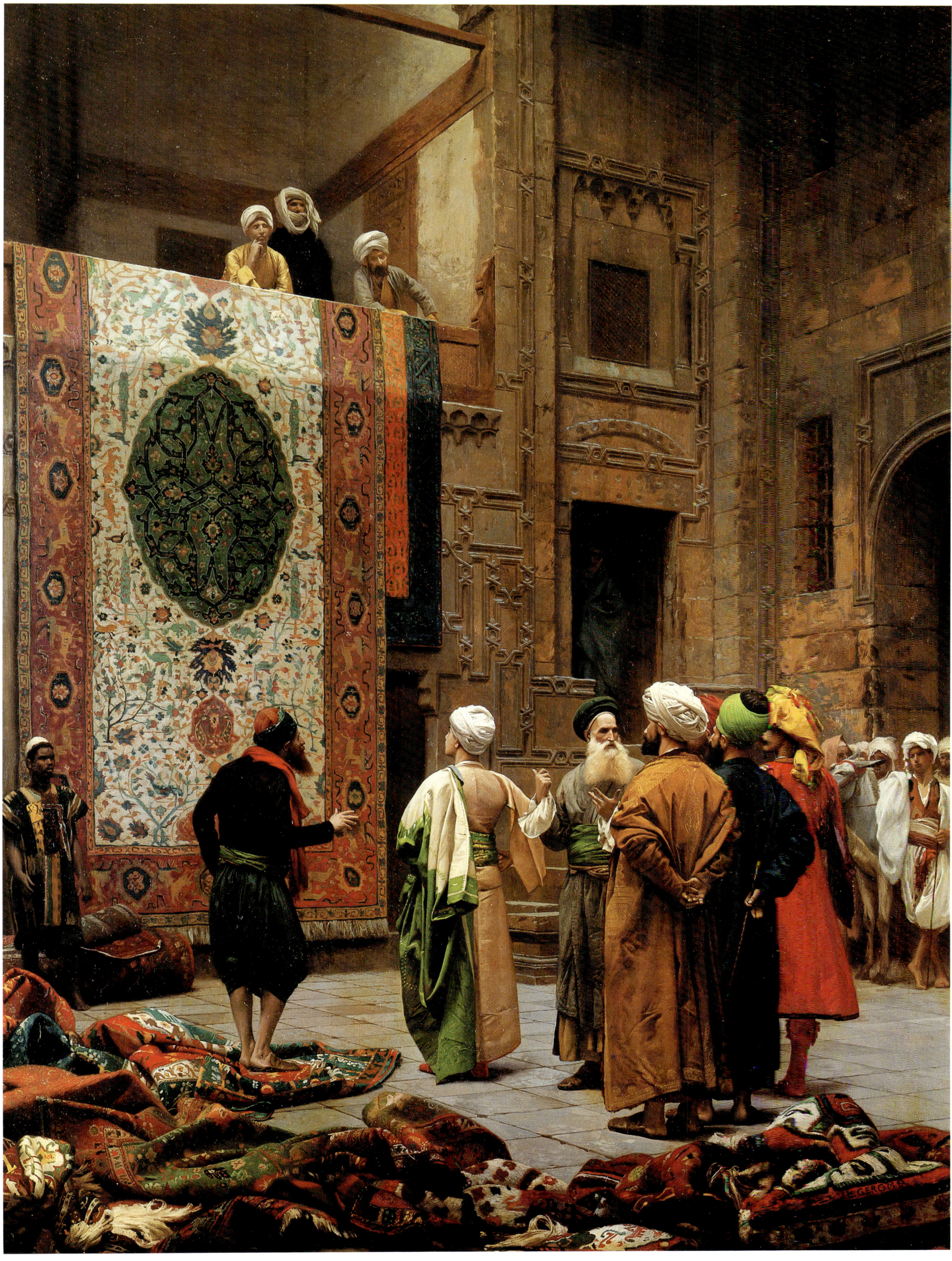

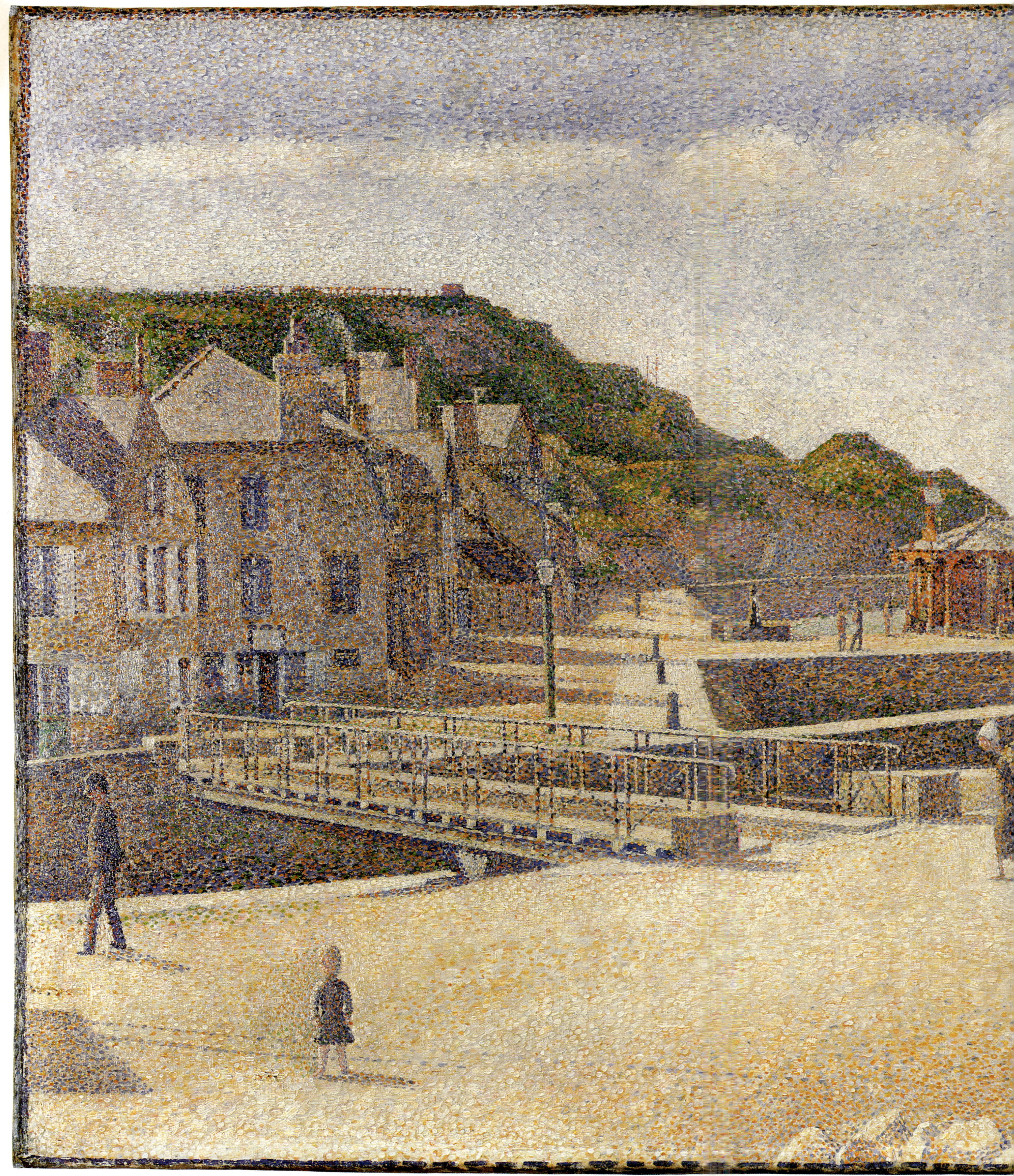

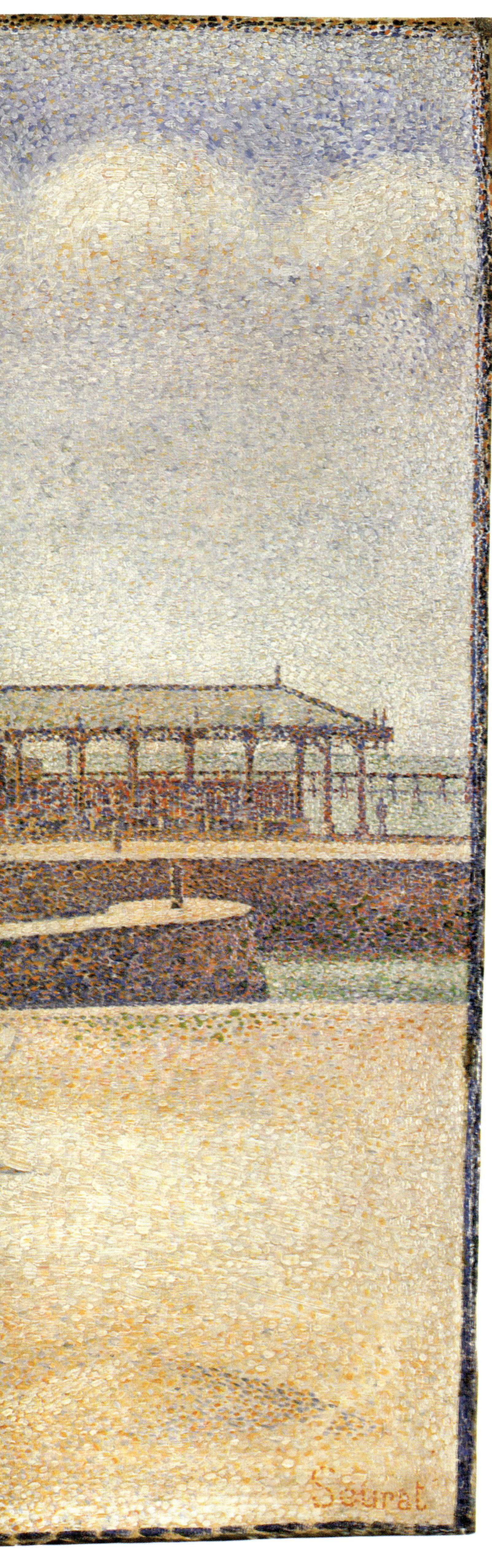

Georges Seurat

FRENCH (1859–1891)

Port-en-Bessin (1888)

In his lamentably short career Seurat produced relatively few major paintings. Clearly, however, this vibrantly crystalline vision of a small fishing village is one of his masterworks.

Seurat wanted to regain the sense of structural solidity neglected by the impressionists in their concentration on light and atmosphere. He turned to then-current scientific theories and divided his surfaces into minute points of pure color, which blend in the viewer's eye to recreate the tones and values of nature in shimmering planes of light. He called the process "divisionism," now better though less accurately known as "pointillism." It is a technique that calls for absolute precision and a geometric simplification of natural forms. Action is frozen and surfaces hardened into machinelike rigidity, yet the results of this tediously painstaking technique are nothing short of extraordinary.

Oil on linen 25½ x 32½" (65 x 83 cm)
The William Hood Dunwoody Fund, 1955

Vincent van Gogh

DUTCH (1853–1890)

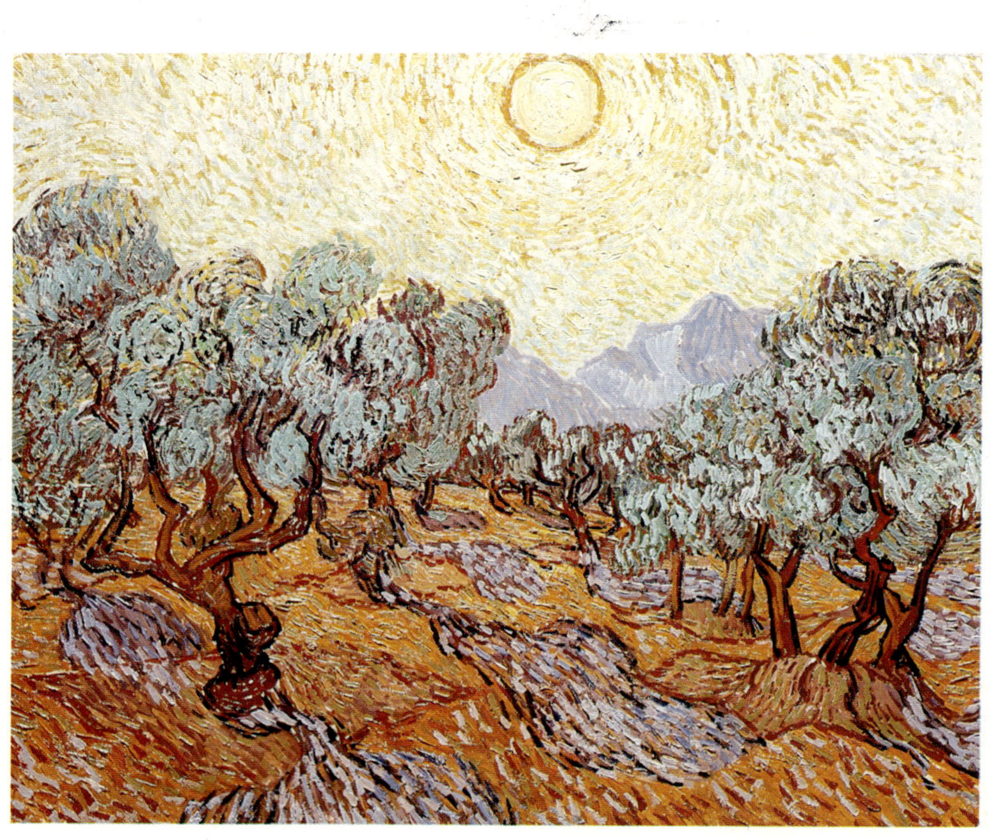

The Olive Trees (1889)

The emotional turmoil of van Gogh's later years led eventually to his confinement in the asylum at Saint Rémy in southern France. The following year, he painted this scene of its olive orchard, one of several variations on the same theme. The gnarled trunks and brittle, glistening leaves appear as the embodiment of a tormented exuberance of nature, as well as of the artist's soul. Yet beyond the violently pulsating surface there is a sense of tranquility in this desolate and sunbaked spot.

In 1913, the Armory Show in New York heralded a new epoch, introducing to America the art of cubism and abstractionism. But the exhibition also included a 'preamble' of earlier masterworks to illustrate the new movements' origins and influences. Appropriately, this painting was one of the masterworks included.

Oil on linen 29 x 36½" (74 x [illegible] cm)

The William Hood Dunwoody Fund 1951

DETAIL

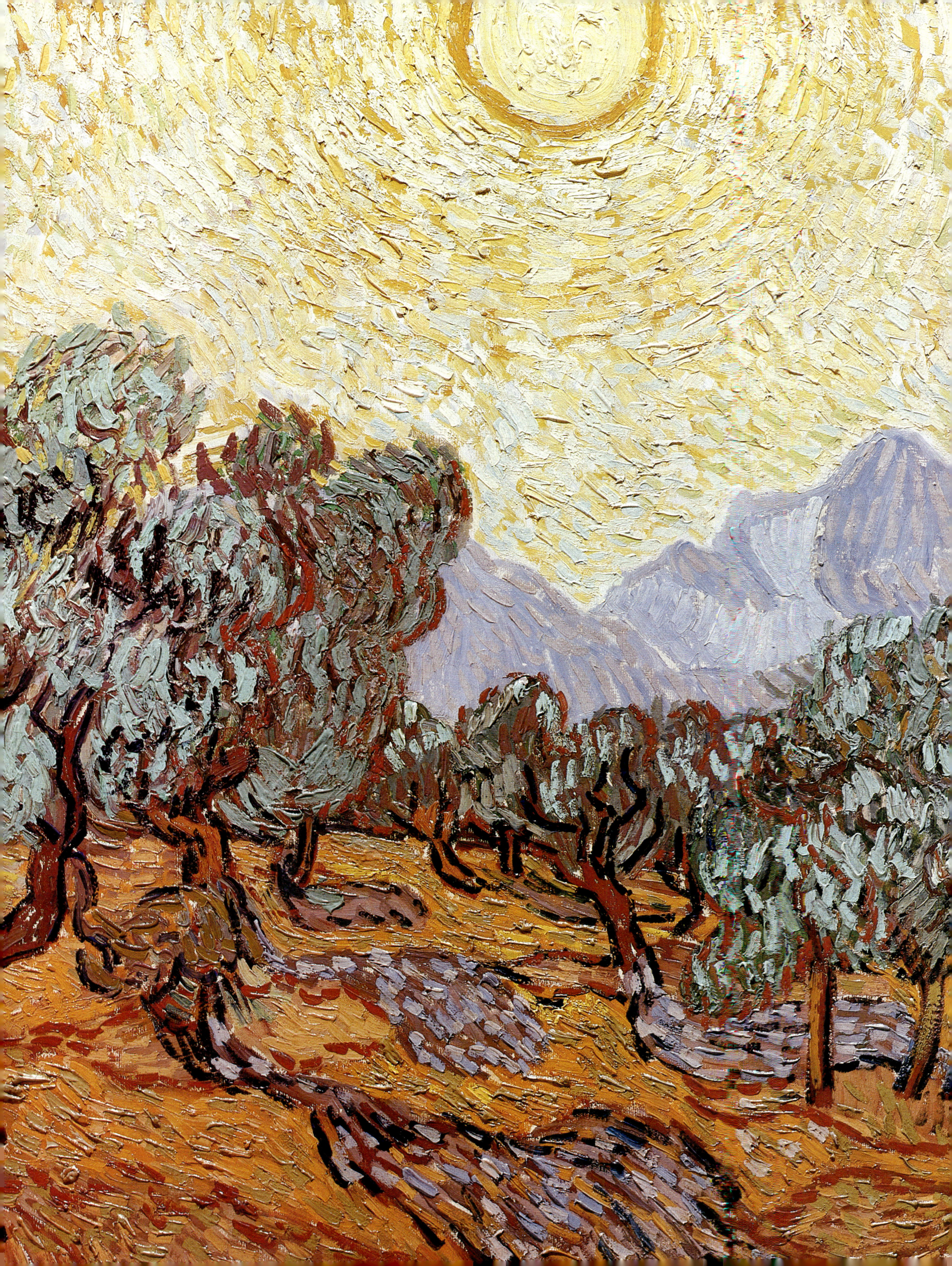

Paul Gauguin

FRENCH (1848–1903)

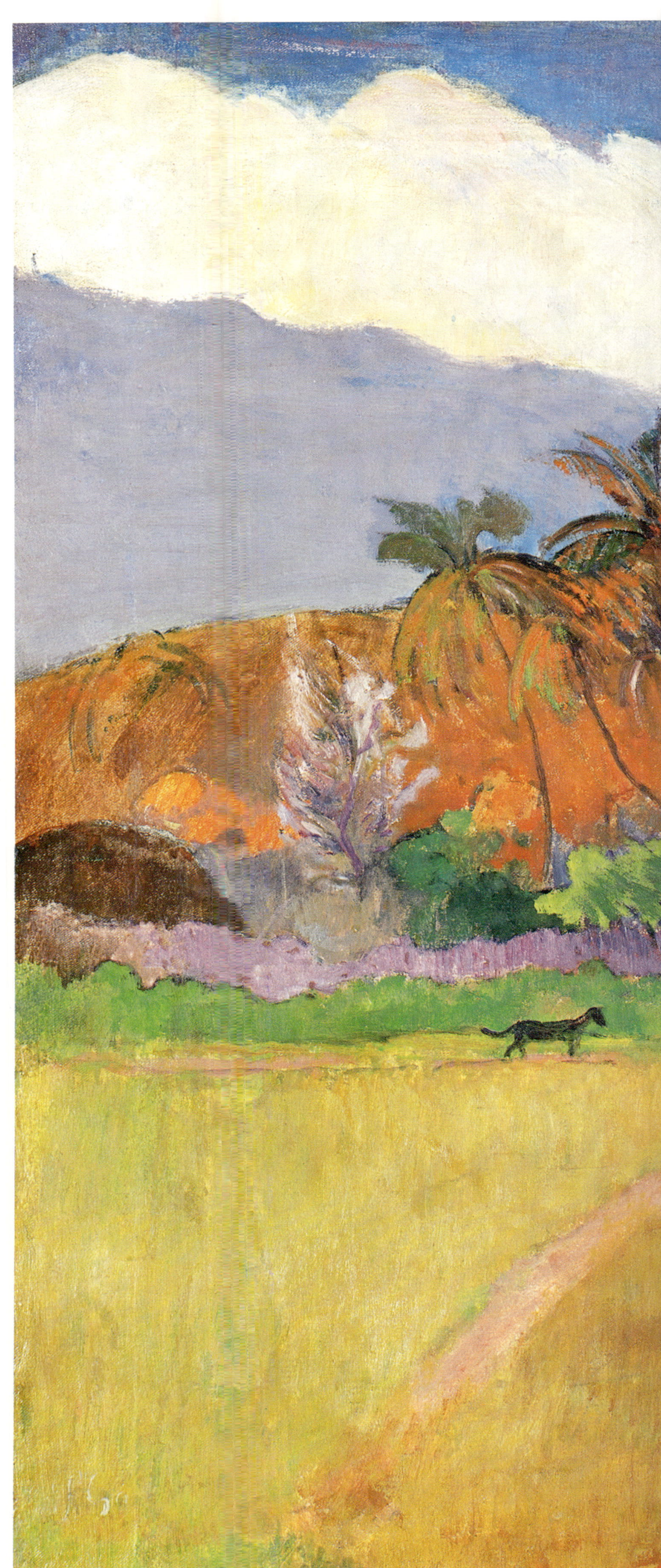

Tahitian Landscape (ca. 1891–93)

Of the many colorful characters who trod the stage of nineteenth-century art, Paul Gauguin was certainly the most exotic. He devoted his life to a search for primitive innocence and, abandoning his family and a banking career, traveled first to Martinique then later to Tahiti to pursue his idyll. This landscape was painted during his first visit to Tahiti, and while exhibiting some of the flattening of form and color that characterizes most 'primitive' art, it preserves much of Gauguin's earlier impressionistic style. There is a directness of vision here that presages later works, but for all its apparent simplicity the structure is still carefully contrived. Note, for example, how the curve of the path is repeated in the mountain and again in the clouds.

The painting was once in the collection of Henry Clay Frick whose interest lay predominantly with the works of the old masters. The inclusion of this landscape speaks highly, not only of Gauguin's mastery, but also of the infallibility of Mr. Frick's eye for quality.

Oil on canvas 26¾ x 36½" (68 x 93 cm)
The Julius C. Eliel Memorial Fund, 1949

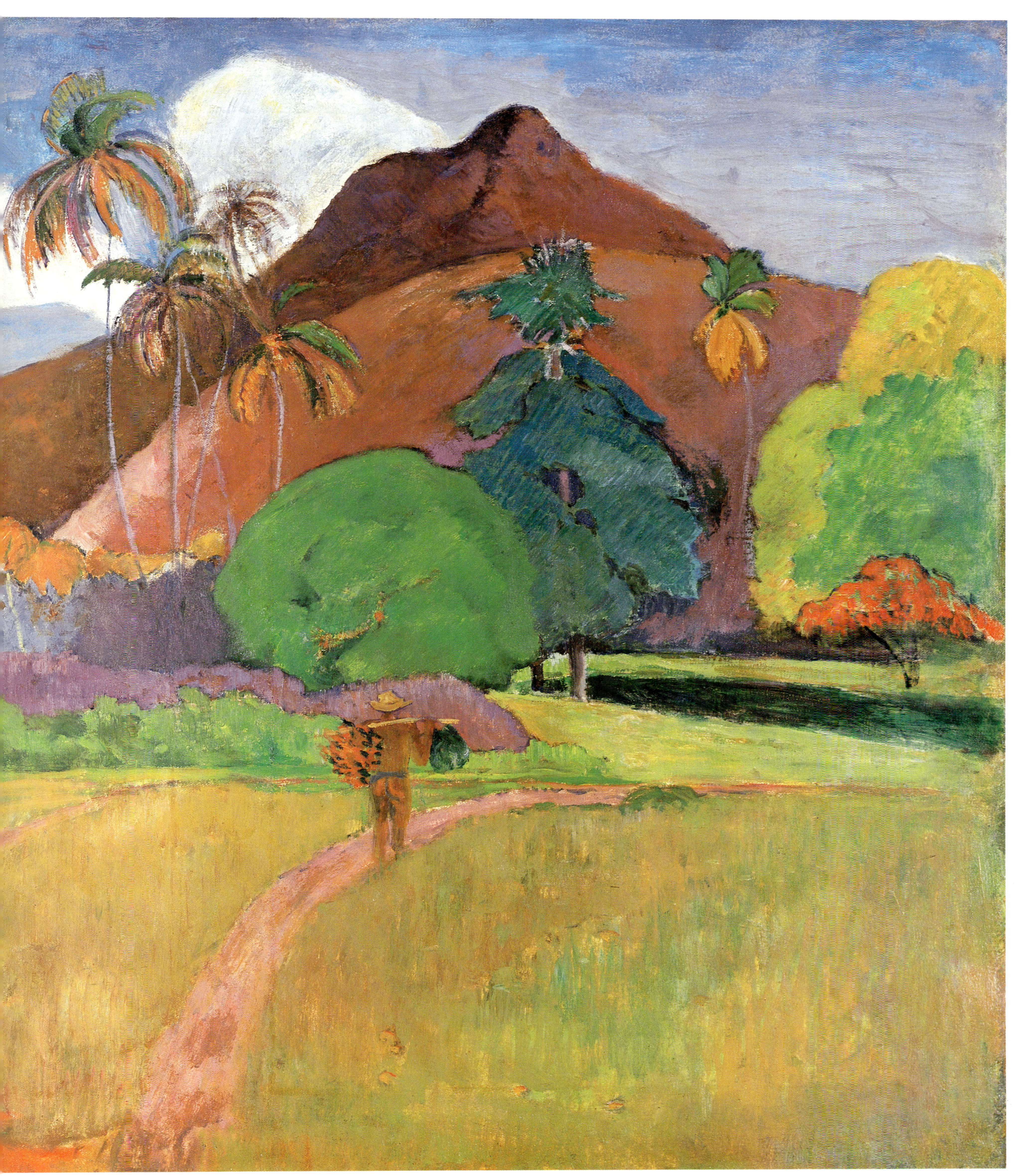

Edvard Munch

NORWEGIAN (1863–1944)

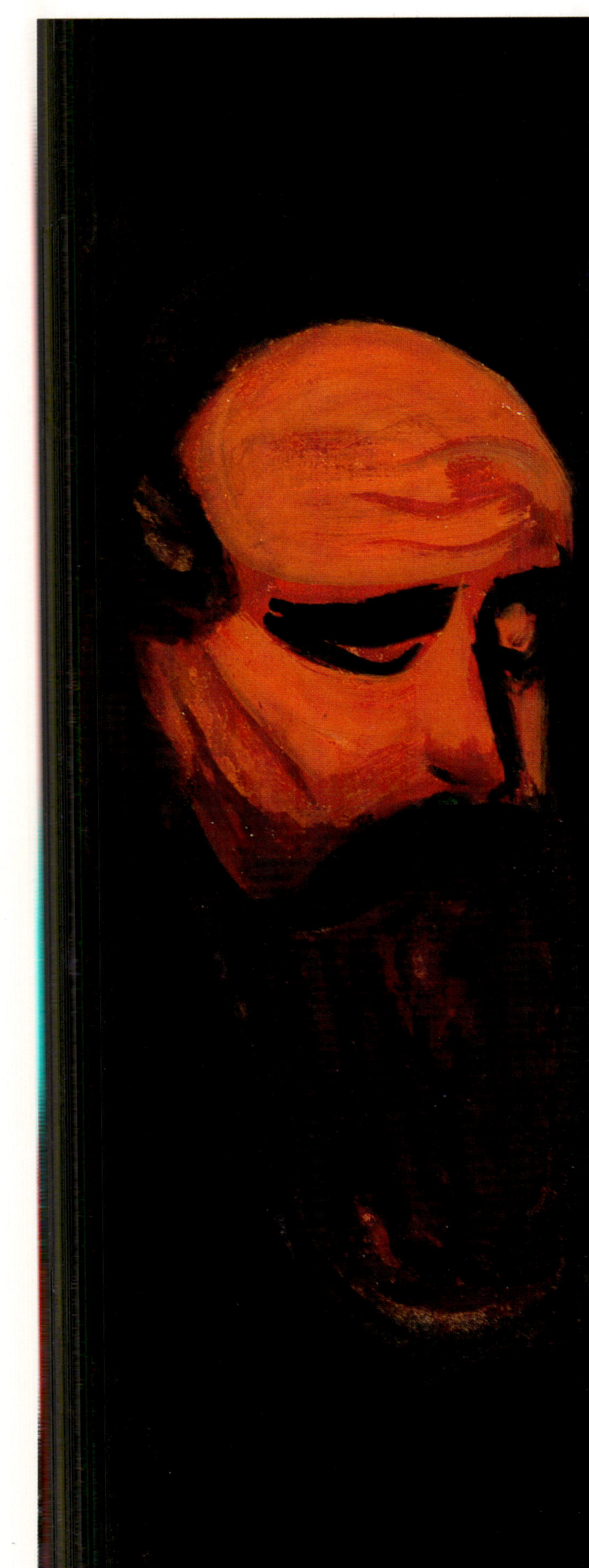

Jealousy (ca. 1897)

Munch's works were frequently the products of deep emotional stress. His childhood was a sickly one; both his mother and his sister died from tuberculosis, and his early years were filled with anxiety. Like Strindberg, he was obsessed with the themes of sexual love, emotional conflict, illness, and death, and he tried to express through his painting the psychological insights that he felt art had previously ignored. His simplified forms and coloration show the influence of Gauguin and the symbolists, but his style is much more that of expressionism; he is considered one of the pioneers of that movement.

Jealousy is from a series titled "Frieze of Life" in which the joys and sorrows of humankind are depicted, portrayed by real-life people. The central figure here is the Polish writer Stanislaw Przybyszewski, his wife Dagne, and her lover, who ultimately killed her, on the left. Munch knew Dagne—had indeed been jilted by her—and also knew her husband. His portrayal of the eternal triangle is haunted by foreboding and a sense of tragedy in which Munch himself was deeply and inescapably involved.

Oil on linen 30¾ x 47" (78 x 119 cm)

The Christina N. and Swan J. Turnblad Memorial Fund, 1955

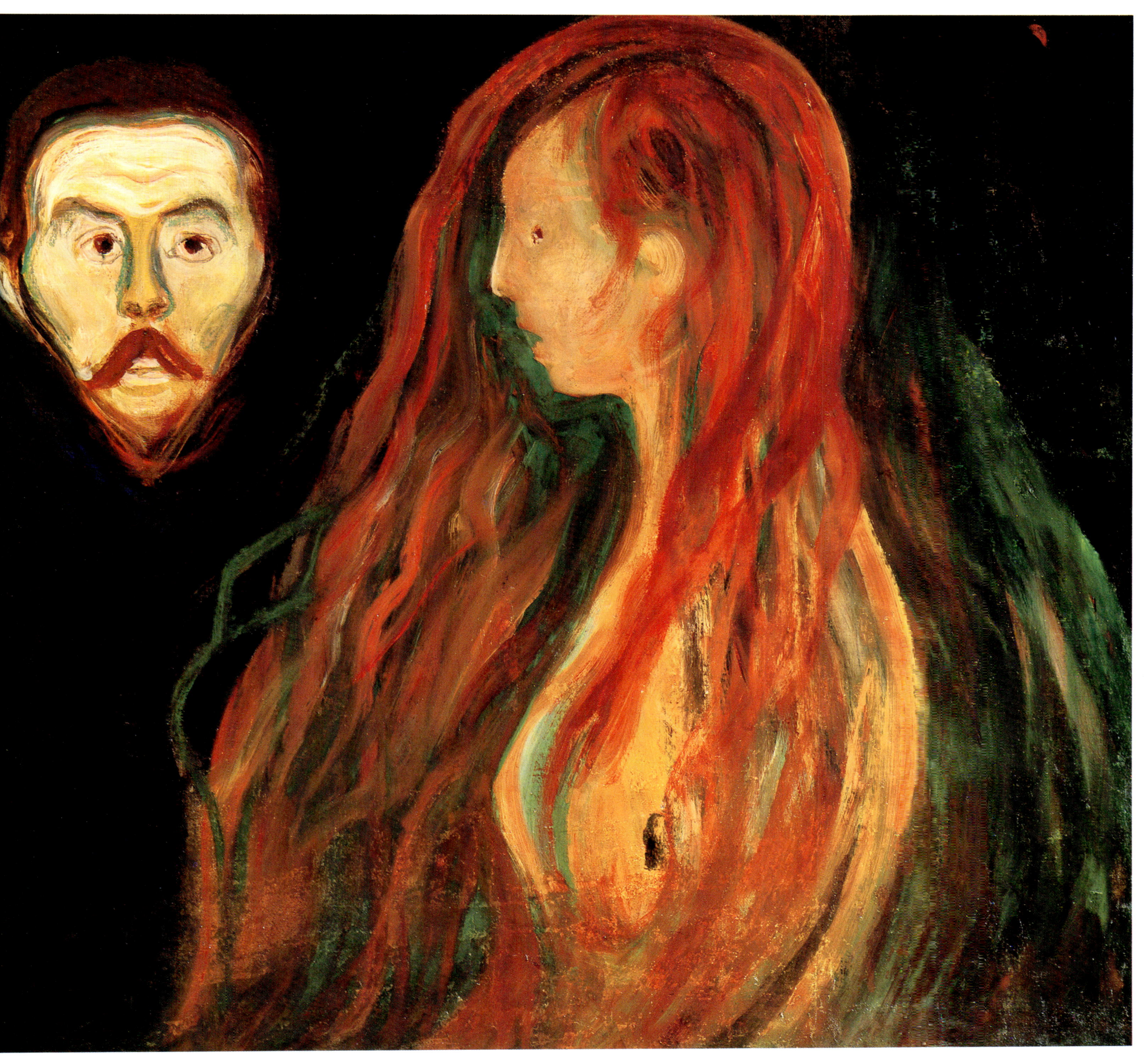

Giovanni Boldini

ITALIAN (1842–1931)

Portrait of Ruggiero Leoncavallo (ca. 1919)

Born in Ferrara, Boldini achieved his greatest success as portraitist to aristocratic Paris. Both he and Toulouse-Lautrec painted there at about the same time, but Lautrec, who came from the aristocracy, painted the low life while Boldini, coming from poorer circumstances, was attracted to the rich and famous.

This lively portrait is of the opera composer Leoncavallo (1858–1919) whose most famous work, *Pagliacci*, was one of Boldini's favorite operas. The active brushstrokes lend a theatricality to the work that is most appropriate to its subject; it captures not only the appearance of the maestro but something of his presence as well. It captures, too, a hint of sadness. Leoncavallo was cheated in the production of his first opera and, aged twenty, found himself destitute. He made a living playing piano in cafés, all the time planning a series of operas of overwhelming dimensions. But the times were wrong for a project of this scale and *Pagliacci*, a small-scale production dashed off almost casually, proved to be his only commercial success. Even this did not pay well enough to support him and he died in Tuscany, a defeated and disillusioned man.

Oil on canvas 24 x 29" (61 x 74 cm)

The Christina N. and Swan J. Turnblad Memorial Fund, 1974

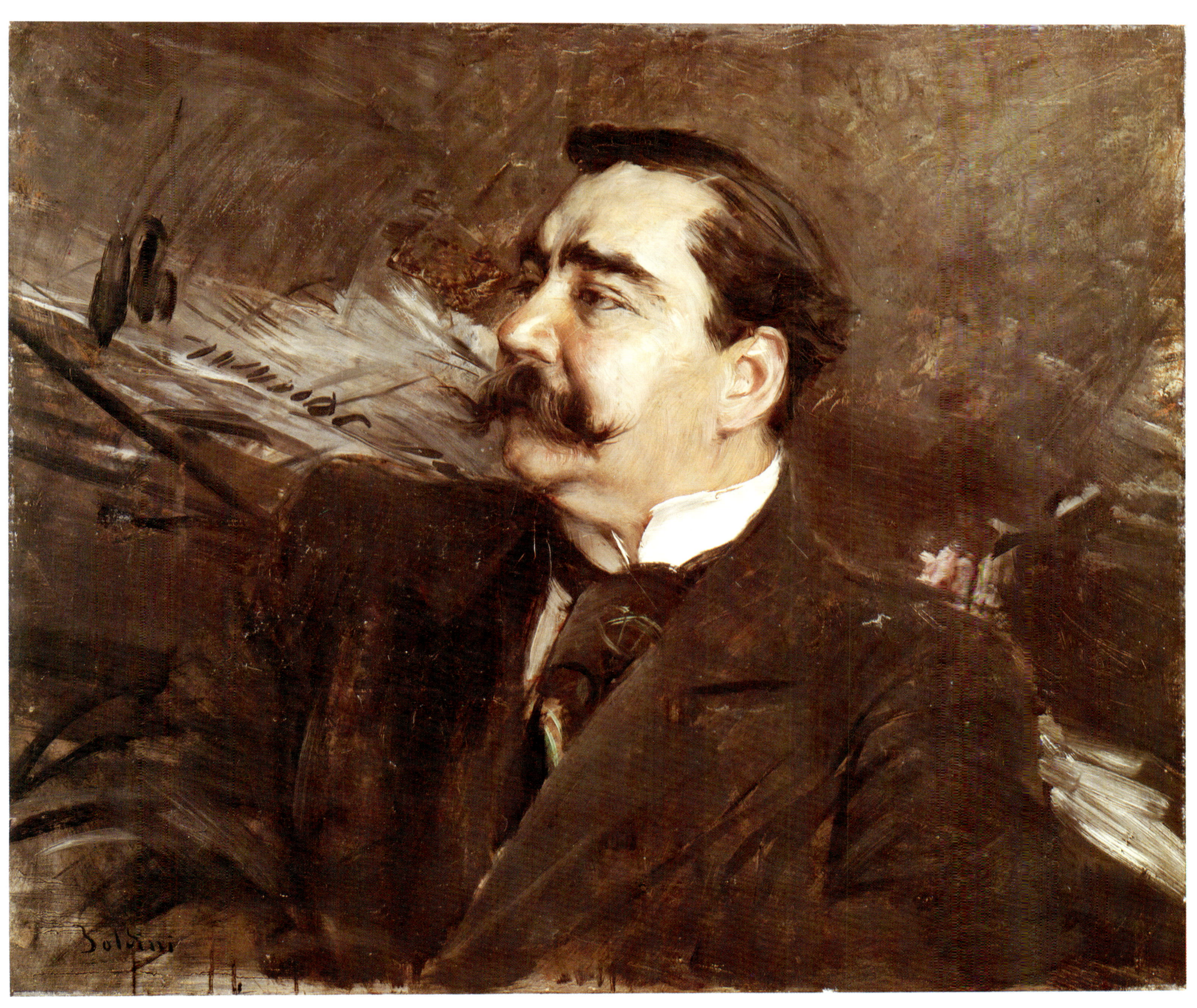
Boldini

Ernst Ludwig Kirchner

GERMAN (1880–1938)

Seated Woman (1907)

Subjective expressionism flourished in Germany from about 1905 to 1930 and found its beginnings in a small group of artists in Dresden who called themselves *Die Brücke*—The Bridge. Their style was harsh, strong, and colorful. It was also subjective, emotional, and occasionally violent, paralleling very closely the work of Matisse and the French fauves but strongly influenced by the northern expressionists and surrealists, notably Munch and Ensor.

Among the group was a young architect, poet, printmaker, and painter, Ernst Ludwig Kirchner. Compulsively creative, he soon became one of its leaders. *Seated Woman*—colorful, decorative, strong, and emotional—is an embodiment of the movement's style.

The "woman" is actually a young girl. Her name was Franzi. She was a street urchin who attached herself to the painters' studio, modeling and perhaps performing other services in return for her food and lodging. At the time of this portrait, she was about twelve years old.

During World War I, Kirchner suffered a breakdown and retired to Switzerland where he continued to write and paint often feverishly. The Nazis disapproved of his work and, as they came to power, his paintings were removed from German museums. Some were sent to Switzerland, others, destroyed. In 1938, following an acute illness, he committed suicide.

Seated Woman had always remained in Kirchner's possession and passed directly from his estate to the Institute. It is one of his finest surviving paintings. Attempts to trace Franzi failed; she disappeared during World War II.

Oil on canvas 31¾ x 36" (81 x 91 cm)
The John R. Van Derlip Fund, 1952

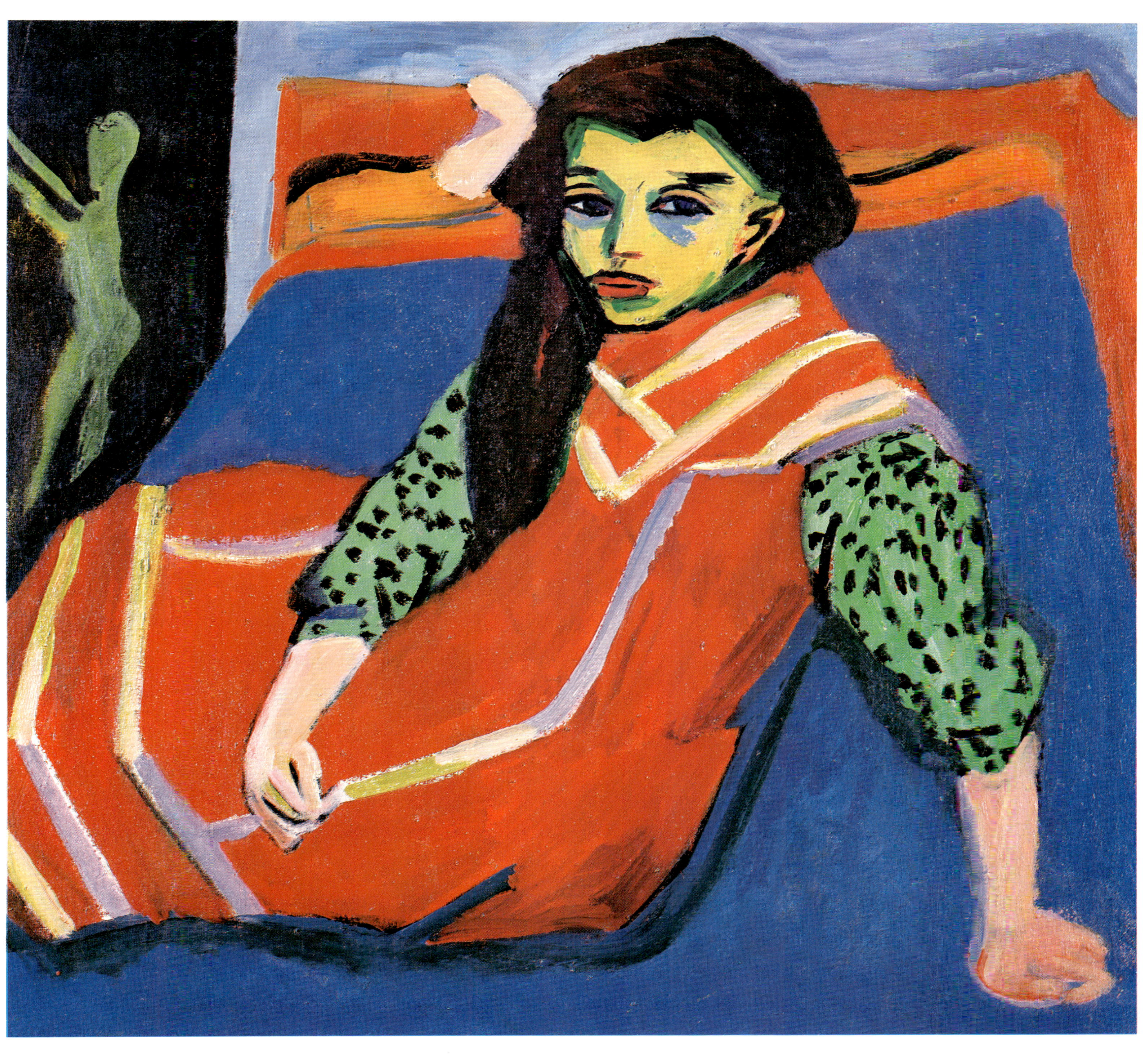

Maxfield Parrish

AMERICAN (1870–1966)

Dream Castle in the Sky (1908)

Parrish, for many years one of America's most popular illustrators, painted in a photographic manner that presaged the airbrush technique of the photo realists. He was a meticulous craftsman, laying on his colors in a series of thin glazes straight from the tube rather than running the risk of muddying them by mixing them on a palette. The deep luster of his pigments, achieved in this way, is quite unique; "Parrish blue" is a term still used to describe the vivid, electric color of his skies and lakes.

The apparent naturalism of detail in this painting is illusory. Parrish is a master of contrasts, not only of light, shade, and coloration, but of scale as well; the foreground elements here are deliberately enlarged in order to heighten the sense of dramatic perspective. At the turn of the century it was a popular pastime to photograph people dressed up as mythical, biblical, or historical characters. The realism of the photograph, contrasted with the fantasy of costume, often produced extraordinarily surrealistic results. A similar thing is happening here: Parrish's Dream Castle is a dreamlike vision rendered even more surreal by his use of subtly distorted realism.

Oil on canvas 6 x 11' (1.83 x 3.33 m)
The Putnam Dana McMillan Fund, 1971

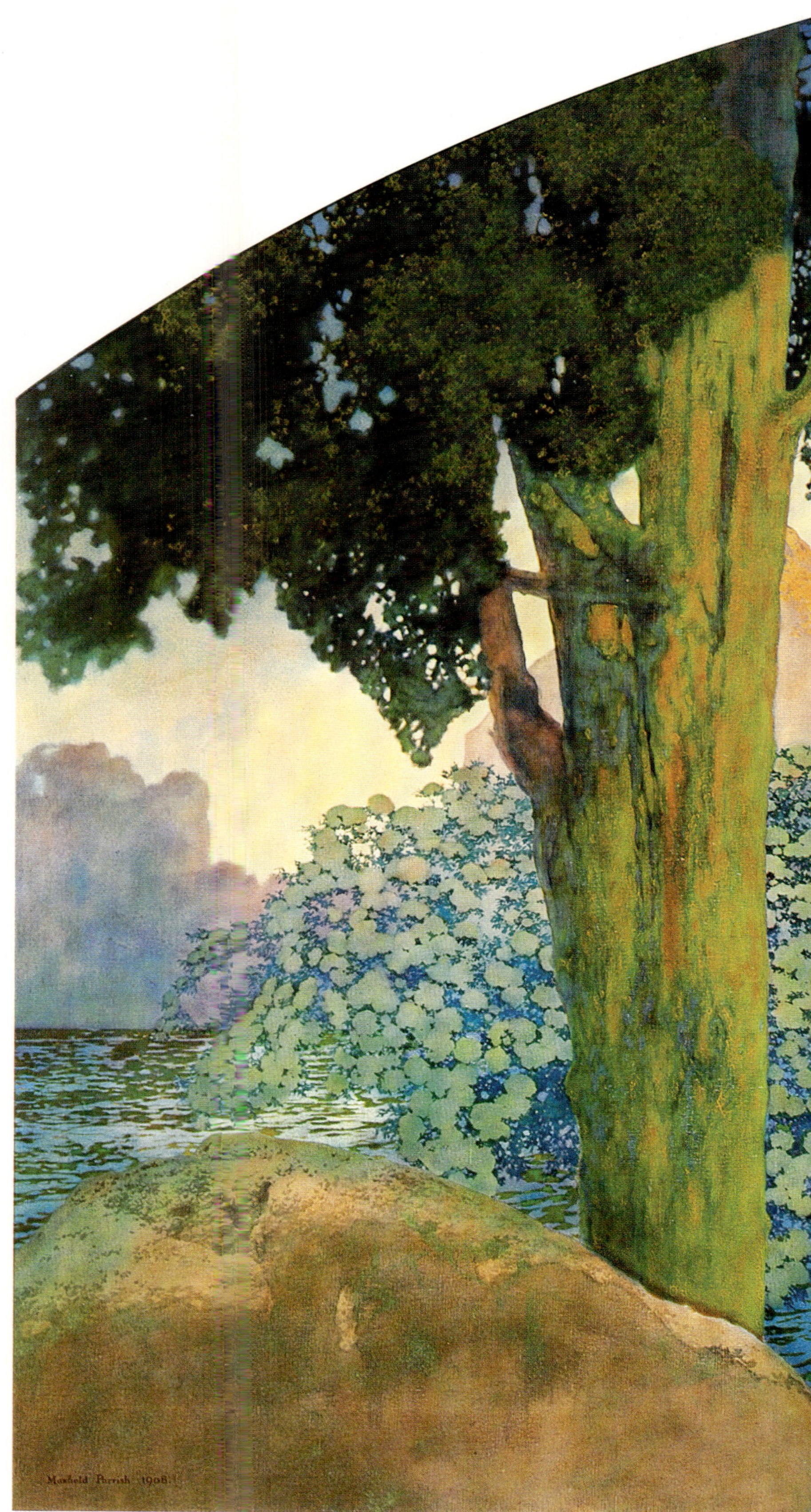

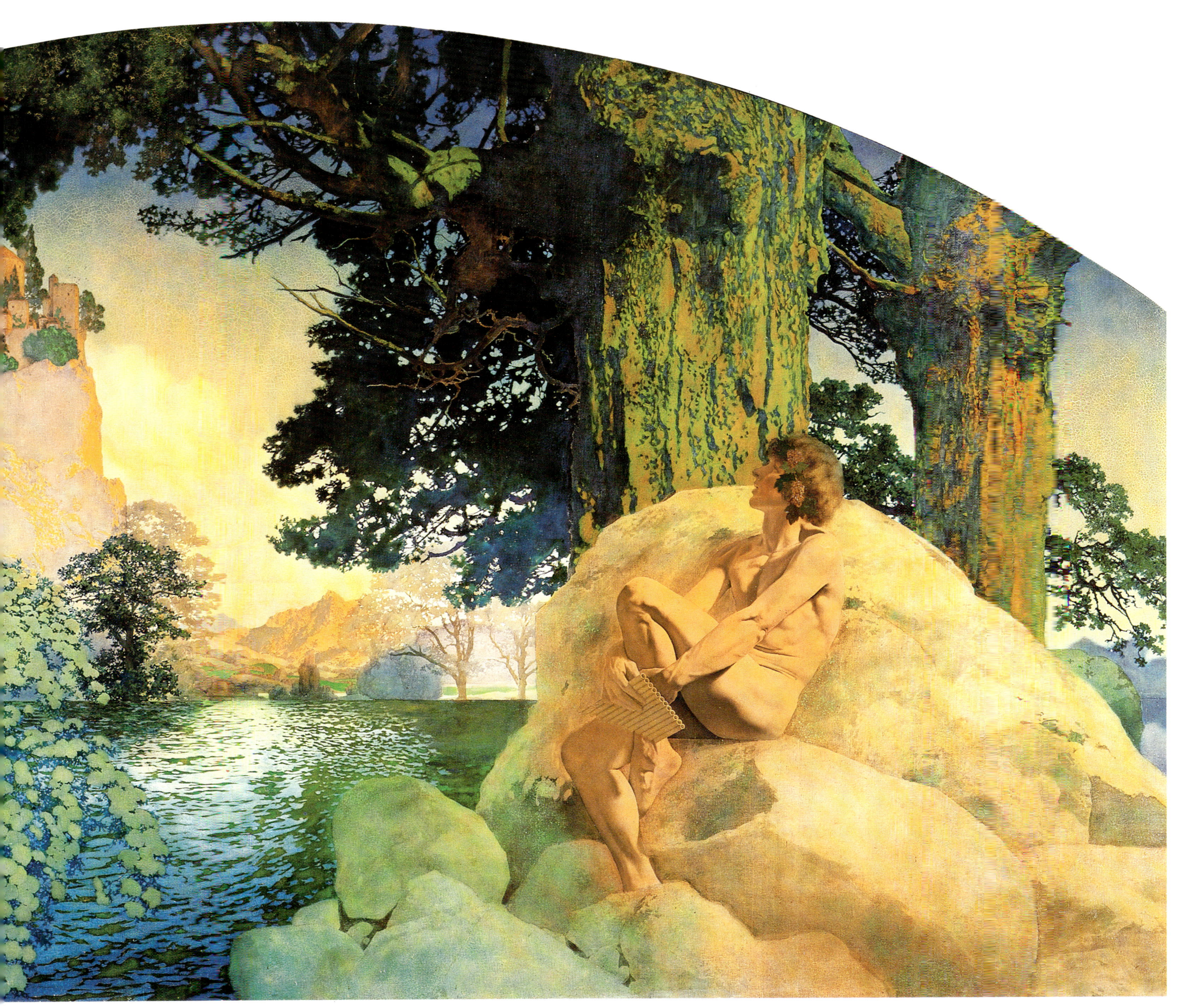

Wassily Kandinsky

RUSSIAN (1866–1944)

Study for Improvisation V (ca. 1910)

Kandinsky emigrated to Germany where he founded the highly influential *Blaue Reiter* (Blue Rider) expressionist group in Munich in 1911. This painting, done during the previous year, represents the transition between recognizable subject matter and pure abstraction. As such, it heralds the birth of a major era in the history of modern art.

Here, Kandinsky hovers on the brink of non-representational painting. The scene, at first glance totally abstract, resolves itself on closer inspection into a garden in which a woman in a blue cloak leans forward in the lower right-hand corner while two horsemen vault a hedge behind her. The suggestion of flower beds, shrubs, and ornamental trees completes the gardenlike surface of this painting, which appears alternately flat and two-dimensional or a solid construction in space.

Oil on pulp board 28 x 28" (71 x 71 cm)
Gift of Mr. and Mrs. Bruce B. Dayton, 19[illegible]7

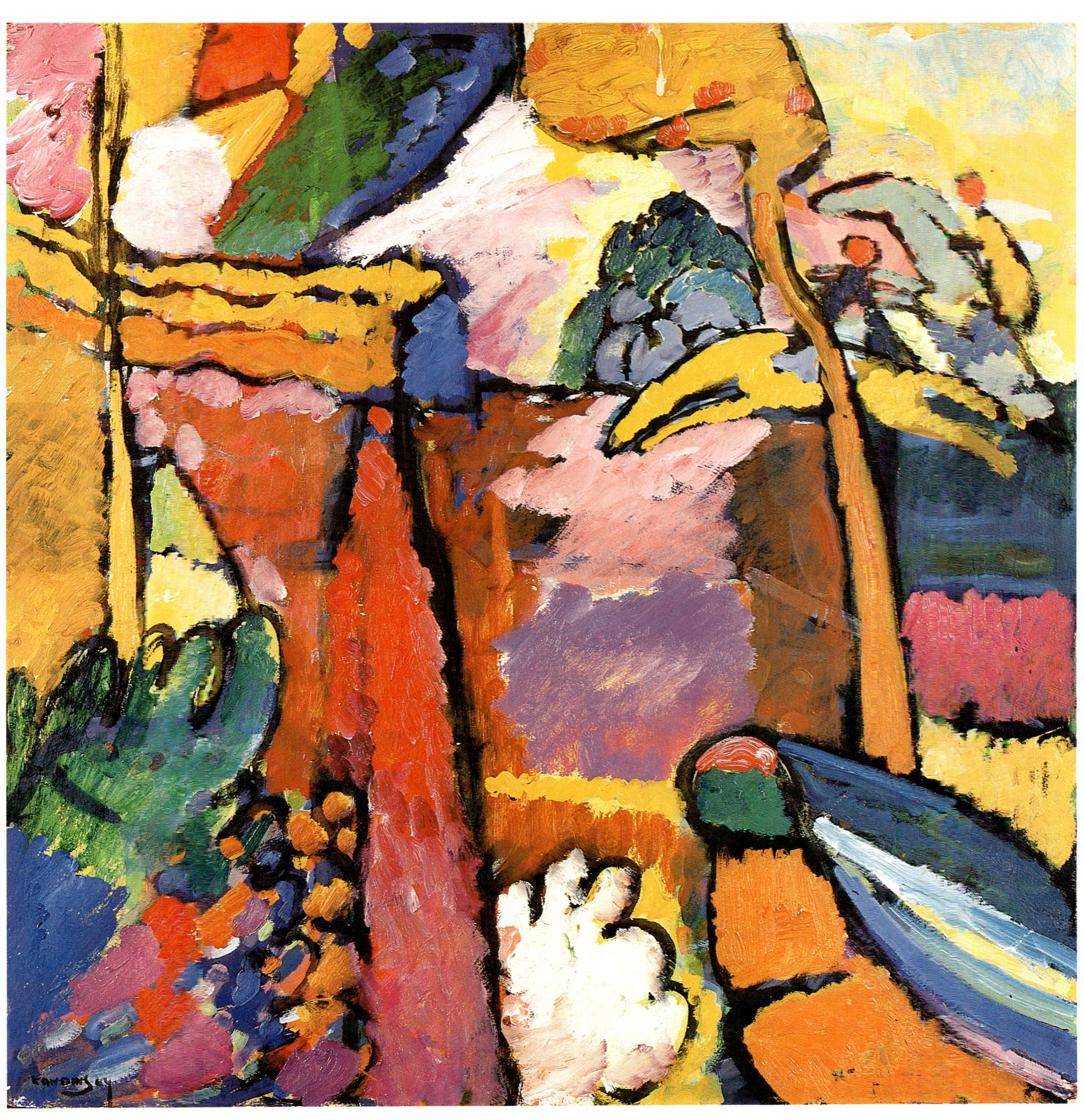

Pierre Bonnard

FRENCH (1867–1947)

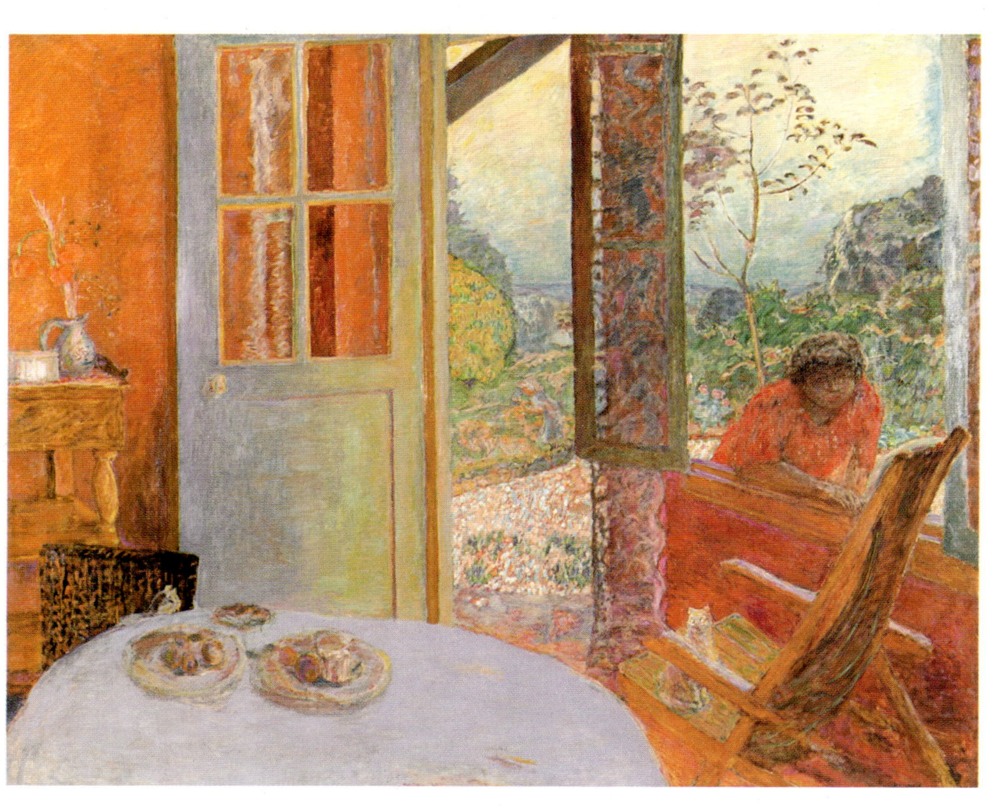

The Dining Room in the Country (1913)

Bonnard, a founder of the group called the *Nabis* (from the Hebrew word for "prophet") was a highly influential figure in nineteenth- and early twentieth-century French art. He was a shy and retiring man who soon broke with the *Nabis* movement and developed his own style, called *Intimisme*, devoted to highly colorful renditions of everyday scenes.

This stunning view was painted at Bonnard's country house, Ma Roulette (a *roulette* is a gypsy caravan), and combines softness of focus and concentration on atmosphere, which was the forte of the impressionists, with a flatness and tendency towards decorative pattern more clearly Bonnard's own invention. The joining of indoor and outdoor space and light is accentuated by the figure of Bonnard's wife who appears, momentarily frozen, glancing through the open window into the room.

Considerably larger in scale than most of Bonnard's paintings, this work is undeniably one of his masterpieces.

Oil on linen 64¼ x 80" (163 x 203 cm)

The John R. Van Derlip Fund, 1954

DETAIL ▷

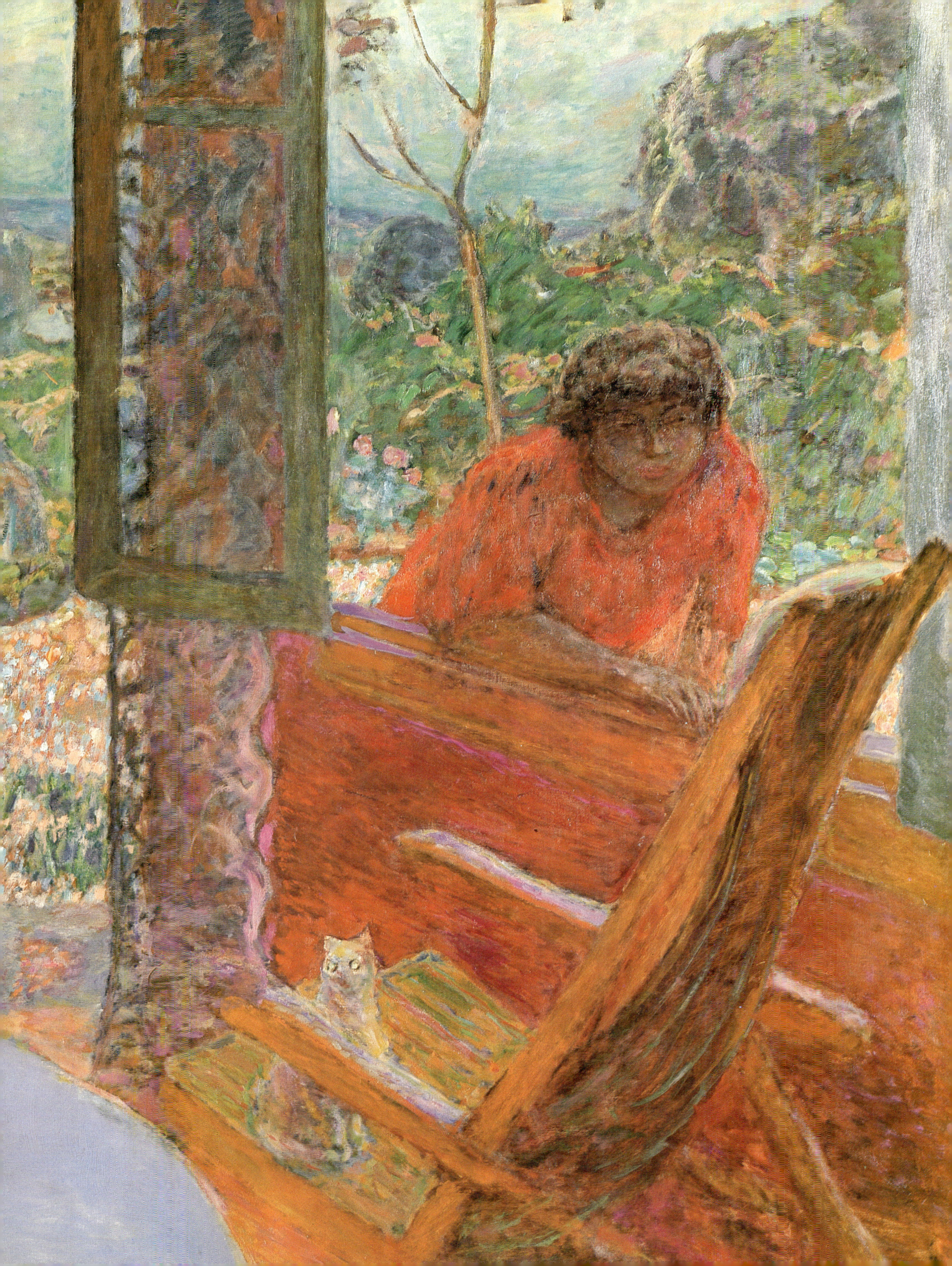

Egon Schiele

AUSTRIAN (1890–1918)

Portrait of Paris von Gütersloh (1918)

Aggressive, hypnotic, and compelling, this work is not so much a portrait as an exploration of the inner personality of both subject and artist. The sitter is Schiele's friend, the multitalented actor, writer, painter, and stage designer, Paris von Gütersloh. The painting's frenzied turmoil reflects the energy of Viennese expressionism but, even more, the anxieties of both sitter and artist at this climactic moment in European history.

This is the end of World War I, a time of despair and disillusion. For Austria, it was the end of an era. This painting, painfully conjured in black, contorted outline out of the golden luminosity of its background, is also an epitaph for the golden promise of a crumbled empire.

Schiele trained with the art nouveau artist, Gustav Klimt, but it was only with the development of his own distinctly angular style and intense palette that he started to attain popularity. This painting, the first by Schiele to enter an American museum, is one of his earliest and most powerful works in his new style. It is also one of his last; in the same year both he and his wife died of influenza.

Oil on linen 55 x 43½" (140 x 110 cm)
Gift of the P. D. McMillan Land Company, 1954

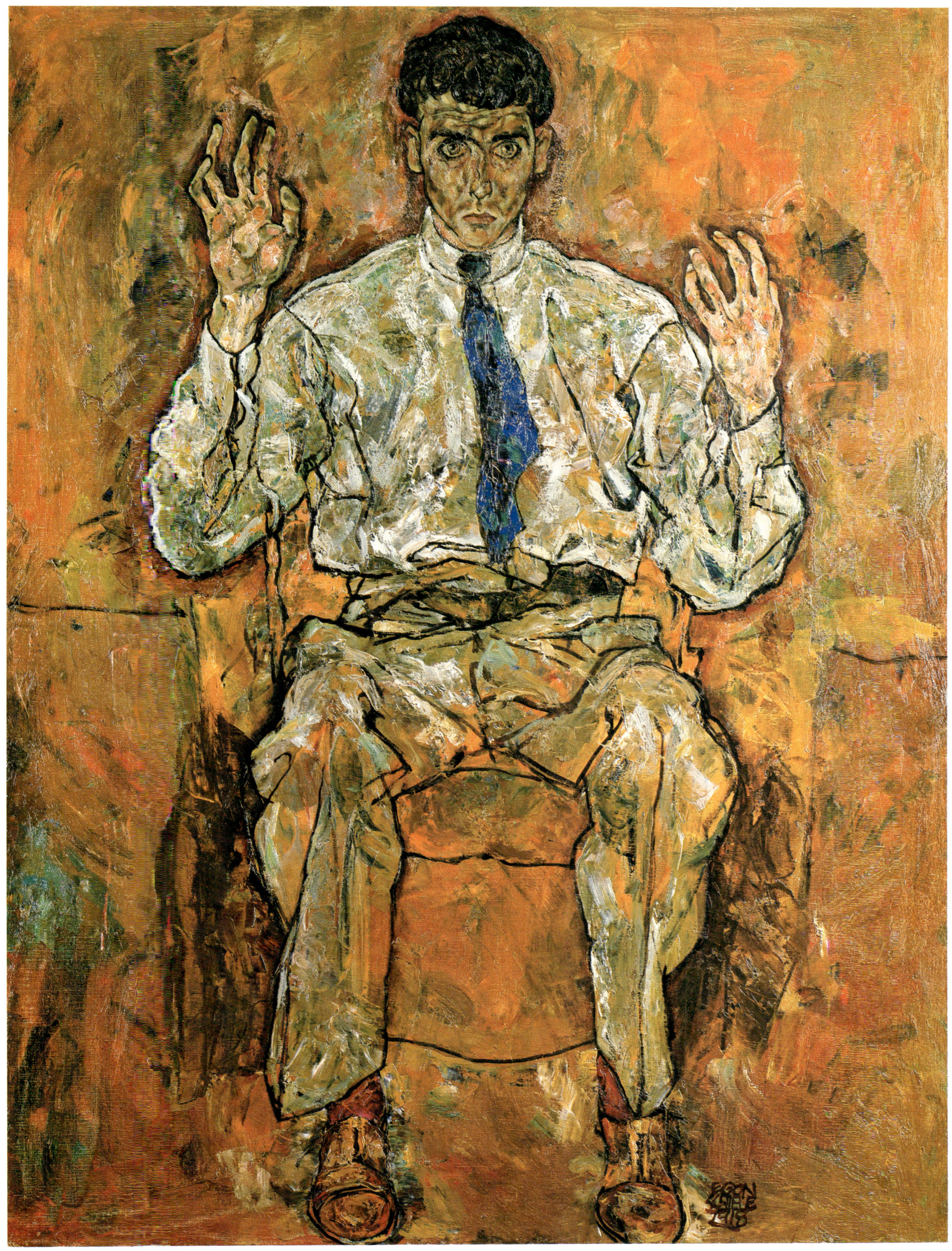
EGON
SCHIELE
1918

Henri Matisse

FRENCH (1869–1954)

The White Plumes (191[illegible])

Matisse was one of the twentieth century's great innovators and brought to painting an extraordinary sense of color and design. The delicate grace of North African art greatly affected the evolution of his style and his highly simplified paintings lack, for the most part, fine detail in their concentration on overall effect.

The sitter here is Antoinette, a young lady Matisse painted many times and for whom he made innumerable costumes. In particular, he enjoyed creating hats but, no matter how bizarre the creation, the final painting always reduced it to its most simplified terms.

The casual informality of this painting is deceptive; Matisse made at least fourteen preparatory drawings, carefully working out the complexity of the design's intertwining lines. The gentleness of the model's expression is enhanced by the subdued background and the black ribbons, and we have a final product of great elegance and style. The work is the antithesis of photographic realism, but its bold abstractions create a compelling and memorable image.

Oil on canvas 28¾ x 23¾" (73 x 60 cm)

The William Hood Dunwoody Fund, 1947

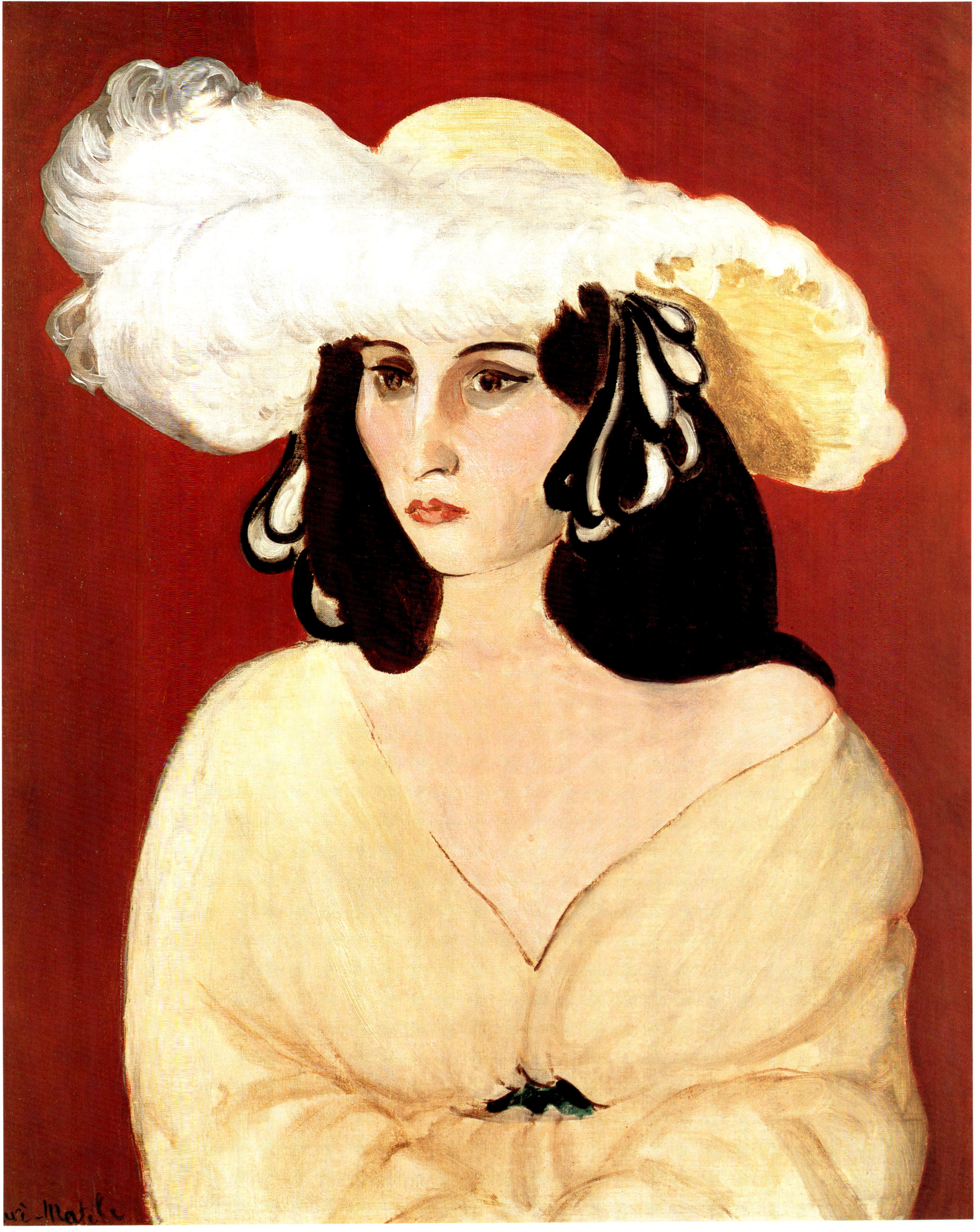

Joan Miró

SPANISH (born 1893)

Head of a Woman (193[illegible])

Miró's frequently playful and humorous images are occasionally charged with the intensity we see here in this agitated and surreal *Head of a Woman.* Painted in his usual highly colored palette, the flailing, upraised arms, the scraggly hair, the mouth reminiscent of a lobster claw and the insectlike proportions seem to reduce the humanity of the figure to a purely animalistic level, a state of bewildered and frightened helplessness.

In spite of its grotesqueness there is nothing aggressive or threatening about this being; it appears, rather, as overwhelmed and terrified by a world not of its own making.

Miró was one of the leaders of the surrealist movement and perhaps the greatest artist to emerge from it. His art sought to mine the riches of the subconscious mind by the "undirected play of thought" to achieve more meaningful realities. As he once said, "For me, a form is never something abstract; it is always a sign of something . . . For me, painting is never form for form's sake." It is this inner realism that makes *Head of a Woman* so intensely evocative and compelling.

Oil on fabric 18 x 21½" (46 x 55 cm)

Gift of Mr. and Mrs. Donald Winston, 19[illegible]

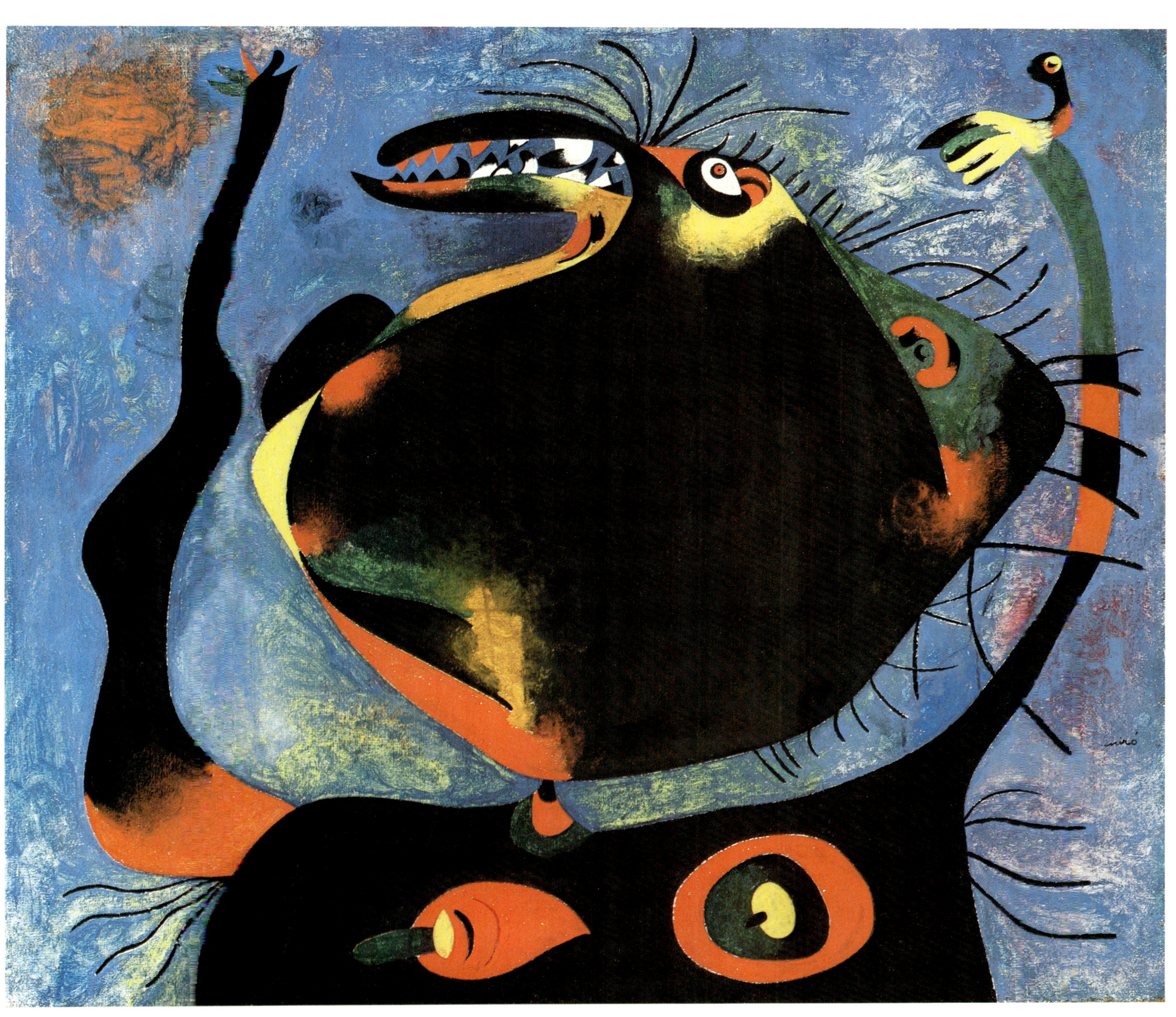

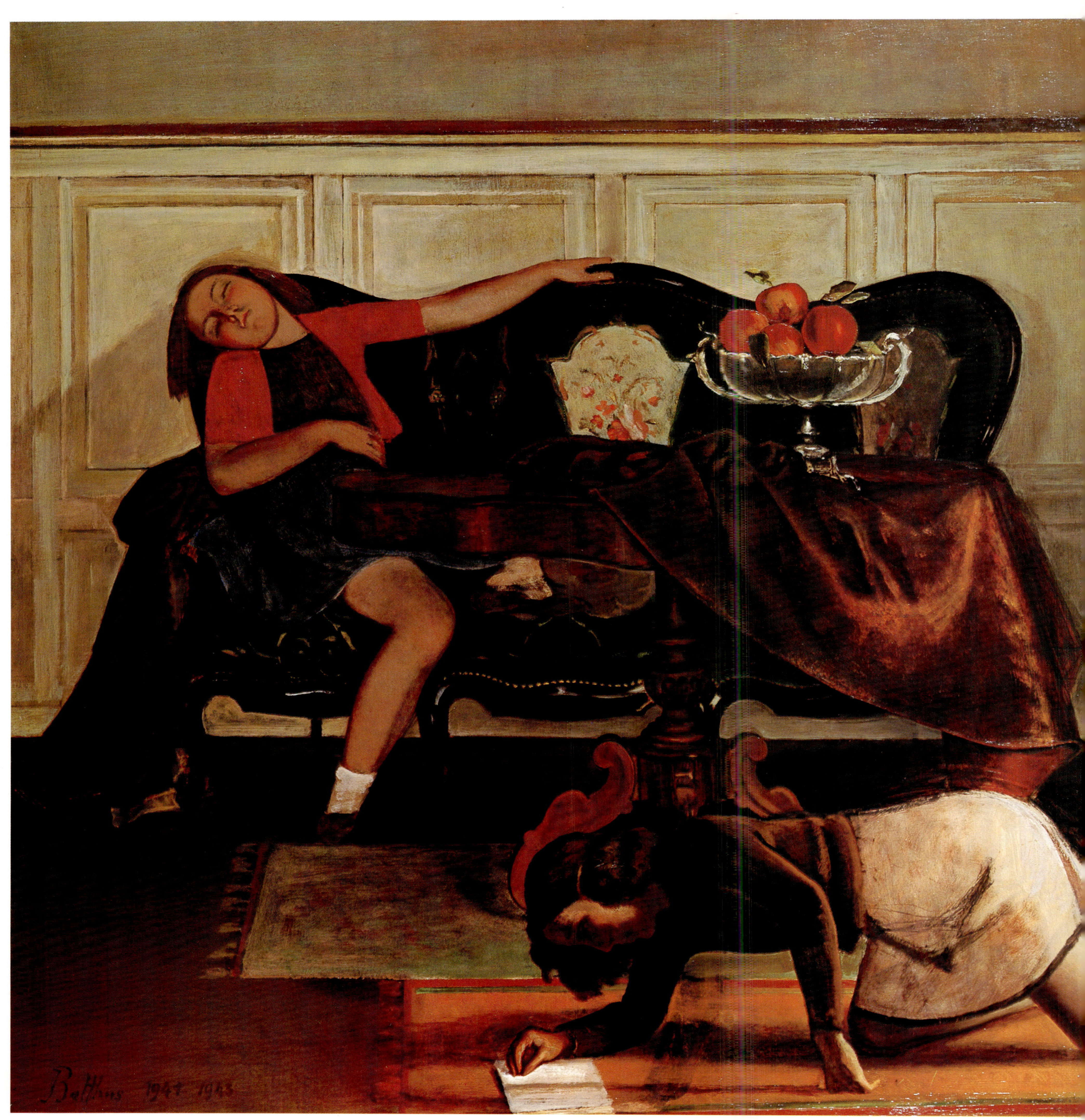

Balthasar Klossowski de Rola (Balthus)

FRENCH (born 1908)

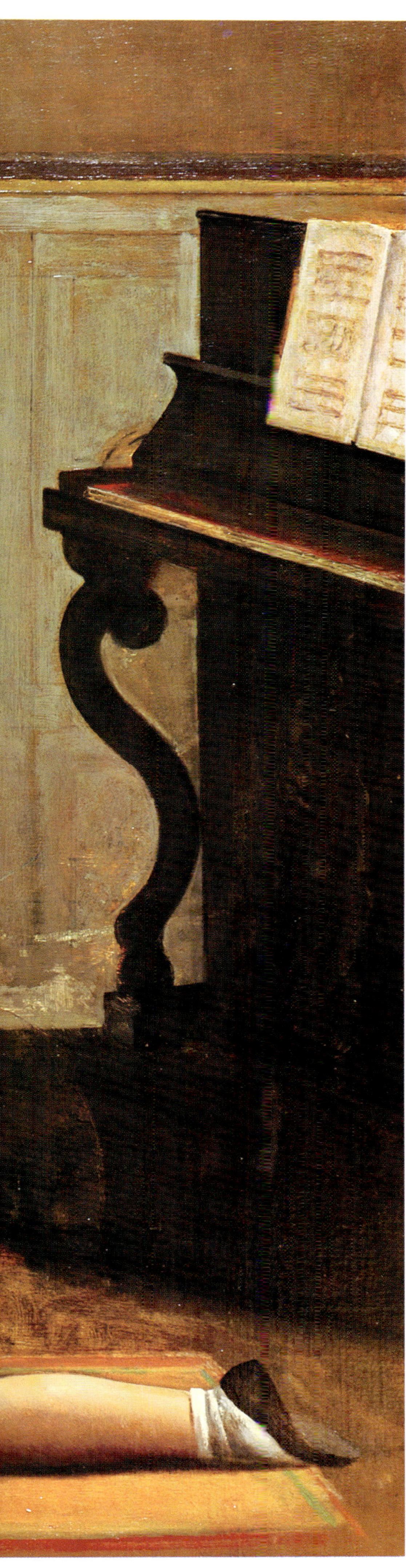

The Living Room (1941–43)

One of two versions of the same subject, Balthus began this painting in 1941. He left it unfinished throughout the following year while he produced the canvas now in the collection of the Museum of Modern Art in New York. He then returned to this painting and finished it in 1943, improving on the composition of this final version.

In this work, with its starkly frontal composition and the number of figures reduced to two, Balthus has created an eerie and somehow uncomfortably erotic scene. Placid and domestic on the surface, it fairly reeks of pubescent temptation, heightened by the voluptuous curves of the sofa and piano, as well as by the allusion to Eve's apple.

Oil on fabric 44¾ x 57¾" (114 x 147 cm)
The John R. Van Derlip and William Hood Dunwoody Funds, 1966

Yves Tanguy

FRENCH (1900–1955)

Through Birds, Through Fire, But Not Through Glass (1943)

The French dadaist poet, André Breton, defined surealism as "the true function of thought . . . dictated in the absence of all control exerted by reason and outside all aesthetic or moral preoccupations." Tanguy's surrealist vision is of the landscape of the mind at its deepest levels. Here there are no names, no purposes, no values, merely *things*. This is as close as we can come to direct apprehension of reality, a fleeting perception of the *noumena* behind the phenomena of our everyday world.

The title of the painting is meaningless, and deliberately so. Meaning has no place in surrealism.

As a young man, Tanguy served with the merchant marine and was drafted into the French army when he was twenty. It was not until the age of twenty-three, when he saw a di Chirico painting in a gallery window, that he decided to become an artist. Despite lack of formal training, his style and technique matured quickly and, by age thirty, he was recognized as one of France's leading surrealists. In 1939 he immigrated to the United States and settled in Connecticut where he continued to paint in a surrealist style until his death in 1955.

Oil on canvas 40 x 35" (102 x 89 cm)

Given in tribute to Richard S. Davis by Mr. and Mrs. Donald Winston, 1975

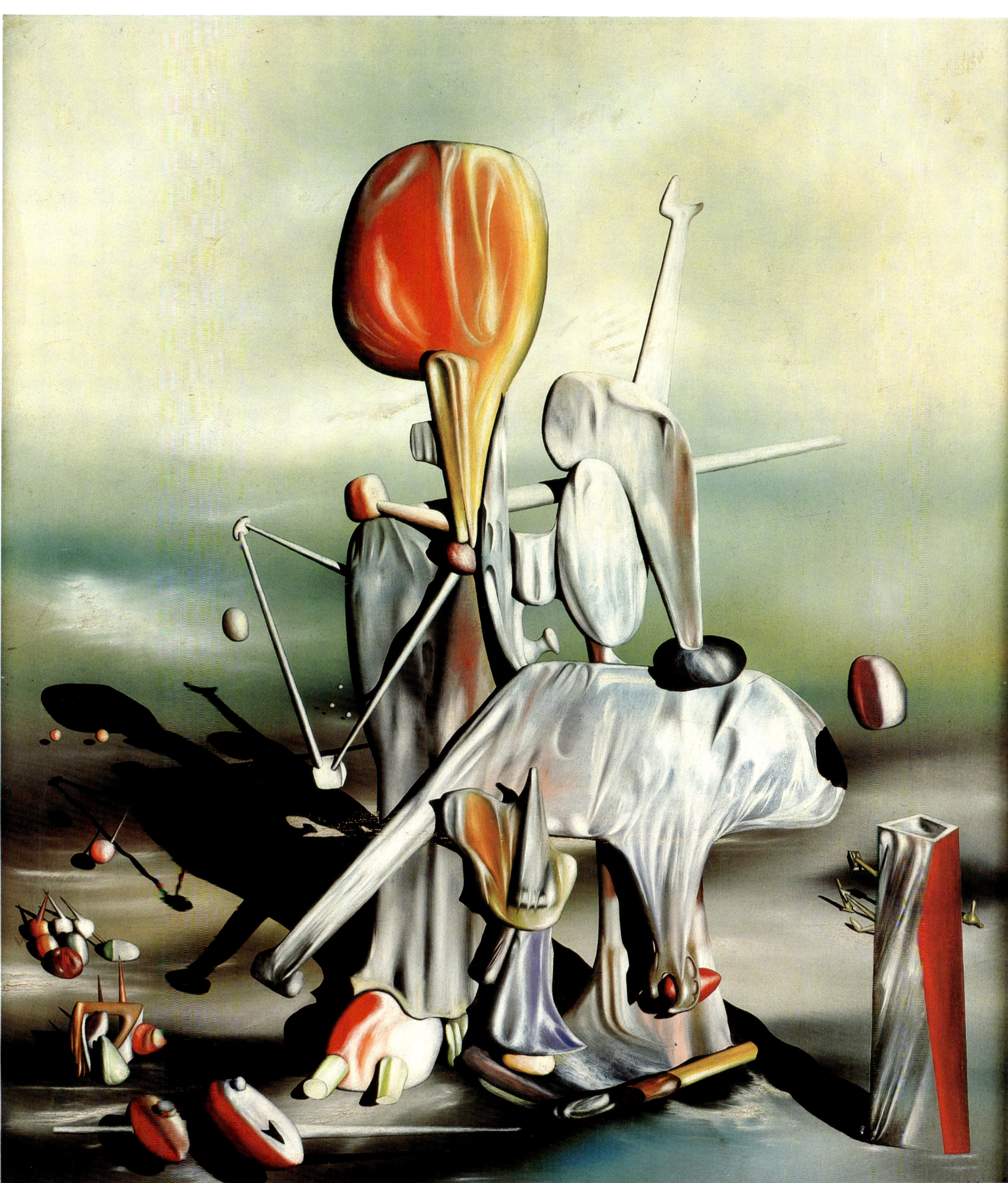

Max Beckmann

GERMAN, (1884–1950)

Blindman's Buff (1945)

In 1937, Max Beckmann found himself among the many great German modernists (including Klee, Kokoschka, Moholy-Nagy, Albers, and Kandinsky) whose works were condemned by the National Socialists. The one-time paperhanger, Adolf Hitler, had declared in 1935 that art should be comprehensible to the people; in 1937 he forbade German painters to use colors that "the normal eye could not apprehend." Severe penalties were laid down for artists who refused to paint in the approved Nazi style. Beckmann fled to Amsterdam.

It was there, towards the end of the war, that he painted a series of five triptychs, of which this is the last. They were made during the Nazi occupation of Holland—a time of violence, deprivation, and constant danger. The triptych itself is a direct reference to the form often used in religious paintings during the late Middle Ages and early Renaissance, and indeed a cynic might point out that the theme of this work is religious, too—the chaotic, mid-twentieth-century scramble for spiritual values in a pagan world.

As with traditional triptychs, humanity is relegated to the wings. At the right, a blindfolded man reaches out futilely with a candle; at the left, a girl kneels before another candle as if in prayer. Behind them, latter-day demons appear to tempt, to sneer, and to seduce. In the middle panel are the figures Beckmann called "the gods." These are the controllers of human destiny—the pipers of the tune to which we dance. It comes as no surprise that a clock should be included among them. In the background, the horse-headed figure refers to the man-eating Minotaur as well as to the legend of Zeus who assumed the shape of a bull in order to carry off Europa. Like Picasso's *Guernica*, which Beckmann seems to quote here, the work stands as a powerful indictment of a world gone mad.

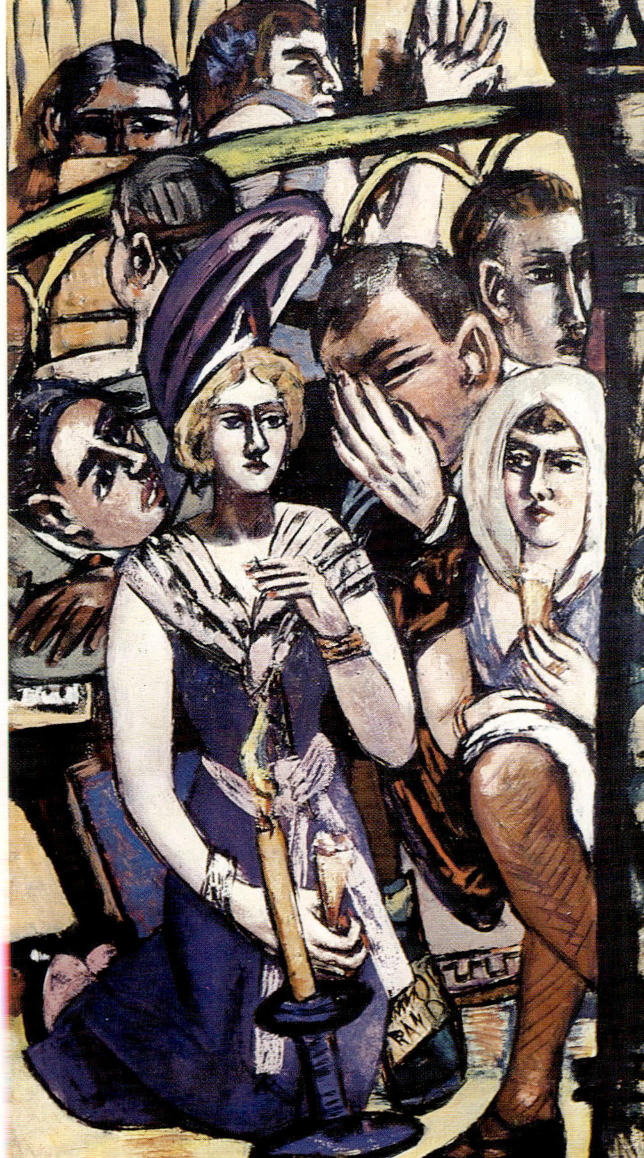

Oil on linen 74½ x 42½" (189 x 108 cm) side panels
80 x 90" (203 x 229 cm) center panel
Gift of Mr. and Mrs. Donald Winston, 1955

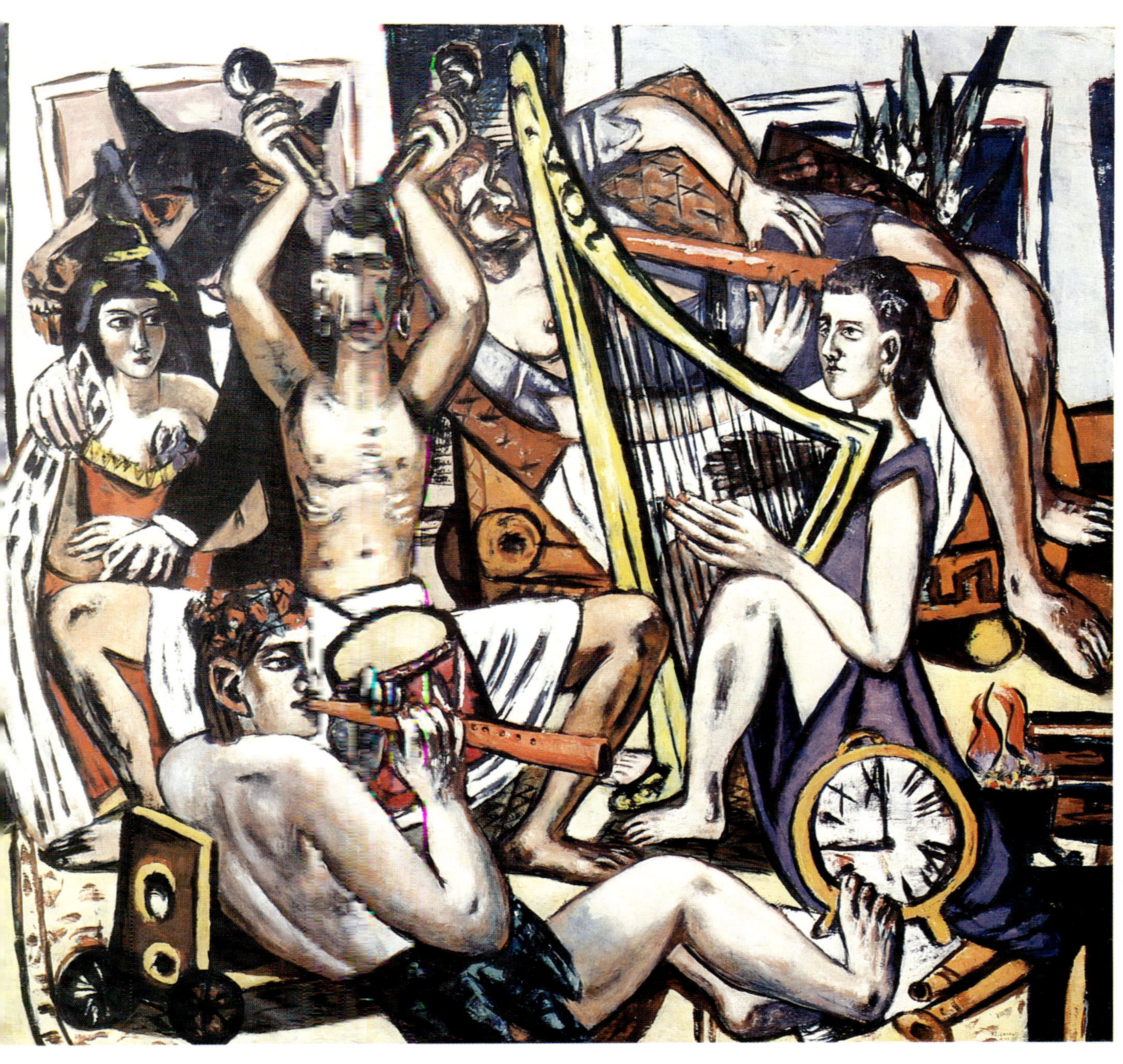

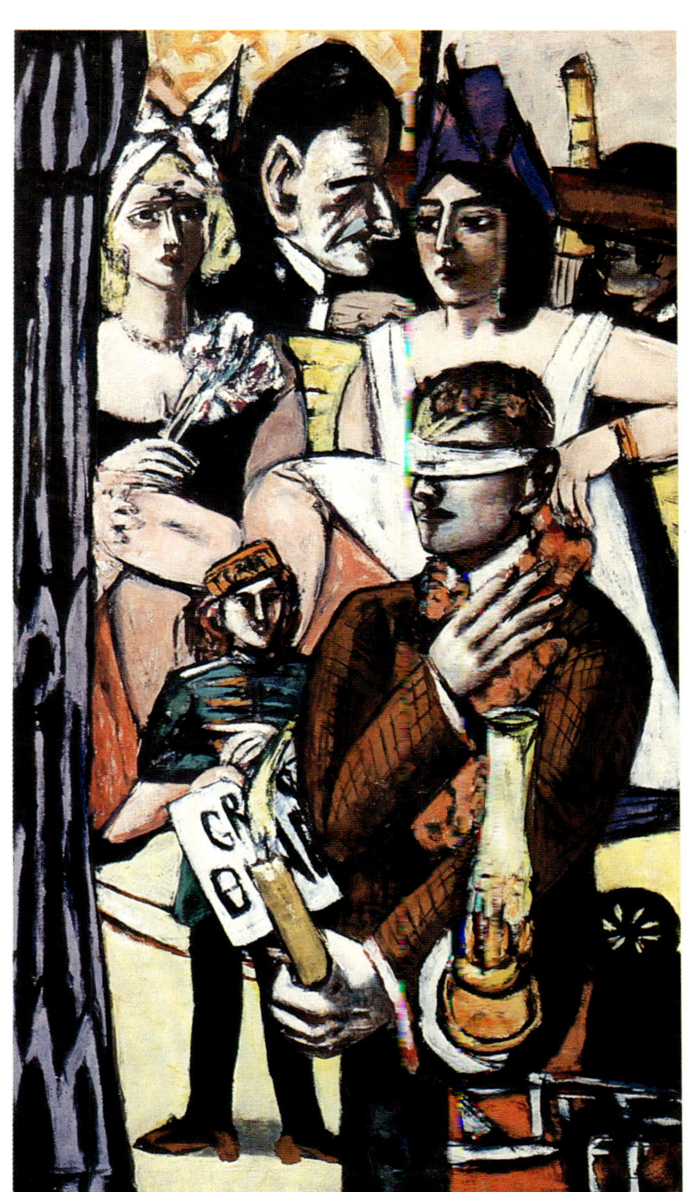

René Magritte

BELGIAN (1898–1967)

Les Promenades d'Euclide (1955)

Surrealism as an international art movement flourished in the 1920s and '30s but continues to the present day. René Magritte was one of its greatest practitioners, and he continually forces his viewers to reevaluate the reality that they believe confronts them. Here, at a casual glance, we see simply the interior of an artist's studio with a finished canvas in front of a window. This perception, however, is quickly interrupted by our realization that this painting of a painting is more than meets the eye.

Is the canvas transparent or is it painted upon? If painted, is the scene on the canvas the same as the scene behind it? And if so, what does "the same" mean? Does it mean that their appearance is similar—like the tower and the road in the painting (or the painting of the painting) . . . ?

Magritte's works evoke an intellectual rather than an esthetic response, but the subtly shifting values of his universe defy rational analysis. In spite of its apparent reality, this is a dream world. However, one should beware of trying to define *too* closely the differences between this world of dreams and the world we call "real."

Oil on canvas 64 x 51" (163 x 130 cm)

The William Hood Dunwoody Fund, 1968

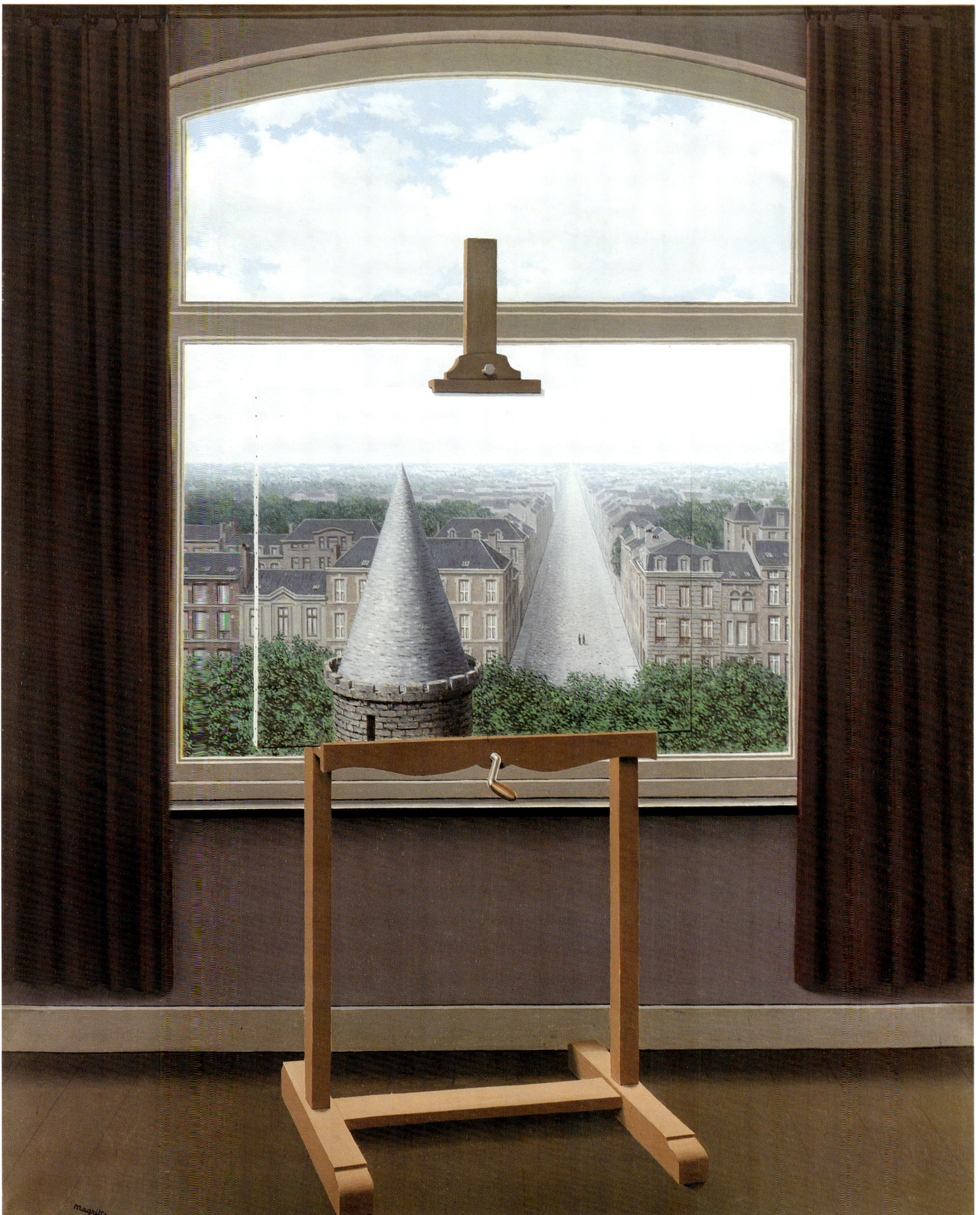
magritte

Chuck Close

AMERICAN (born 1940)

Frank (1969)

Beginning with its ancestor, the *camera obscura* of the sixteenth century, the camera has provided artists with technical assistance, inspiration, and a source of extreme frustration. Perhaps more than any other factor, the ease with which the camera captures surface appearances led artists to search for other, less immediately apparent kinds of reality. Photographic realism, once art's highest aim, became almost a term of derogation in the postphotographic art world. However, the American school of photo realism (of which Close is a prominent member) prompted a reevaluation of the function of photography and, at the same time, the way in which we actually see the world around us.

This monumental portrait took about six months to complete. Starting with an ordinary black-and-white photograph, its surface divided into a grid of small squares, Close enlarges the image onto a correspondingly squared-off canvas using acrylic paint sprayed on freehand with an airbrush, the highlights produced by scratching away the paint.

The result is neither photographic nor painterly, rather, something beyond the two. It is an exploration of the process of seeing simultaneously through the dead eye of the camera and the living eye of the artist.

Acrylic on canvas 9 x 7' (2.74 x 2.13 m)
The John R. Van Derlip Fund, 1969

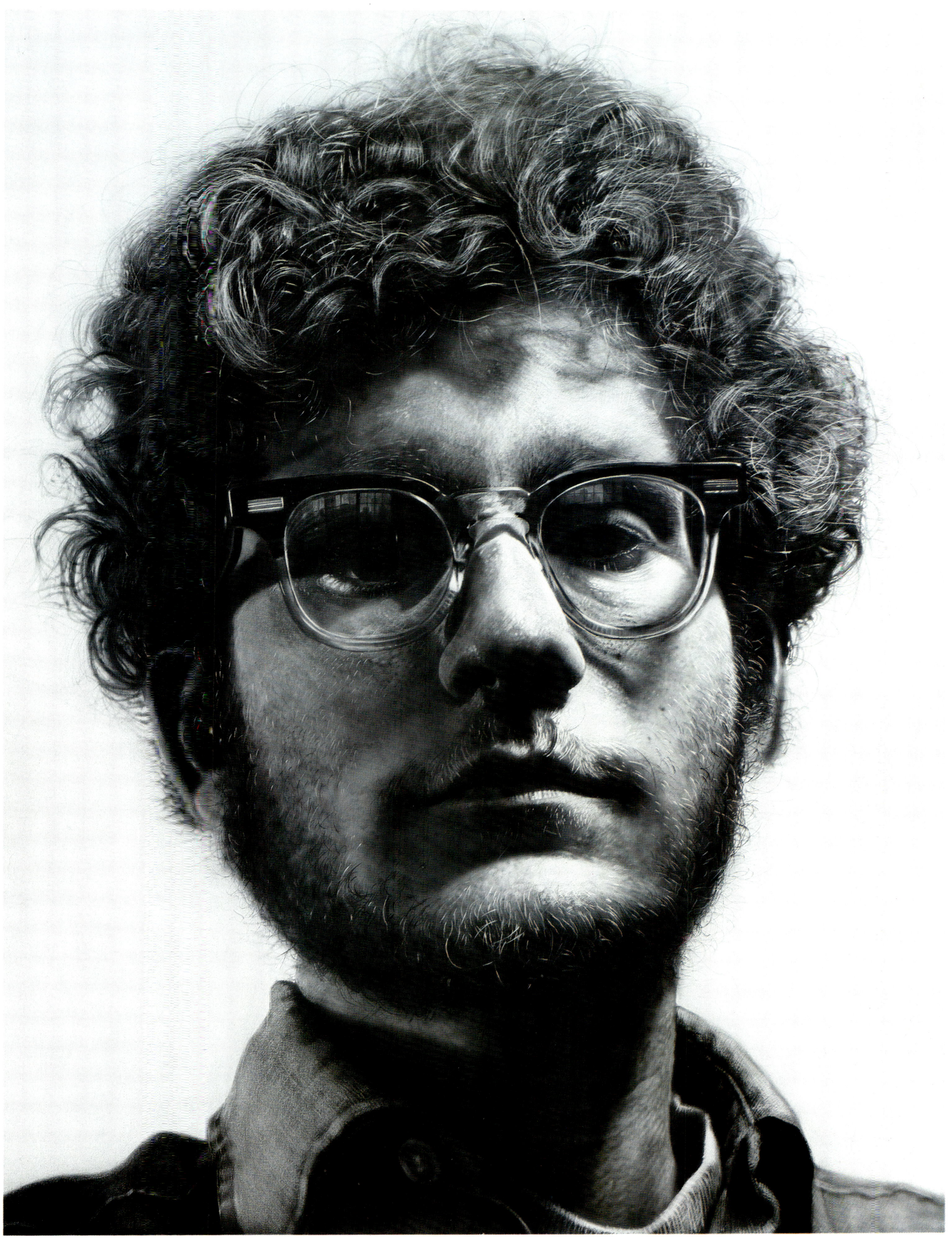

ON THE FRONT COVER

André Derain FRENCH (1880–1954)

St. Paul's from the Thames (1906–07)

Derain was one of the exhibitors in the 1905 Salon d'Automne whose bold, slashing strokes and unnatural colors earned them the name of *fauves* or "wild beasts." Like Matisse, he developed a vocabulary of color, using it as a structural element in his paintings rather than as a means of imitating natural appearances. With flat surfaces of raw color, decorative and rhythmic form, this view of St. Paul's Cathedral is Derain's last work in the fauve style and stands as a culminating statement of its principles. With this painting, he set fauvism aside and followed Picasso and Braque into the realms of the style Matisse dismissed as "only cubist"; his colors became more restrained, his forms more geometric and rectilinear.

Derain was never a leader. His paintings broke no new ground, his ideas were never highly original. Yet his sensitivity and his unerring instinct for the very best of contemporary style and vision have made him into one of the most important of the French modernists.

Oil on canvas 39¼ x 32¼" (100 x 82 cm) Bequest of Putnam Dana McMillan, 1961

ON THE TITLE PAGE

Jean-Baptiste-Siméon Chardin FRENCH (1699–1779)

The Attributes of the Arts (1766)

In 1766 it was assumed by many that Chardin, after a long and successful career, was over the hill and no longer able to compete with younger artists. His entry of a painting in the Salon of that year aroused considerable ridicule— ridicule that abruptly faded when his entry was revealed and then awarded the grand prize.

This is the winning entry, its magnificence giving an immediate lie to any speculation about Chardin's waning powers. He had himself been a great commercial success throughout most of his life and here he depicts the attributes of the arts and the rewards that are accorded them. We see, from the left: literature, painting, sculpture, and architecture—music apparently taking a lesser place in the artist's esteem. The rewards include medals and honors as well as hard cash.

The center of the scene is given to a plaster cast of Pigalle's *Mercury*. This work was extremely popular at the time, and its inclusion is a form of homage by one artist to another. The tight composition, the careful balance, and the glowing colors dominated by brilliant flashes of red and blue, all bespeak the hand of a great master—and one whose powers, rather than waning, are here seen at their peak. Indeed, Catherine the Great of Russia was so impressed by this work that she commissioned Chardin to paint a second version, which now hangs in the Hermitage Museum in Leningrad.

Oil on linen 44½ x 57¼" (113 x 145 cm) The William Hood Dunwoody Fund, 1952

ON THE BACK COVER

Jean-Baptiste-Camille Corot FRENCH (1796–1875)

The Springtime of Life (1871)

Of Corot's more than three thousand paintings, the great majority were landscapes. Relatively few were figure paintings such as this one. Yet the lightness of his brushstrokes were as well suited to portraiture as to landscape, and the misty and diaphanous atmosphere he created so effortlessly lent itself especially well to this charming vision of a young girl.

Corot studied with two teachers. One stressed the importance of structure and balance, the other taught him to study nature "naively and conscientiously." Their combined influence is seen in this work: a direct and seemingly spontaneous vision of nature, carefully composed to form a perfect spatial balance.

Success came late in life. Corot was fifty-six before his paintings started to sell. Soon, however, there was great demand for his works, and the aging artist became extremely wealthy and influential. He used his wealth and influence to help the younger generation of artists such as Courbet, Millet, and Manet, and his own work became a bridge between the formalism of French heroic and romantic art, and the great breakaway movement of impressionism.

Oil on linen 41 x 29" (104 x 74 cm) Bequest of Mrs. Erasmus C. Lindley in memory of her father, James J. Hill, 1949

AF504184

SAN FRANCISCO

BERLIN

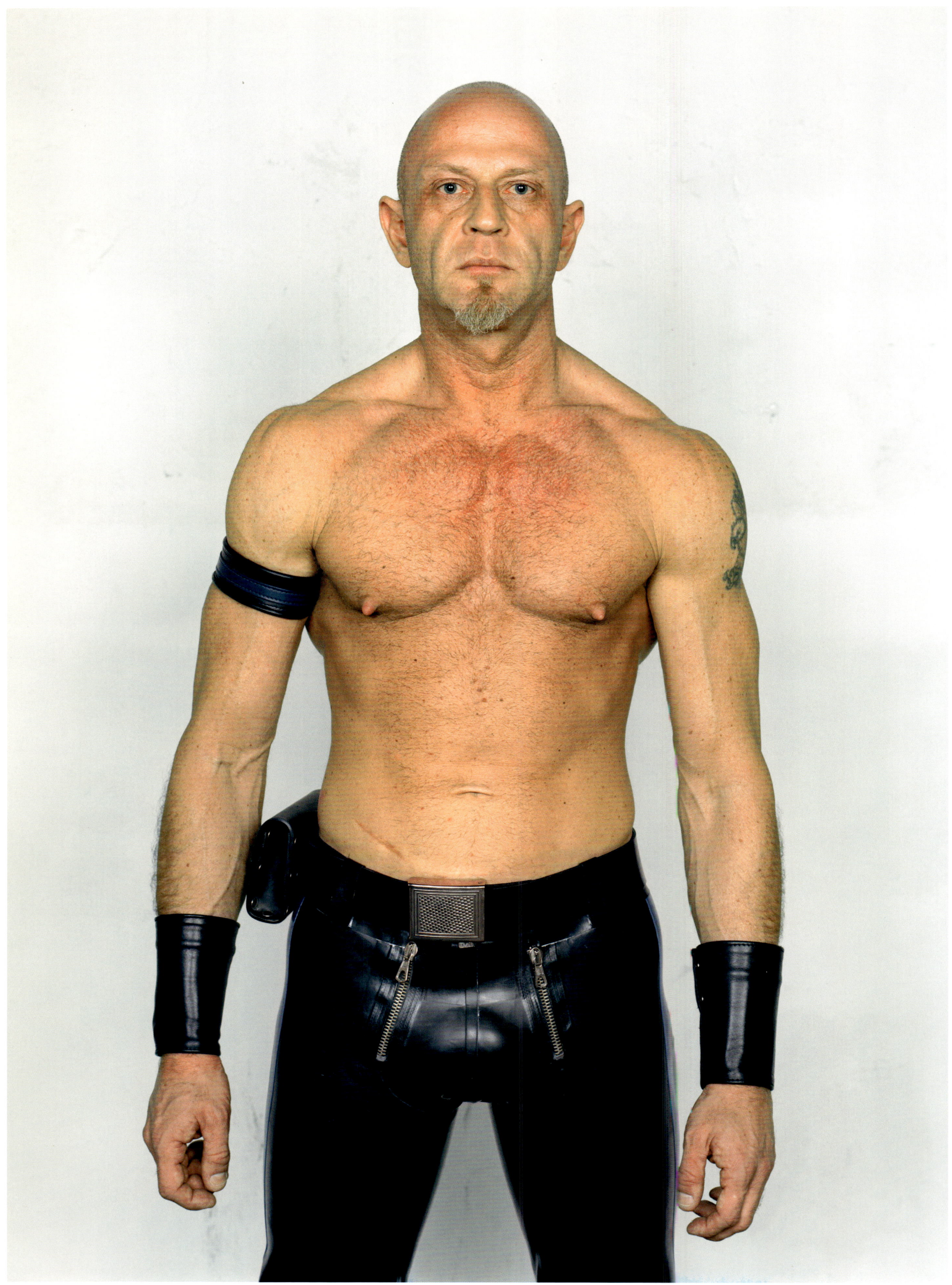

Rough6 Berlin

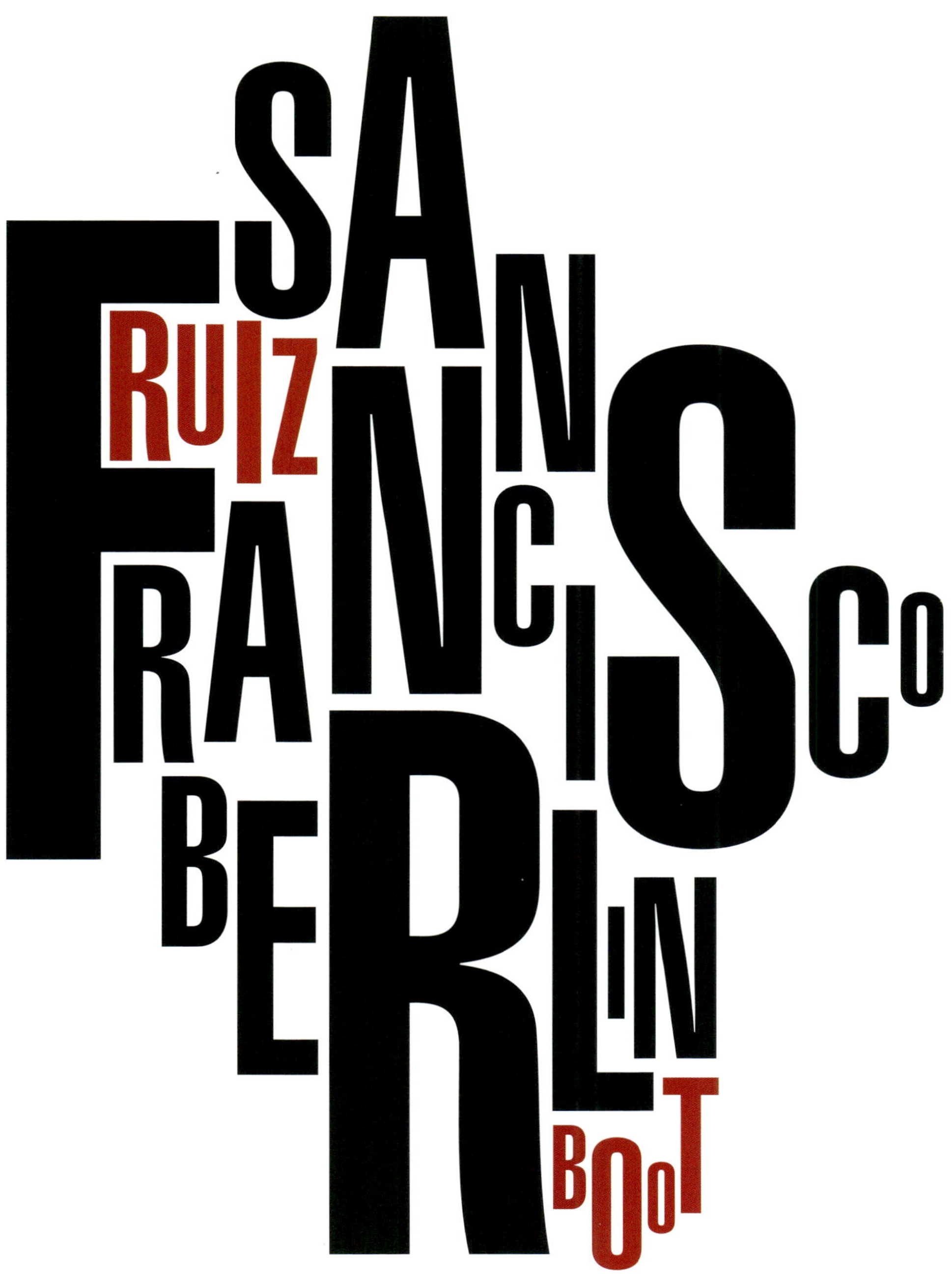

SAN FRANCISCO BERLIN   STEFAN RUIZ

WITH A CONVERSATION: STEPHEN MAYES, STEFAN RUIZ & CHRIS BOOT

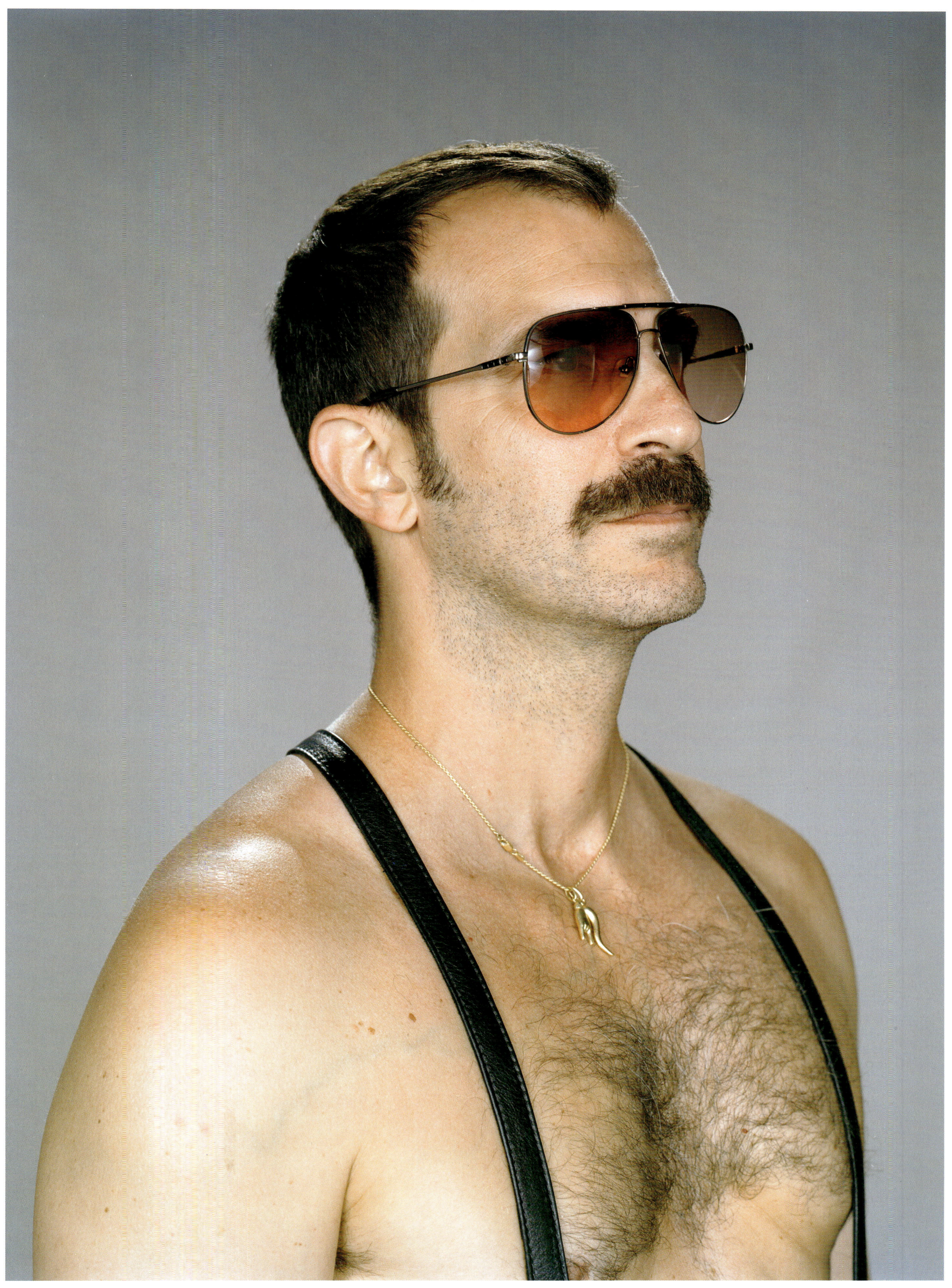

Michael Goffoletti San Francisco

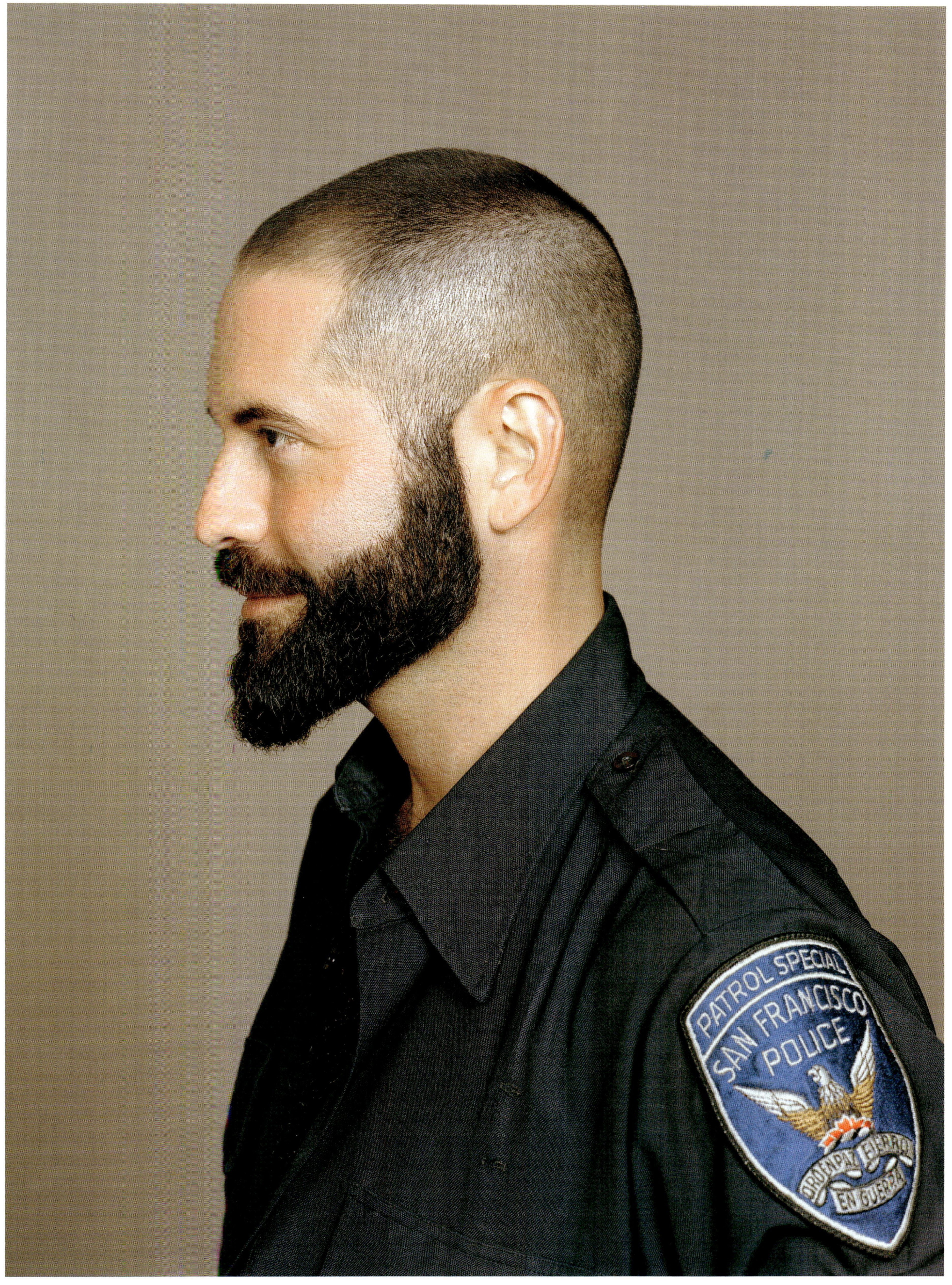

Bearded Wolf San Francisco

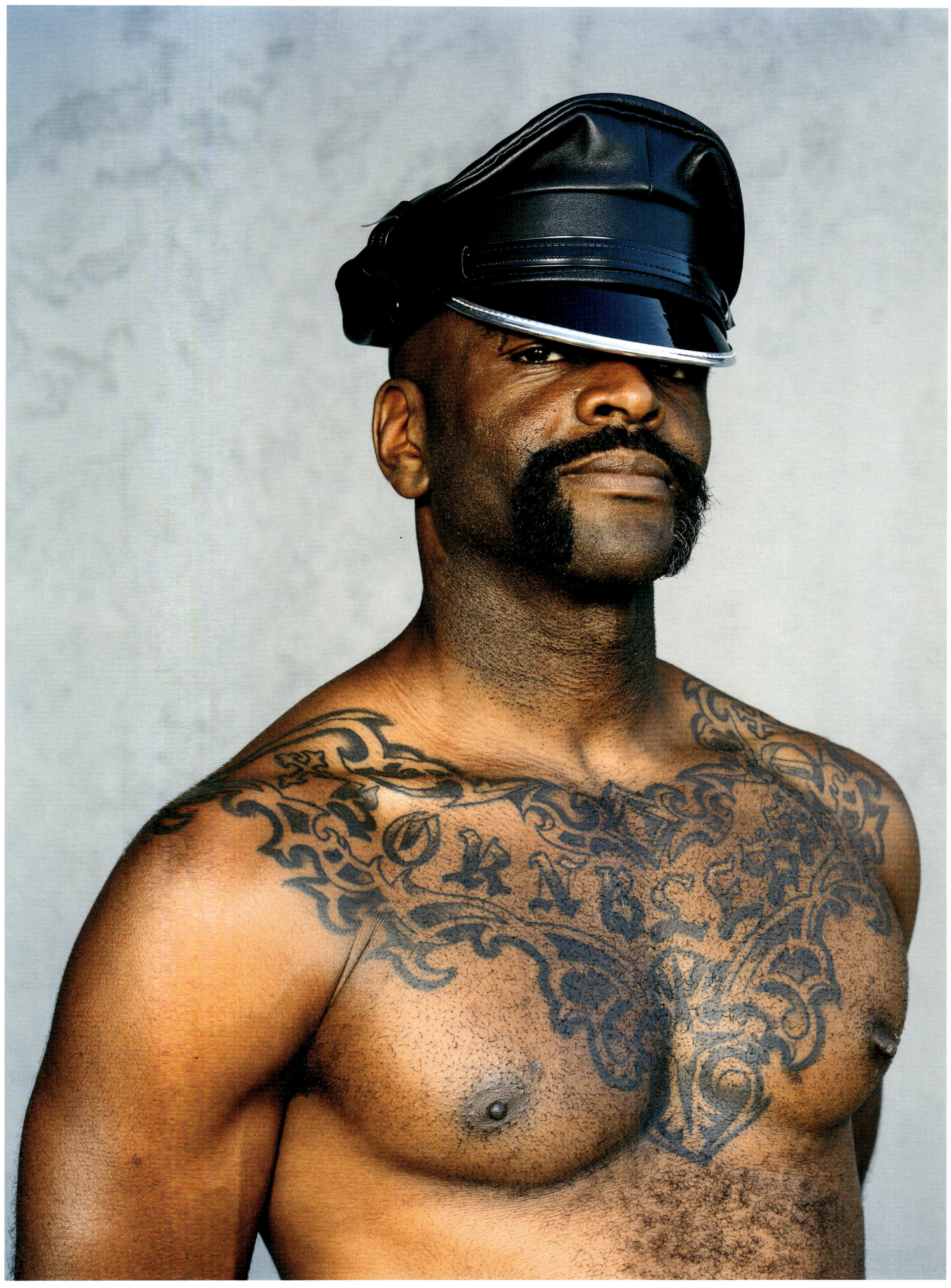

Mr. XL San Francisco

I've only been in San Francisco for going on five years. I moved here from Atlanta, having grown up in the South, in south-east Alabama. I came to San Francisco for the first time in 2004, on vacation. All my friends said, 'Oh, you're going to want to move there, you're going to want to stay,' and I was like, 'Yeah yeah, right.' And of course I moved here nine months after I first visited. It was love at first sight.

In the South, you were always hitting your head on the ceiling, but then you come to a place like San Francisco and there is no ceiling. Especially in regard to sexuality and exploration and that sort of thing. There's something in the air here. I feel like people are invigorated, their minds are clearer. I don't know why. It just felt new and good and progressive and right.

I don't really consider myself a fetishist to any degree. I guess it's something you just kind of go along with. The Folsom street fair has this kind of reputation. I wouldn't say I was nervous the first time I went, but I went with this heavy sense of expectation, like it was going to be really dark – definitely sexy, but with an edgy undercurrent. I think in the past it probably had more of that undercurrent. Now it feels mainly like a celebration. People are laughing and carrying on. All the gay boys all come in to town to= celebrate their kink. There is definitely that sexy edgy air, but it's not the heavy dark thing that it's made out to be. It's very light, considering how dark it could be!

Of course I like to dress up... At Folsom that time, a big group of friends were staying with me. We all got dressed up and went out. It's really the one time of year I put on leather and work that part of my psyche. I can get into the leather scene, this whole environment, and maybe that spills into my nature, but I have to be able to draw the chalk around it. I'm not just putting on the outfit and going to church. A lot of the guys in the crowd all blur together, all wearing the same harness, with the same muscle tone... I feel like I need to do something to stand apart from it, to tweak it a little bit.

With other costume holidays, I'm there too of course.

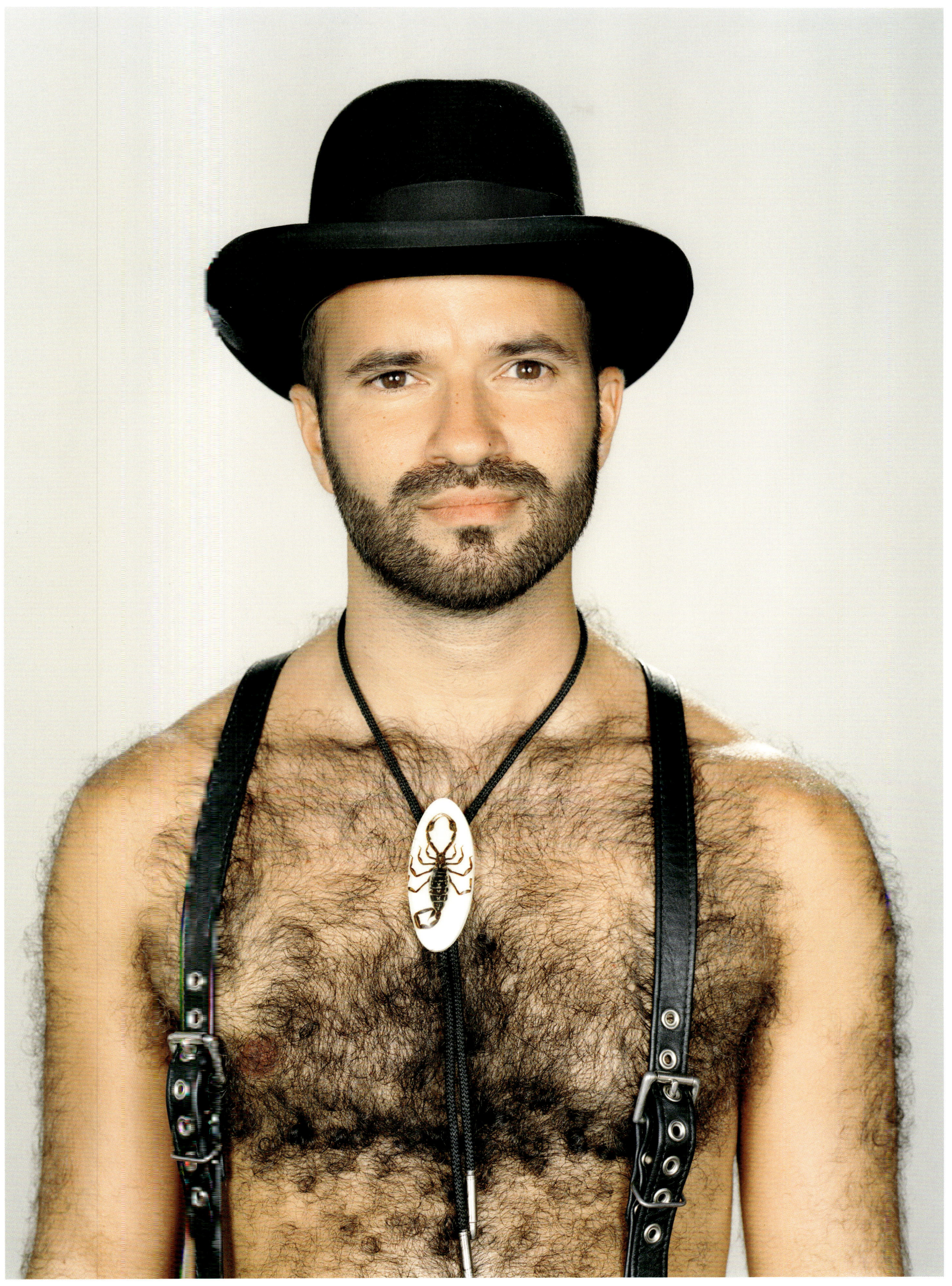

Charles San Francisco

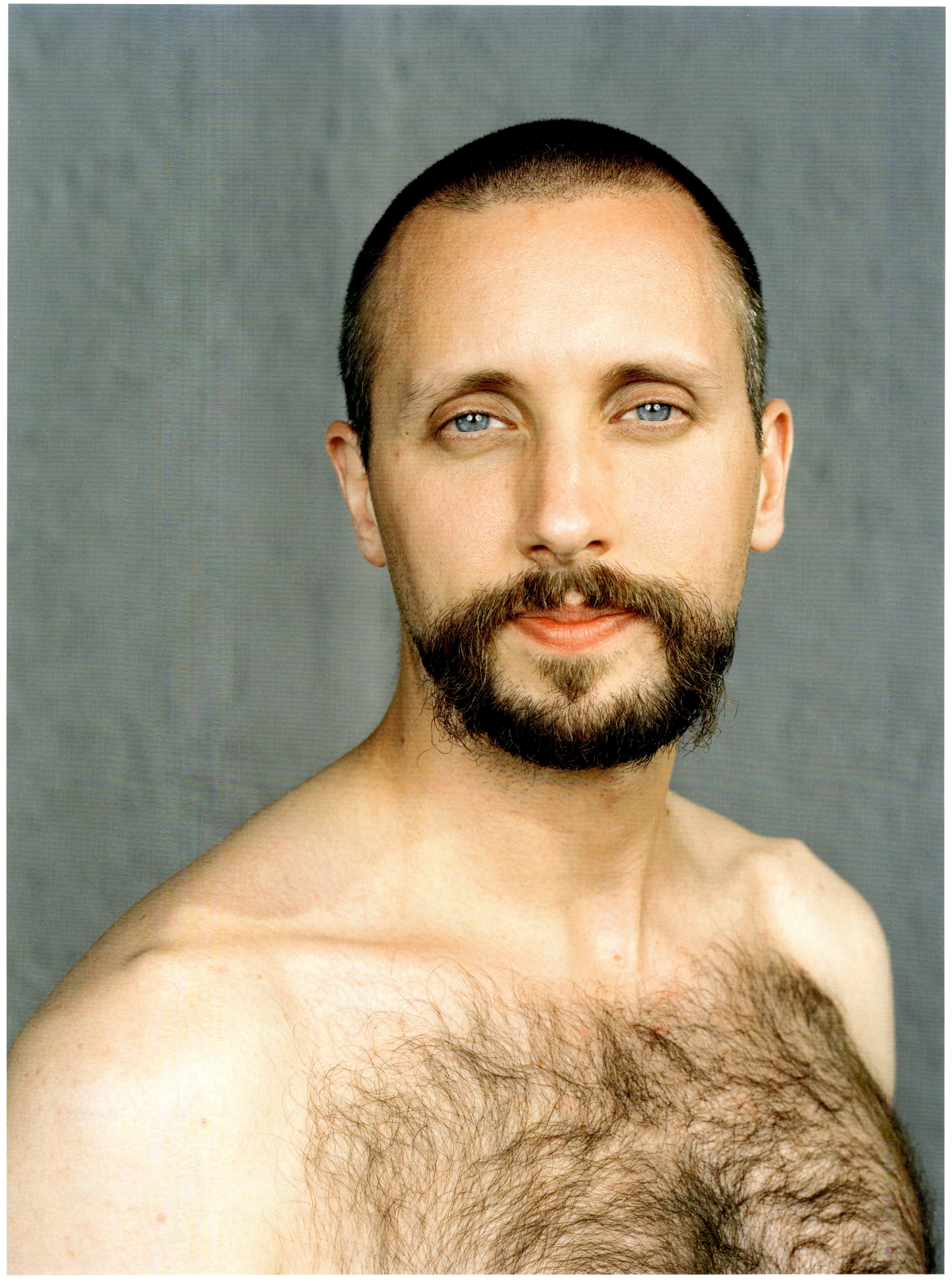

M Arana San Francisco

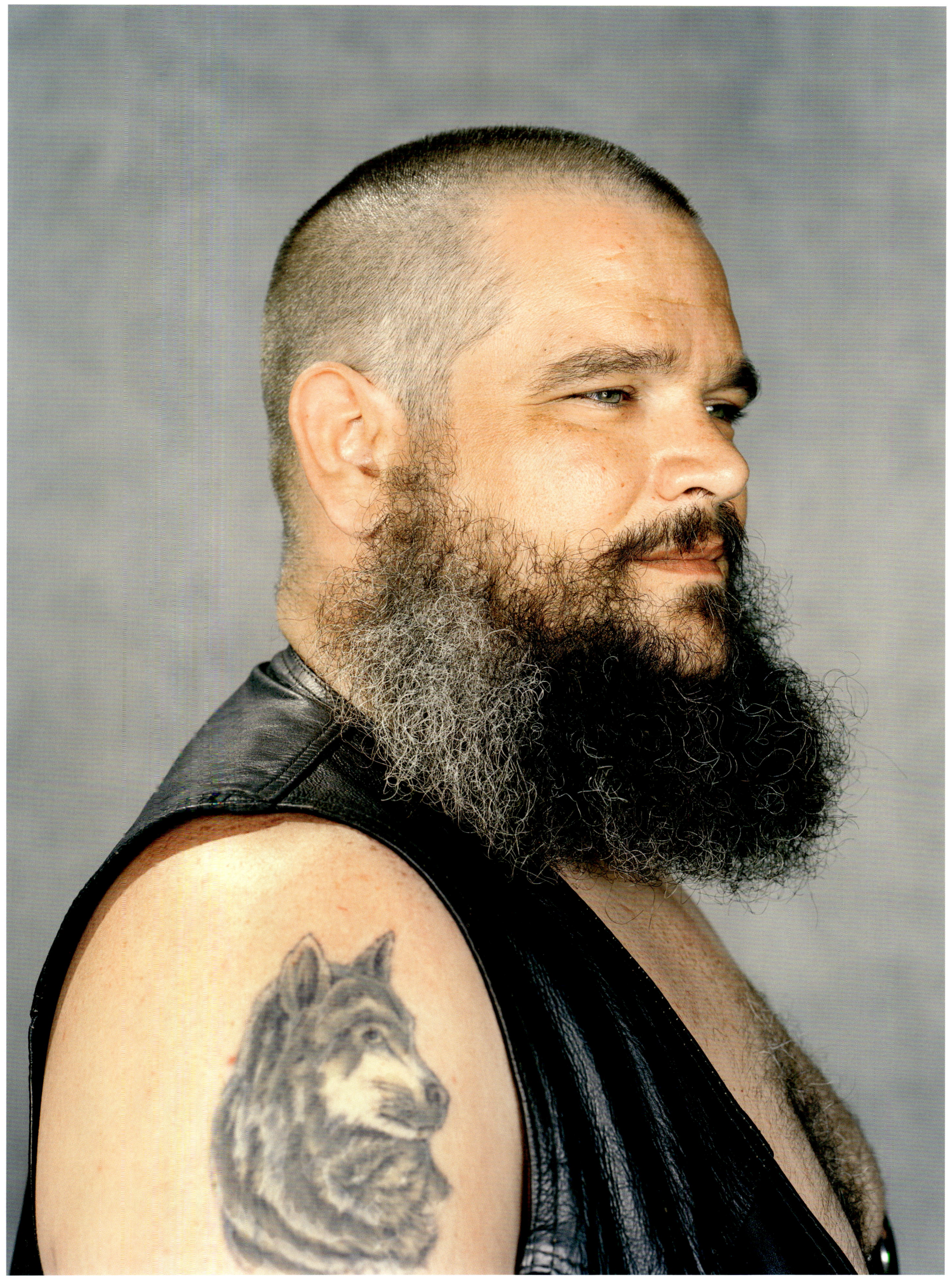

Boy Bryan San Francisco

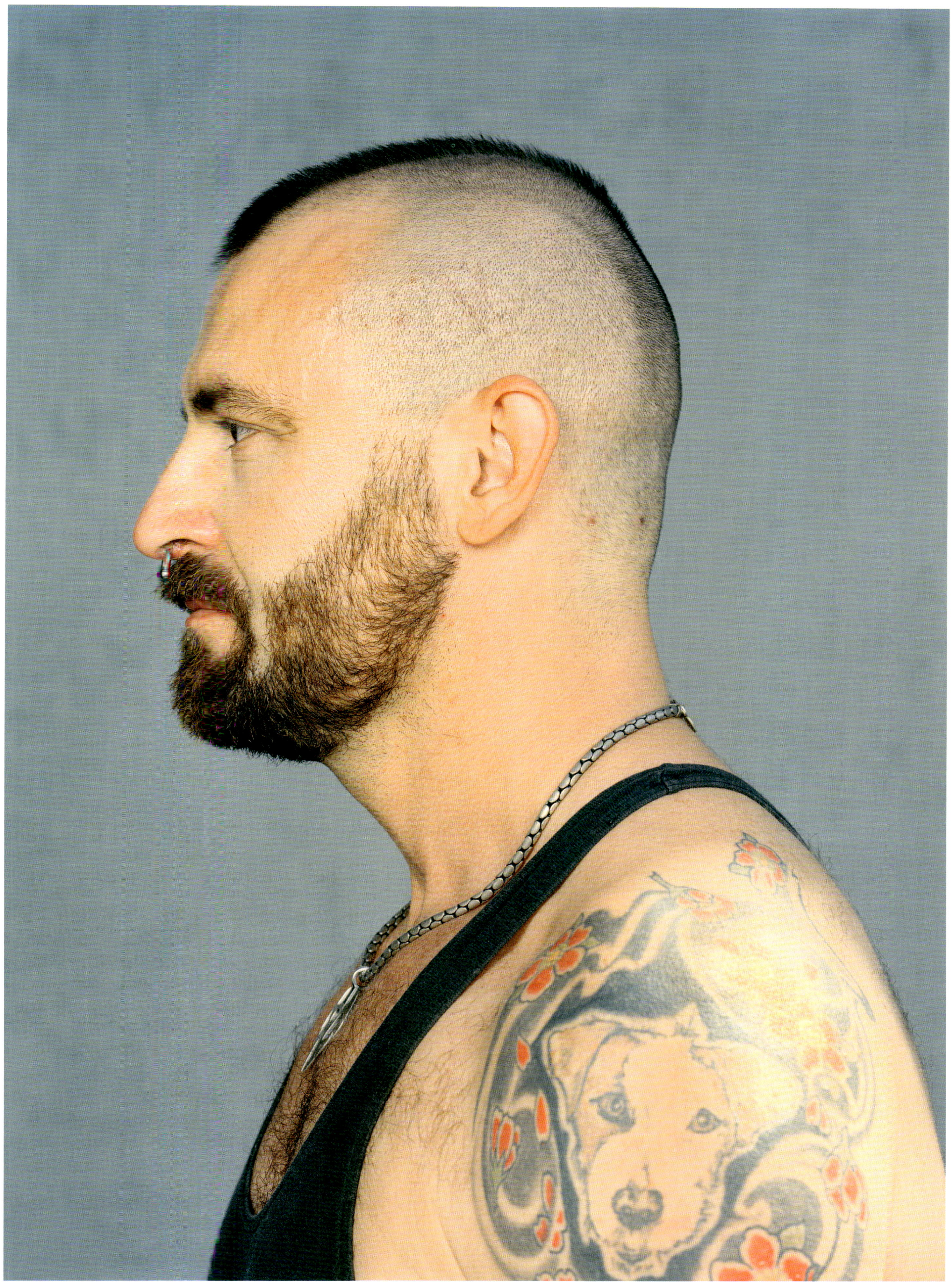

Frank San Francisco

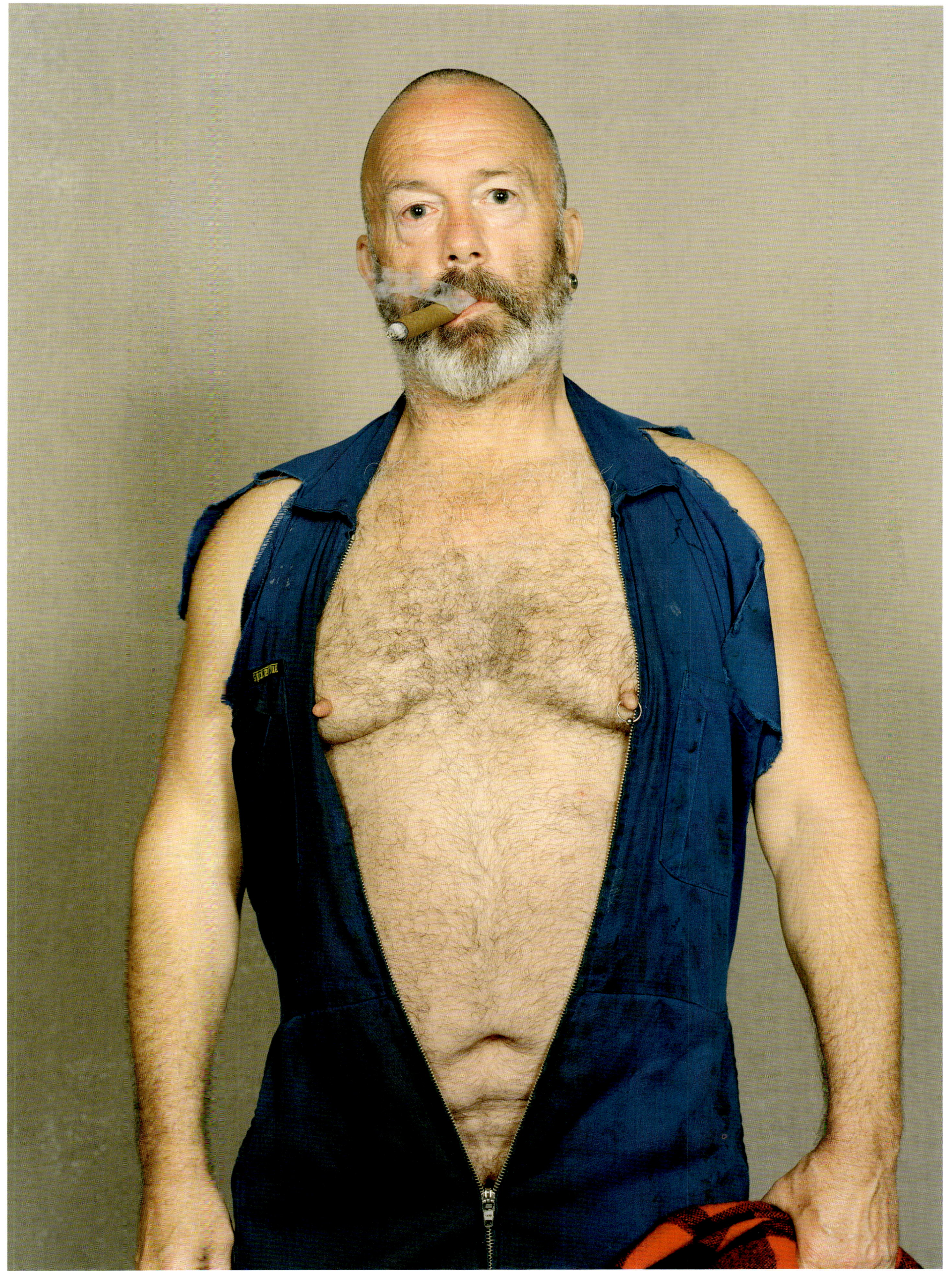

Cigar Daddy San Francisco

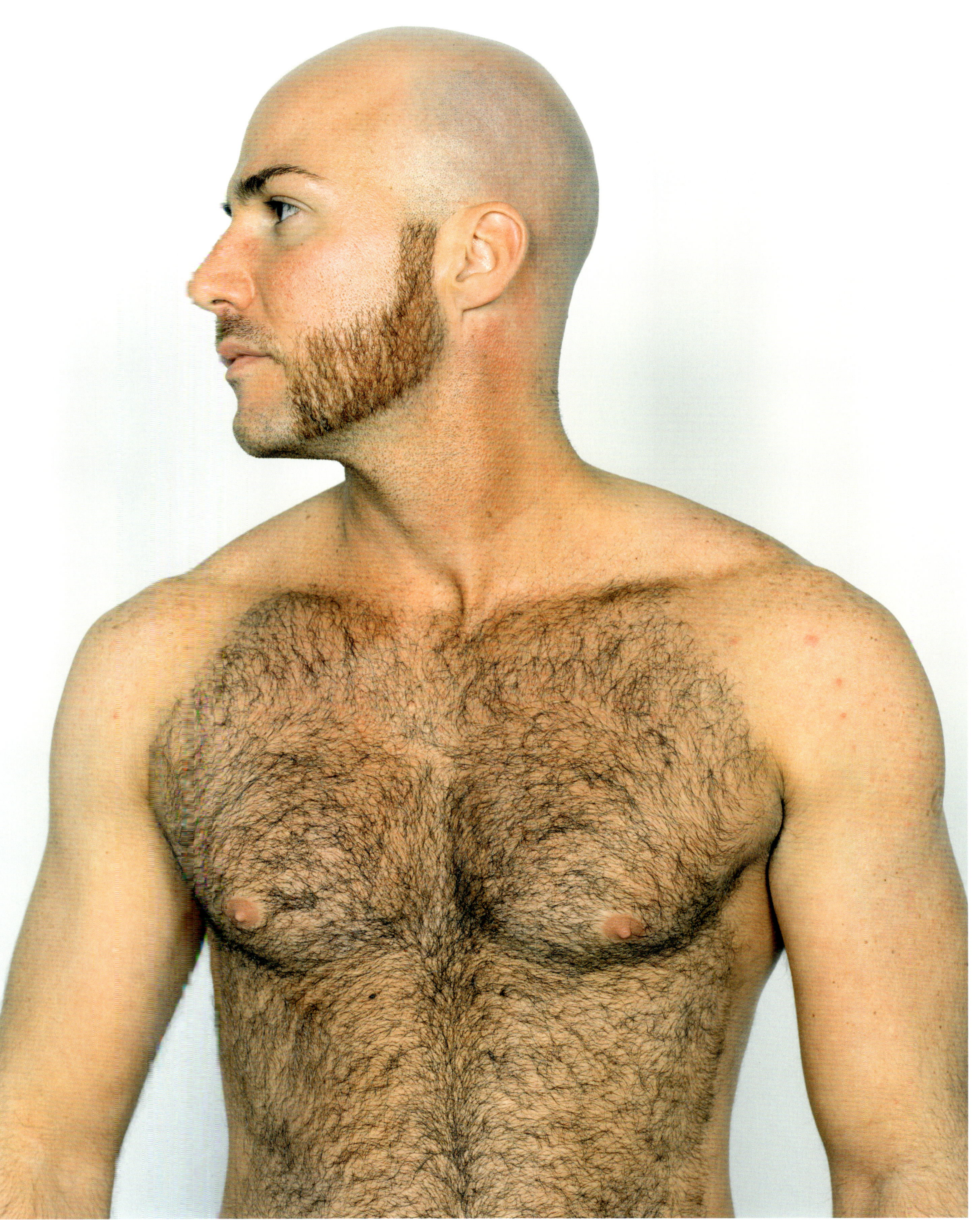

Ivano Spain Berlin

I identify as a trans man. I was born a woman but I transitioned ten years ago. Now I have a birth certificate that says that I was born male. I'm attracted to other men, which is what makes me gay.

I identified as a gay man before I started taking hormones or having surgery, but then people on the street usually read me as a butch woman. It was really hard to be recognised the way I thought of myself, and especially hard to be part of the gay men's community – even though I had a male partner, a gay man. We've been together for twelve years now. He didn't have a problem, but very few others got the concept.

These days I pass as male. When it comes to sex of course there are always issues of disclosure – *do* I tell? *when* do I tell? *how* do I tell? A trans guy can pass for a man and go into a dark room and give somebody a blow job, and not disclose that he was born biologically female. But for me, I feel comfortable if I'm able to talk about it first. I don't want to get involved with people who might be disapproving or prejudiced. I don't want to make a connection and then get negative feedback later on.

In ten years, things have totally changed. There's more of an understanding that gender and sexuality aren't fixed categories, and people are open to different interpretations of 'gay' or 'queer'. Years ago, men I met would say, 'Yes, I can accept a trans man socially, I can accept his gender identity, respect him... But I can't interact with him sexually if he doesn't have a dick.' Now I find men are much more open, more curious. Of course, it depends on the particular scene. I'm part of a community in Berlin that's focused on SM play rather than casual sex. Here, I find the attitude is that SM guys *should* be creative, *should* be open to different possibilities and try new things.

Berlin is rather important to me, for lots of reasons. There are several other communities I'm connected to – punks, redskins, squatters, anarchists w which have all ended up more established here than anywhere else in Germany. Especially the queers. We have a joke here that everybody nice ends up in Berlin.

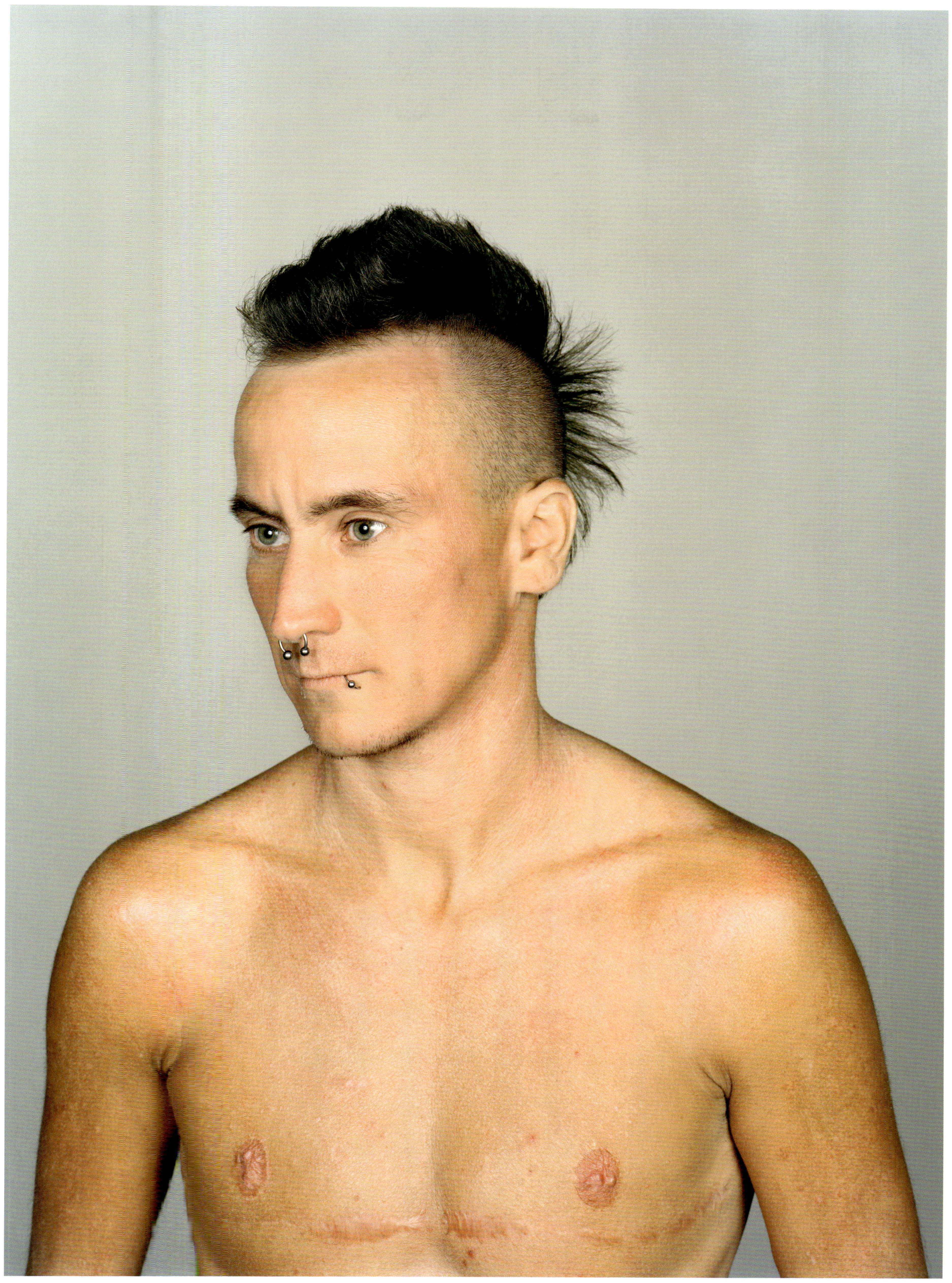

Trans Punk Berlin

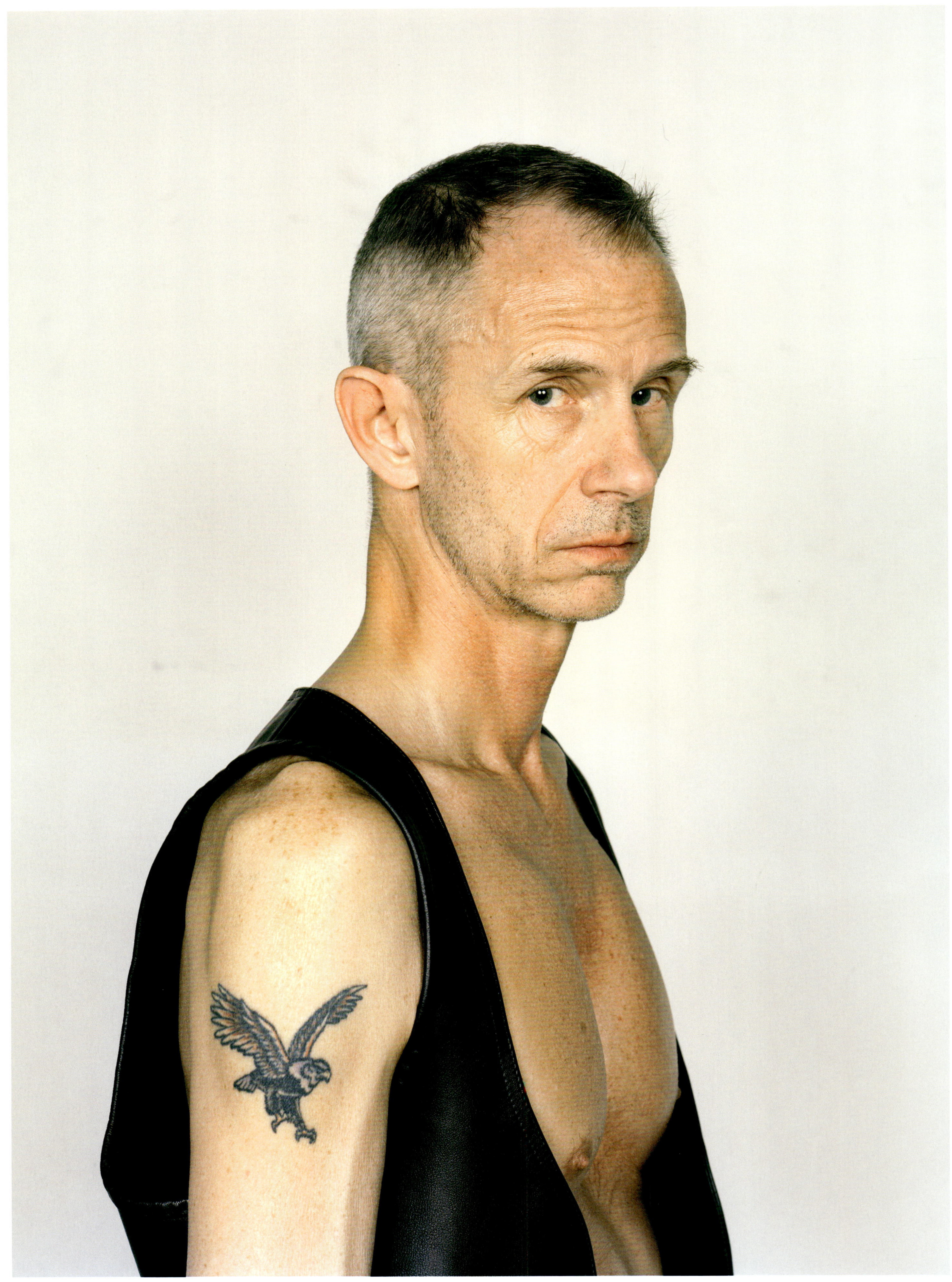

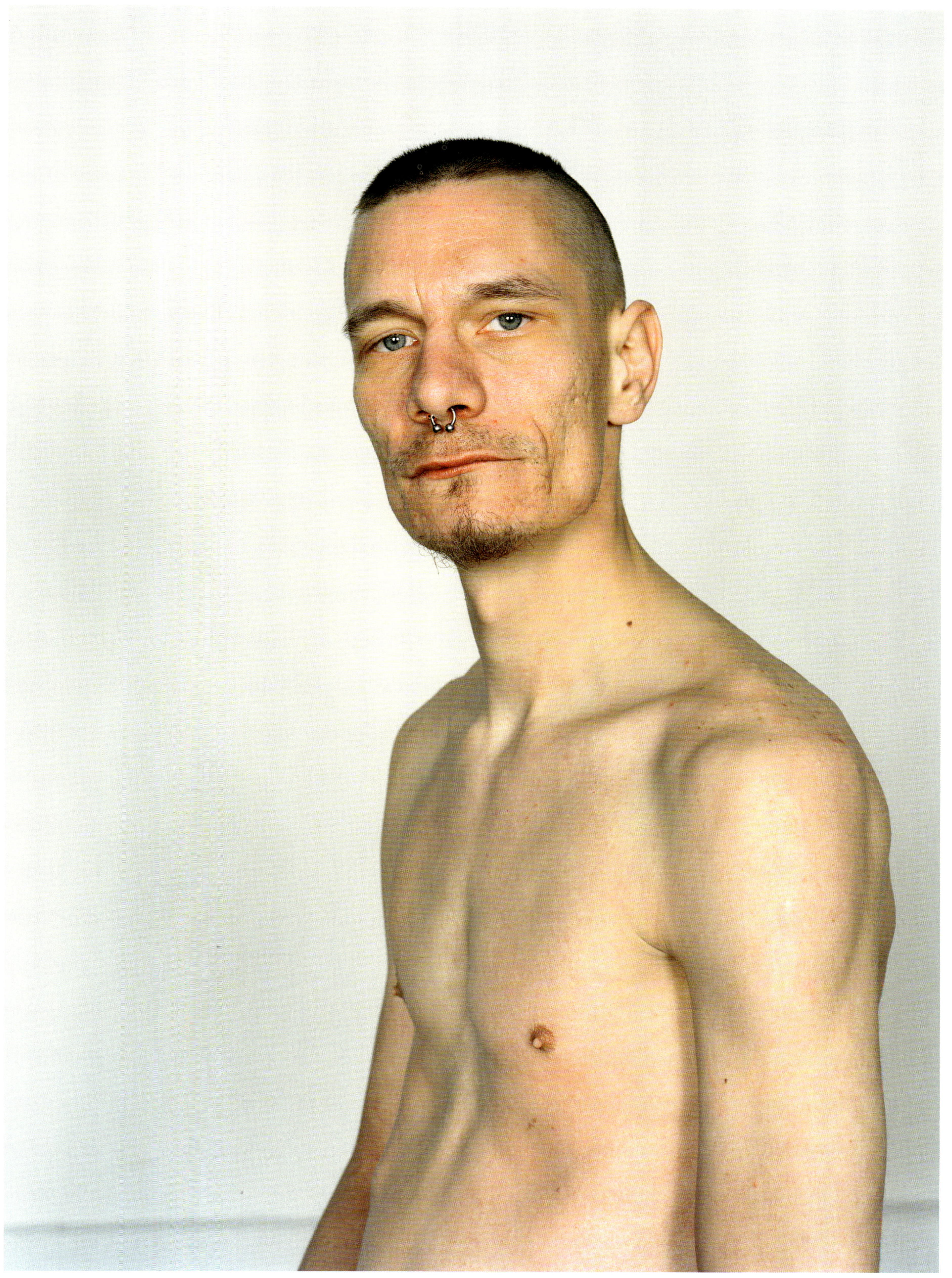

Septum Berlin

My name is Christian. I'm now 24 years old and I'm Swiss. I've finished my studies and I'm working in Geneva. Some friends in Lausanne introduced me to the fetish world and I went to Berlin with them. I had heard a lot of things about Berlin, London and Amsterdam, but Berlin was nearer. So we rented a flat there for the Easter Weekend. That was my first fetish weekend.

When you think of the leather scene, you assume it's for bears, older guys, guys who like unsafe sex, those kinds of things. I went to Berlin to see if I fitted in. What I found was many other men my own age, men like me, who are into rubber and leather. I made many friends there and some have even come to see me in Switzerland.

Of course if you're HIV-positive and if you're clear about that, it's not a problem. I think we have to be clear. I'm not positive, and I want to stay this way. I want to have fun but I protect myself. Those big parties are not always easy for young people. If I find a hot guy, I need to have a minimum of discussion with him before I have sex. You have to talk, not just have sex. That's really important for me.

It's hard for young people, for other reasons also. For a start, leather and rubber gear is very expensive.

If I could, I would go to a fetish party every weekend. I like both leather and rubber. I like parties. It's fun meeting people with the same interests, making friends, dancing and having sex.

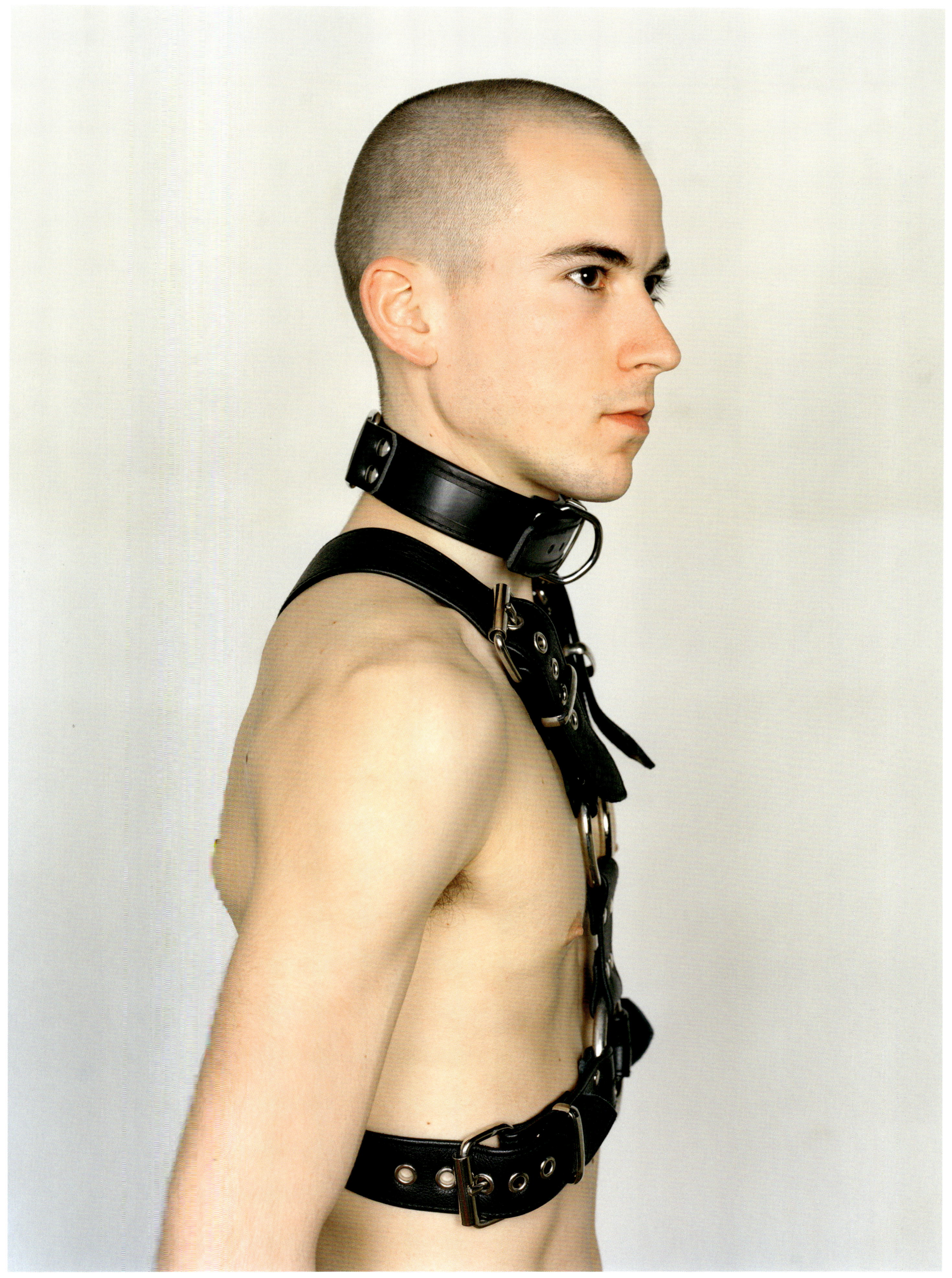

Christian Berlin

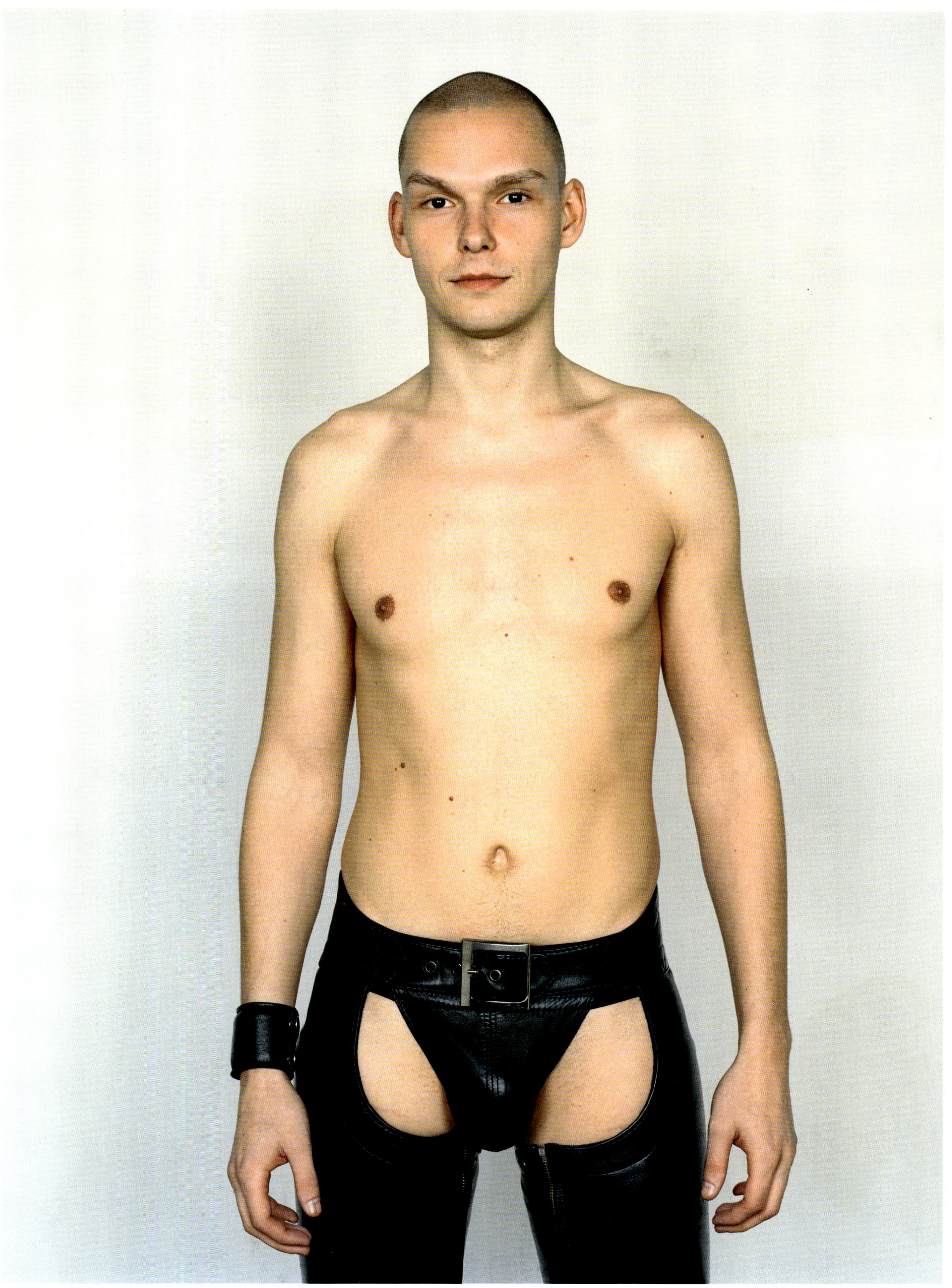

Kristof Berlin

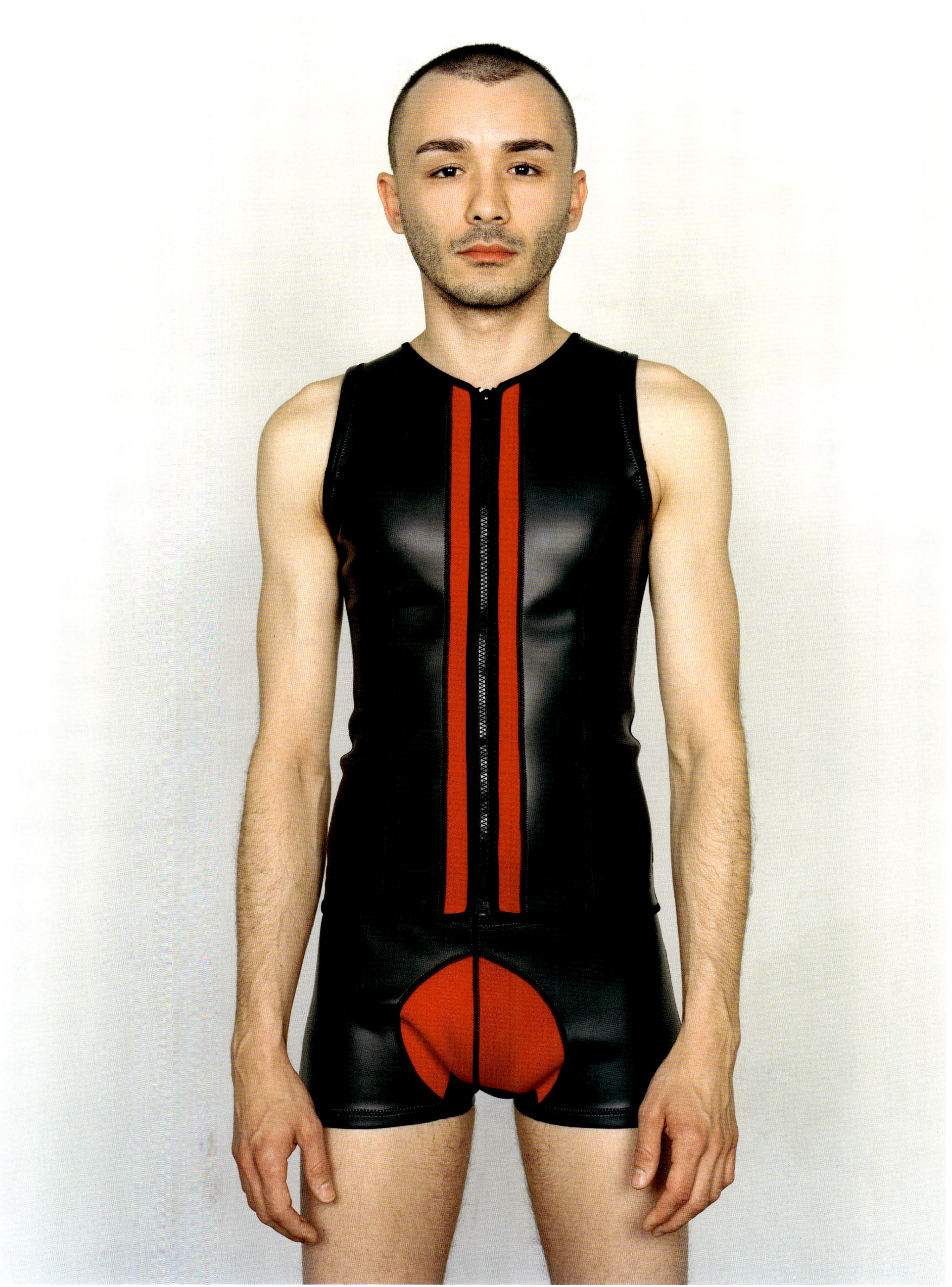

Esteban Berlin

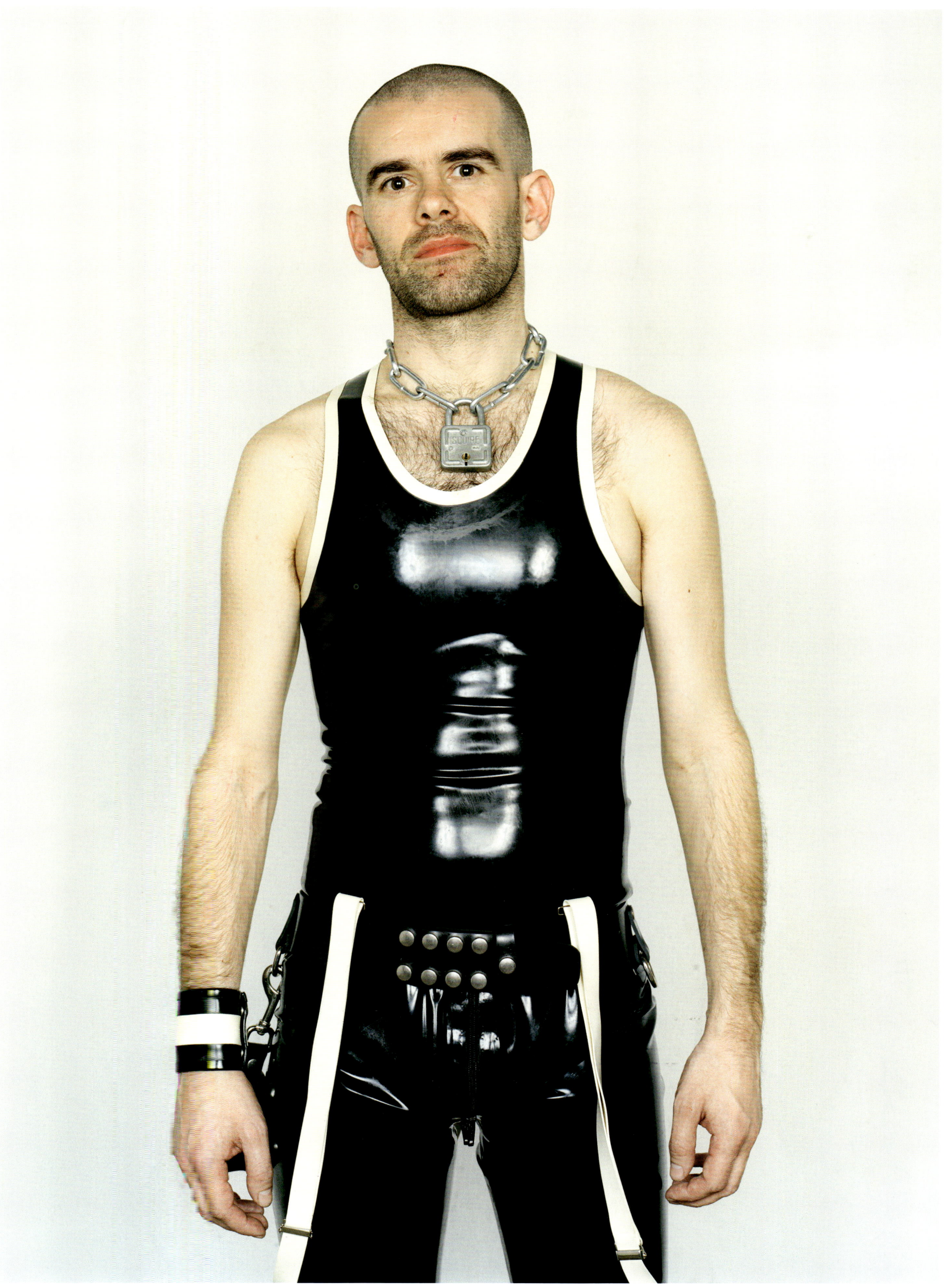

Fotoxy Berlin

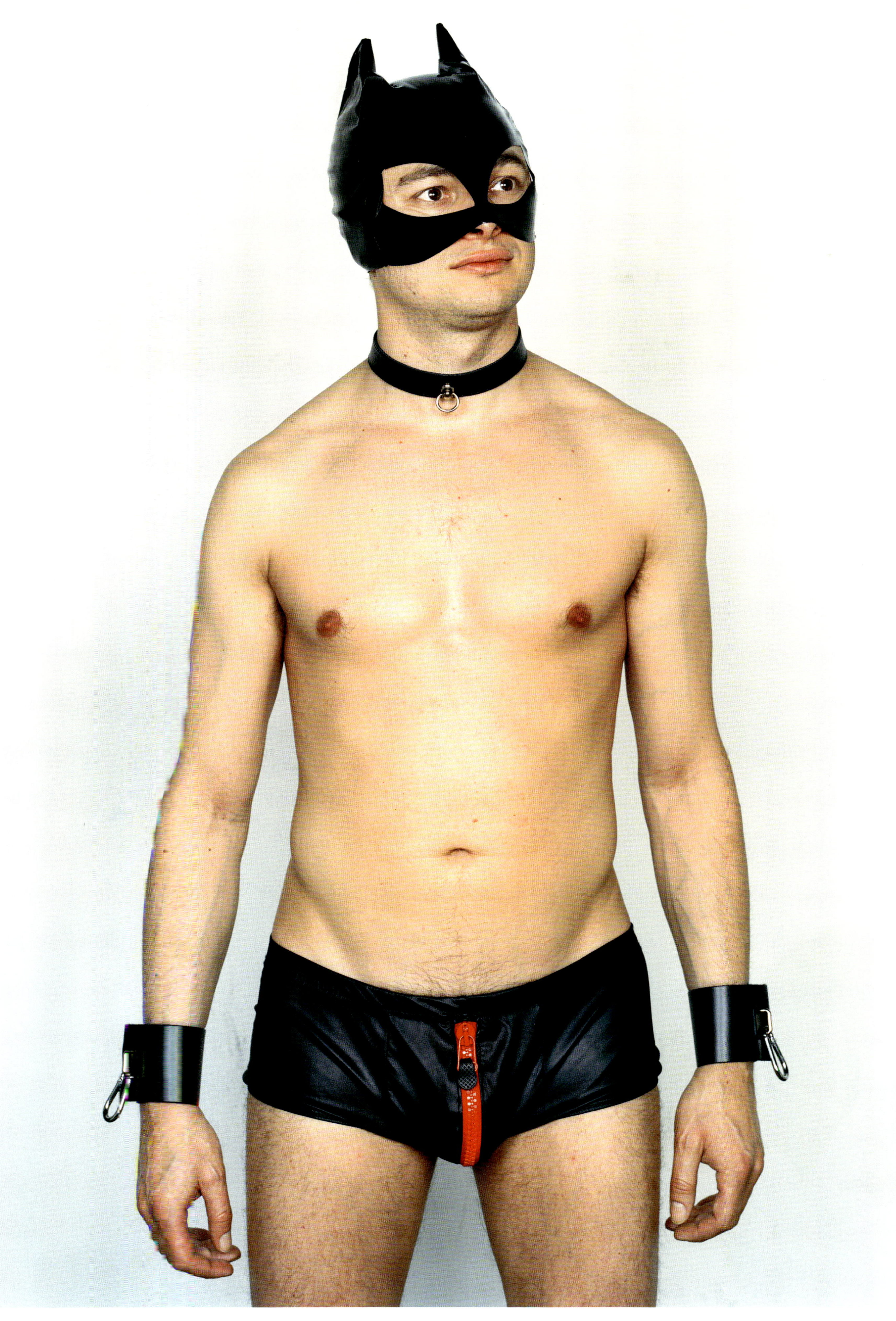

Cat People Berlin

I'm 26 and I live in Manchester. I work as a photographer, plus I work in a couple of gay bars and the Rob gear shop, and at kids' camp during the summer.

I really like the whole piggy kind of punk look and I *love* my rubber look. I like my rubber to be a bit different, so I get clothes made. I don't have a Superman fetish, I just thought it would be a bit geeky, a bit ironic. Plus black, white and red are my favourite colours. I've got lots of rubber – suitcases full! A police uniform, things that are bright and colourful, normal clothes but in rubber... A lot of people who are into rubber are into wearing full rubber suits for sex, and I've got that stuff too, but I like wearing rubber out and about. I like the attention and I love the way it transforms you. You're like someone else. And it's very social. You get into conversations with everybody about it.

It ends up taking up quite a lot of my life. I run the Manchester Rubbermen, a social club where we call each other up when we're going out in gear, and meet up and go on pub-crawls. Part of the reason I like the scene so much is because it's really a community. Everyone gets to know each other. People share their gear. I'm active in church as well, and I see similarities between my church community and the kinky community. The way people are with each other, the way everyone looks out for each other. I absolutely love that whole community vibe. I'm going to run for Mr Rubber UK just to promote that. I don't feel the scene is just about sex.

My church mates all know I'm gay and they're cool with it. I've got a Facebook page which includes some of my rubber pictures – casual pictures, not play pictures – and everyone I know is on there, even kids I've worked with on summer camp. It gets people talking. They say, 'What's that? What's that material? Why would you dress up like that for a photo?' I explain and they're like, 'Oh okay, cool.' I don't think my interest in rubber has to be hidden.

I've only been to Berlin once. Everyone was so friendly, it felt like being part of a family. Like, everyone's got that affinity with each other. Just hanging out. And the ridiculous late nights. Everyone's out every night geared up, then quite happily wearing it the next day just sat on the sidewalk or having food round a cafe. I absolutely loved that. The parties are a thousand times bigger than in Manchester. I was like a kid at Christmas. Yeah, I got a bit naughty over there.

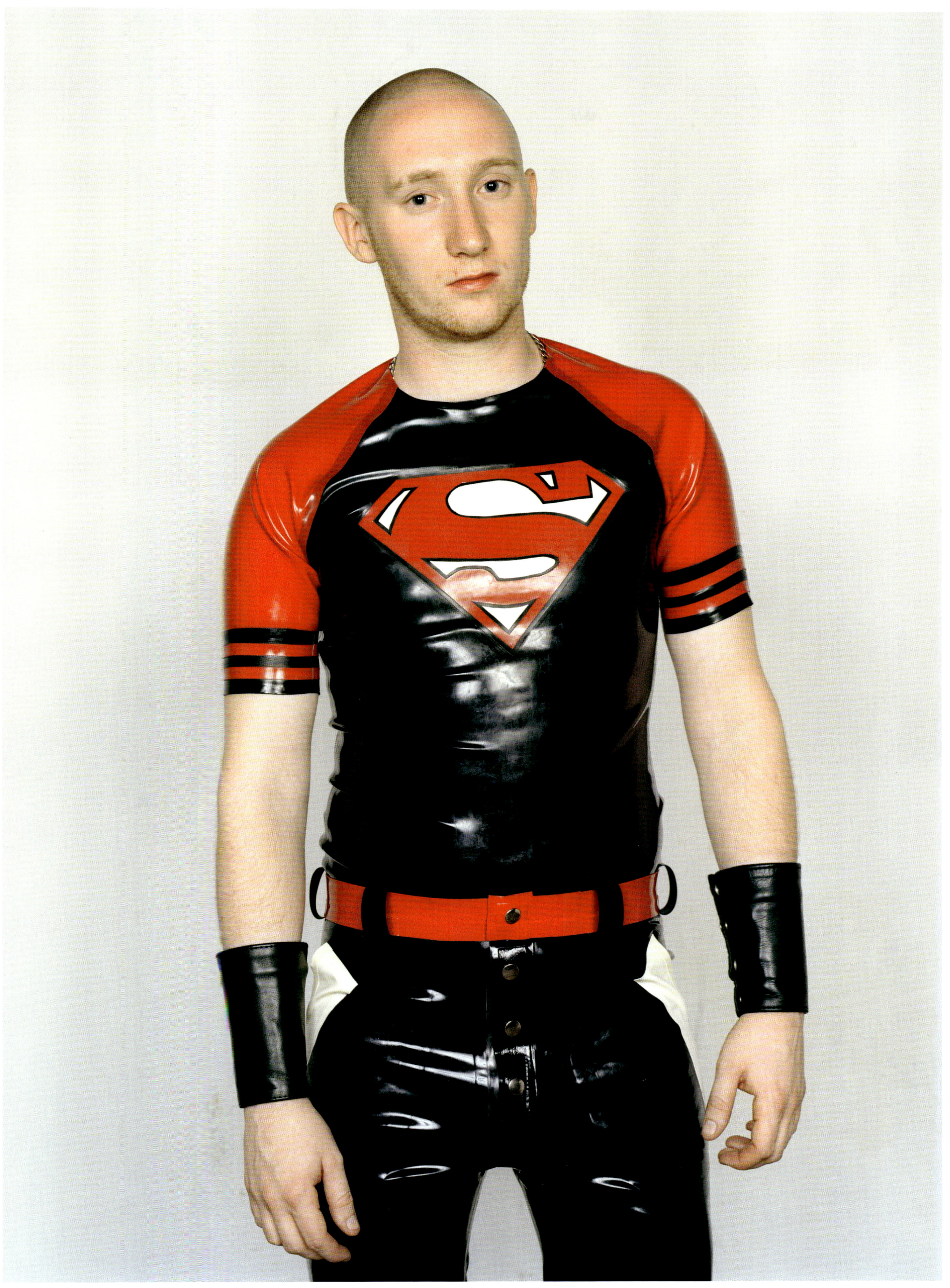

Rubbaboy Berlin

I'm actually a professional, a nurse, in real life. And I have a dinner theatre that I run in my spare time. But I'm based in a part of the USA, in the Bible Belt, where no one lives a Master/slave or BDSM lifestyle.

I really enjoy visiting San Francisco or New York and putting together my 'show'. I first came to San Francisco about thirty years ago. I used to shoot photographs and over time I shared the pictures with friends, and they suggested other people I should show them to. Pretty soon I was being published by *Drummer* magazine, a leather/fetish magazine that went out of business about ten years ago. That got me involved with the fetish community. I did photography for leather videos – lots of friends were porn stars. So I have lots of friends in San Francisco and love to visit. I go two or three times a year.

In my life at home, I tend to be very much a control freak. But it's great to go to San Francisco and play slave – to *be* a slave, to give up control to someone else and have that total change in mentality. Hence the collar around my neck. I didn't have the key to it, Master Taíno did. He's from DC, where he lives with two or three permanent slaves. He's quite well known and has a slave training academy. He and one of his other slaves were staying with me. He put the collar on me for that week, and I loved it. Absolutely loved it. Right now I have another Master who I'm working with. A permanent Master would be great, but it's fun to go to San Francisco or New York and jump into the role for a weekend or a week.

When you have a Master you serve, it's like there's someone that cares about you and is concerned about you. It's like having a little angel on your shoulder, a voice in your head that helps make decisions for you and helps to keep you on the right track. Like if you're out for dinner and you go, 'Oh, I want that piece of pie,' and the Master goes, 'No, you don't need that,' and you go, 'Oh yeah, I don't need that.' There's lots of things the Master has control over, and it's your job to think of him and help serve him. It's very much a relationship.

It's possible to develop these kinds of relationships in San Francisco. They're more open to different relationships and lifestyles than anywhere else.

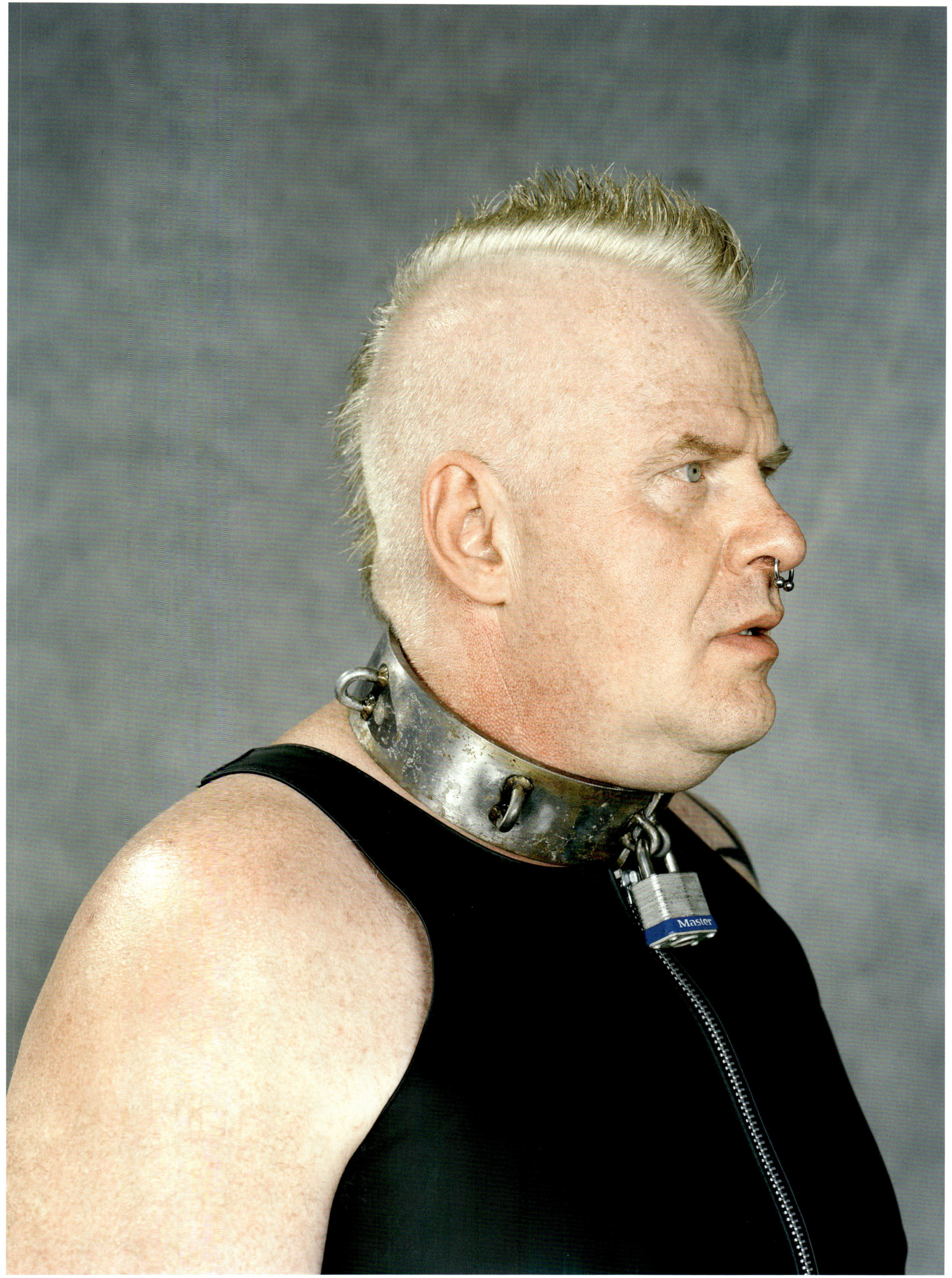

Gummibearid San Francisco

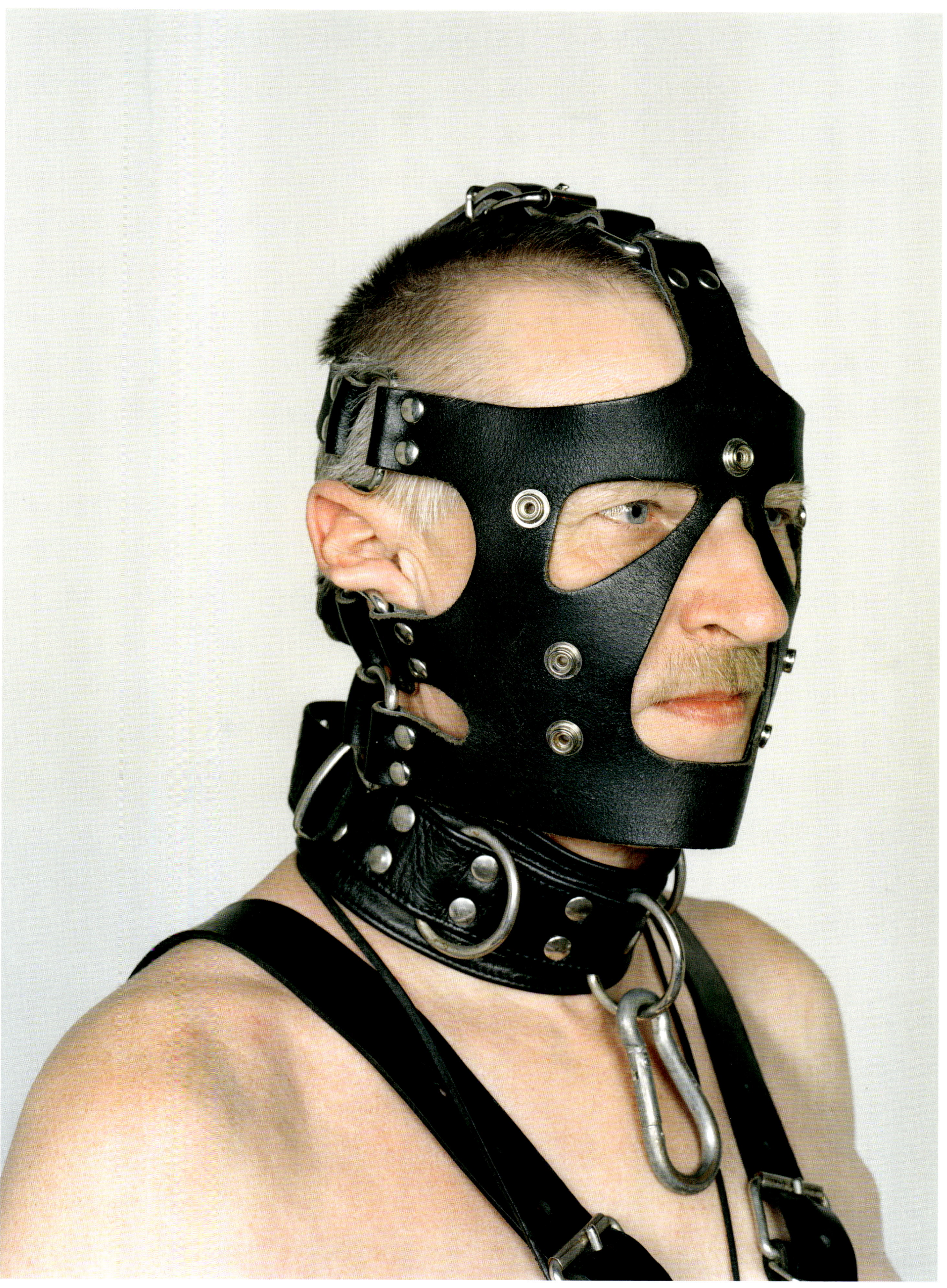

Slave Michael Berlin

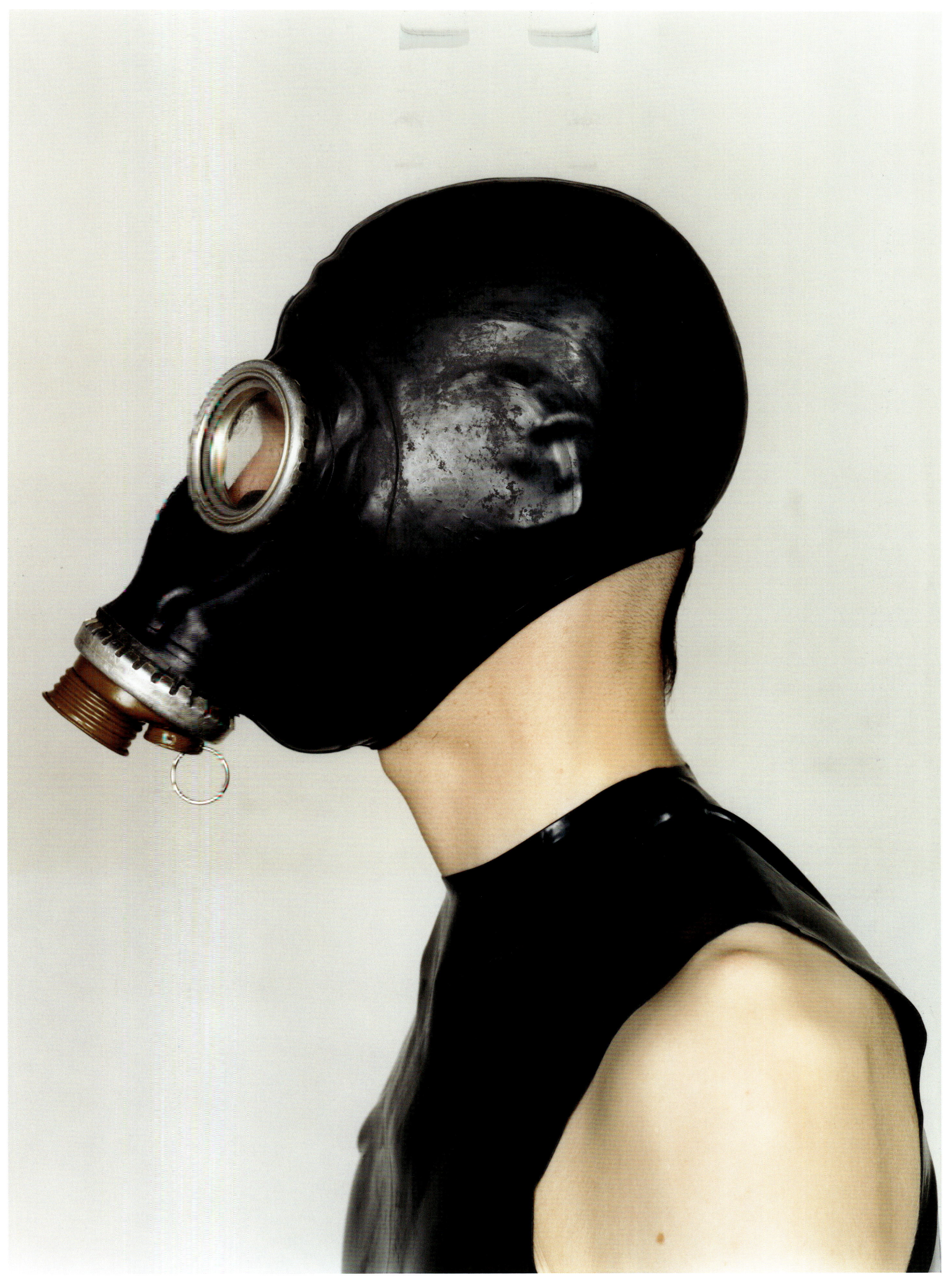

Rubber Total Berlin

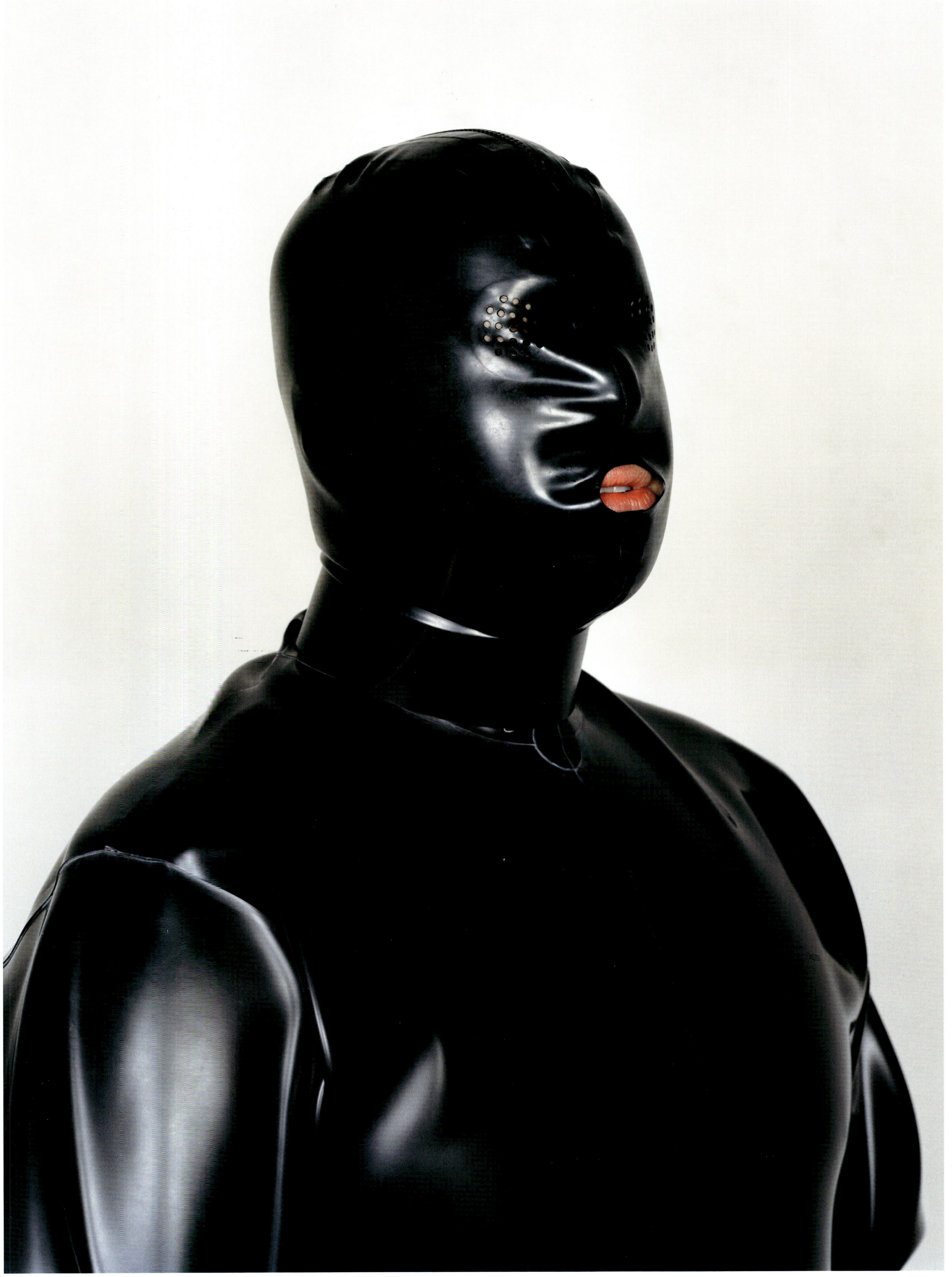

Gasmsk Berlin

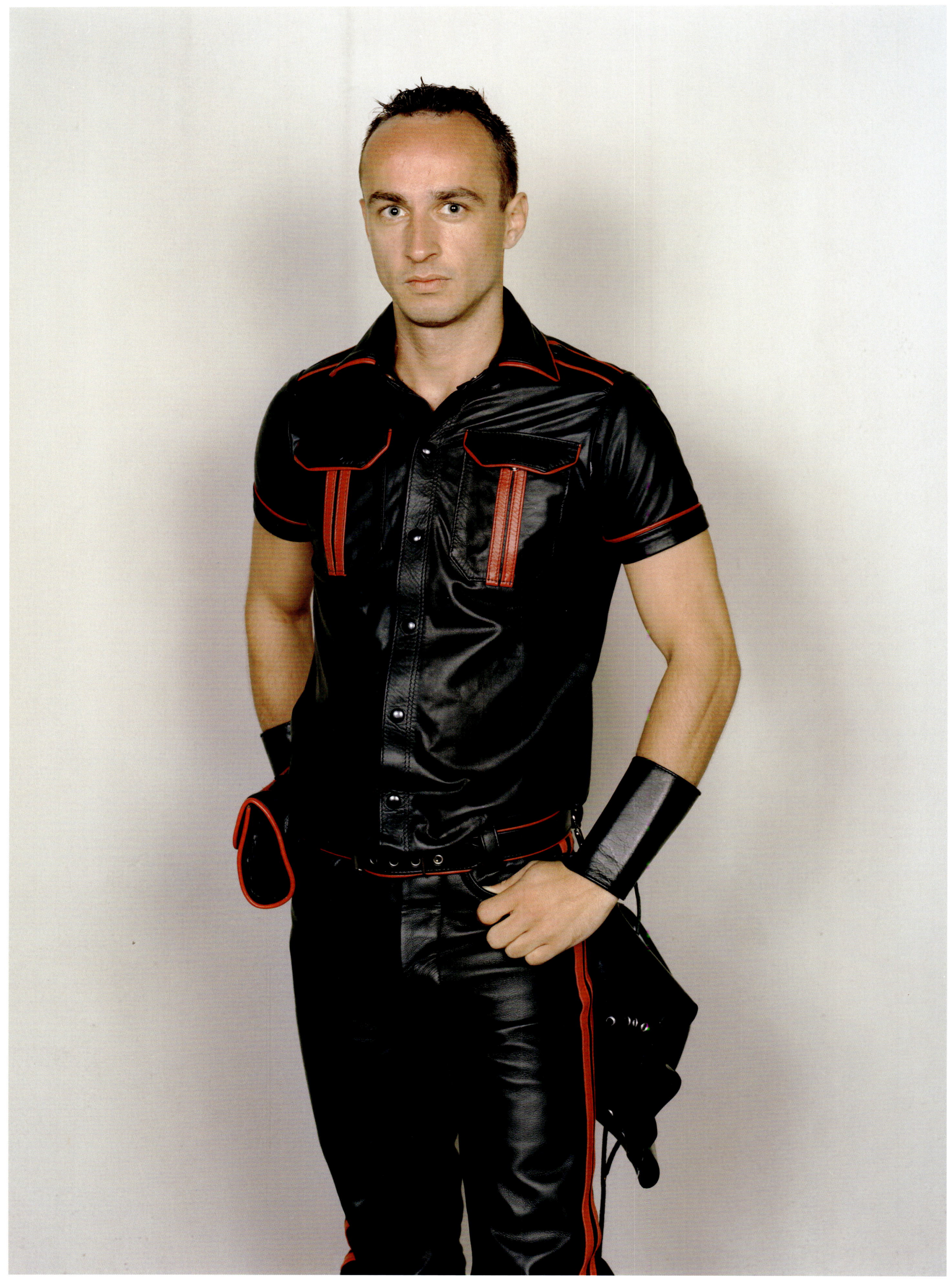

Mucandi Berlin

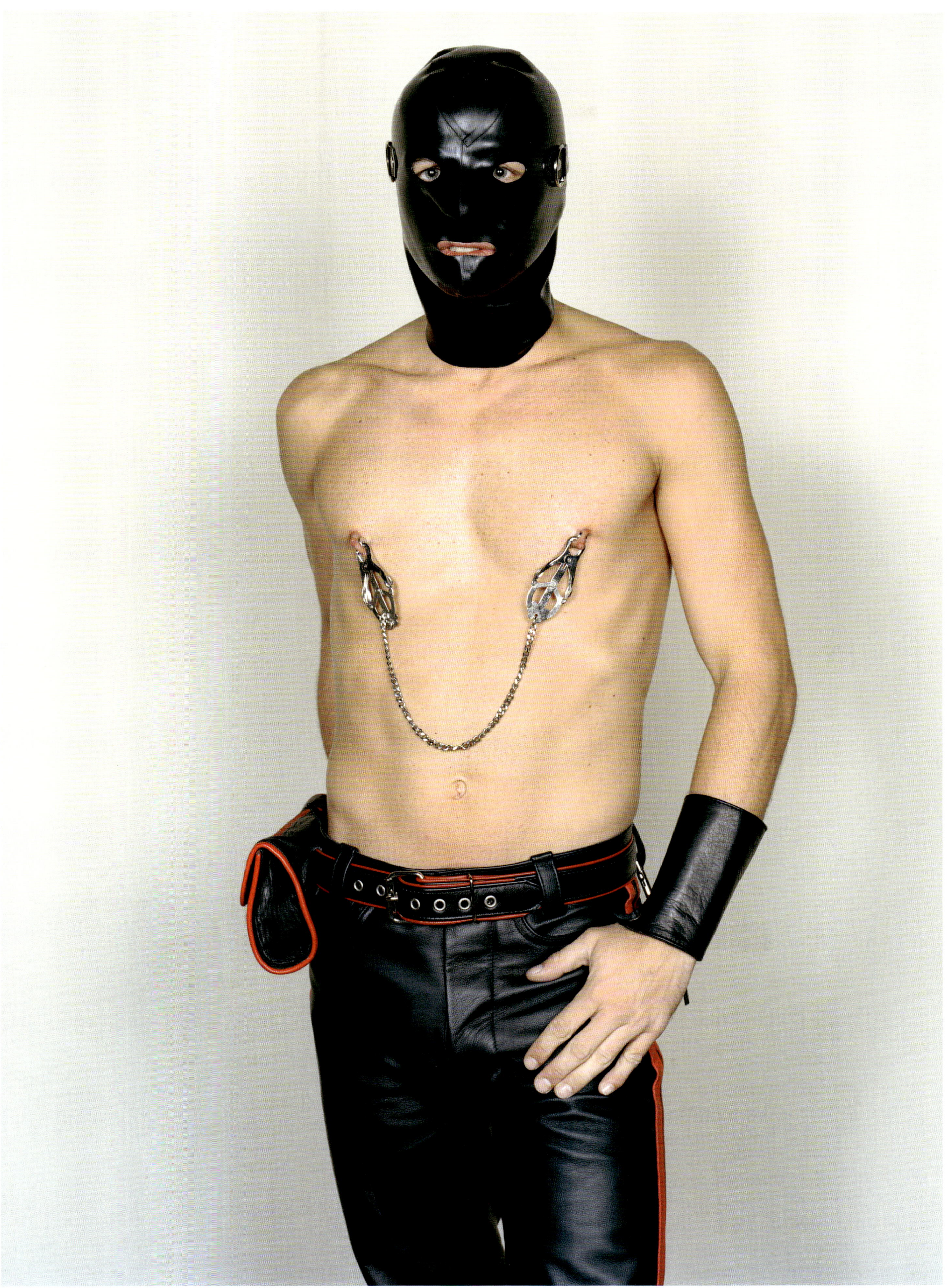

Mucandi Berlin

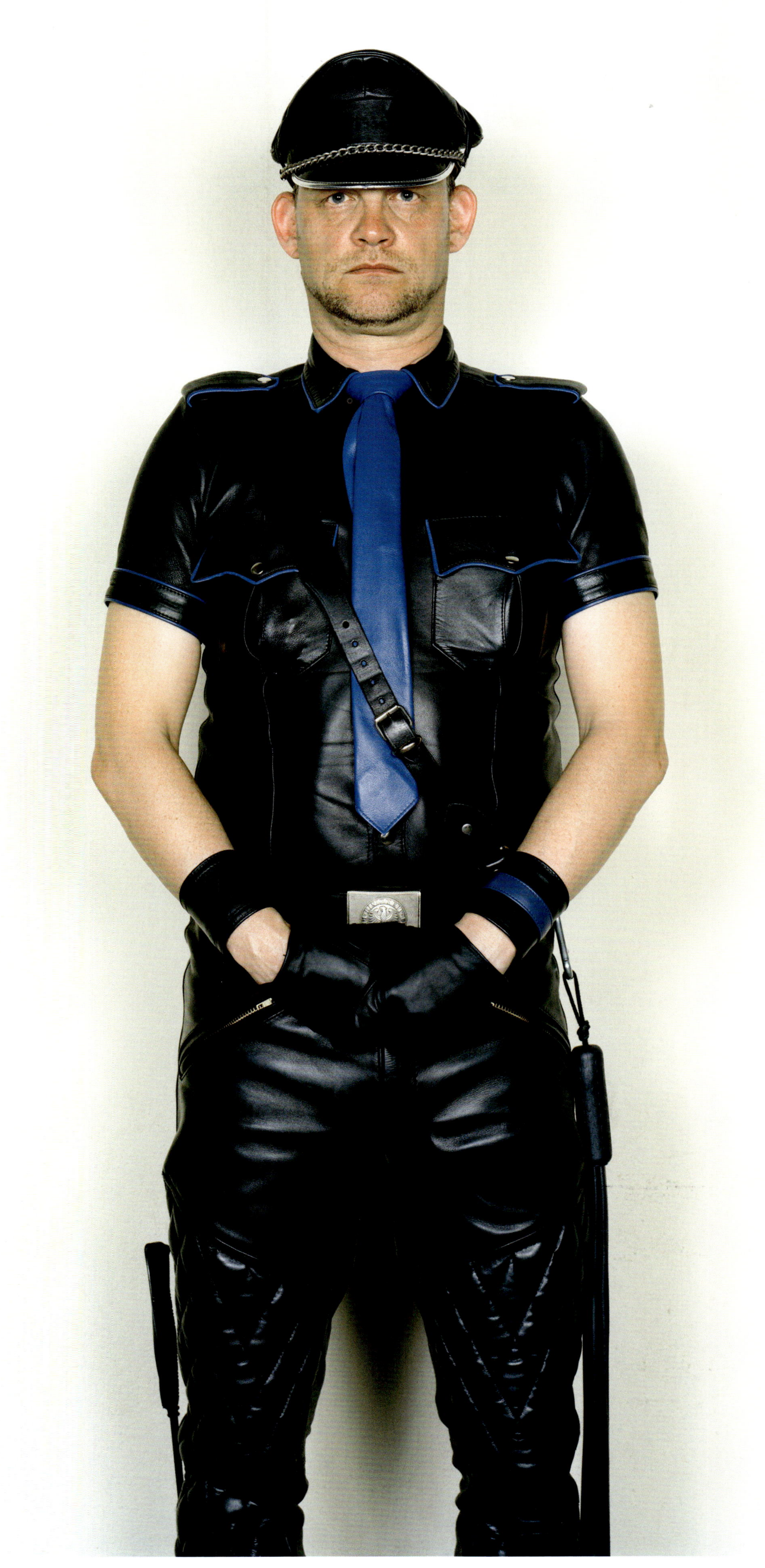

LeatherMate 44 Berlin

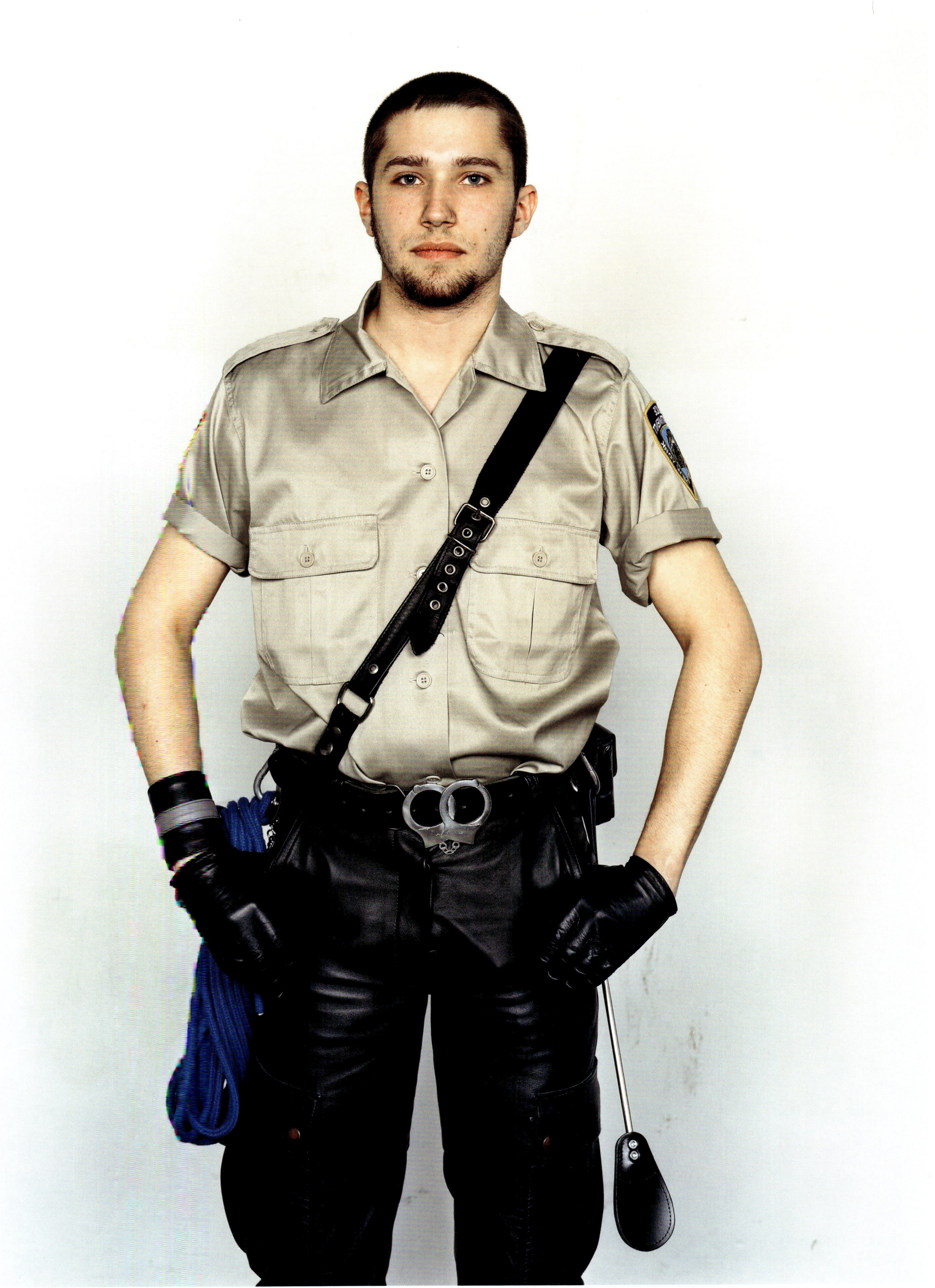

Kevin JJE Berlin

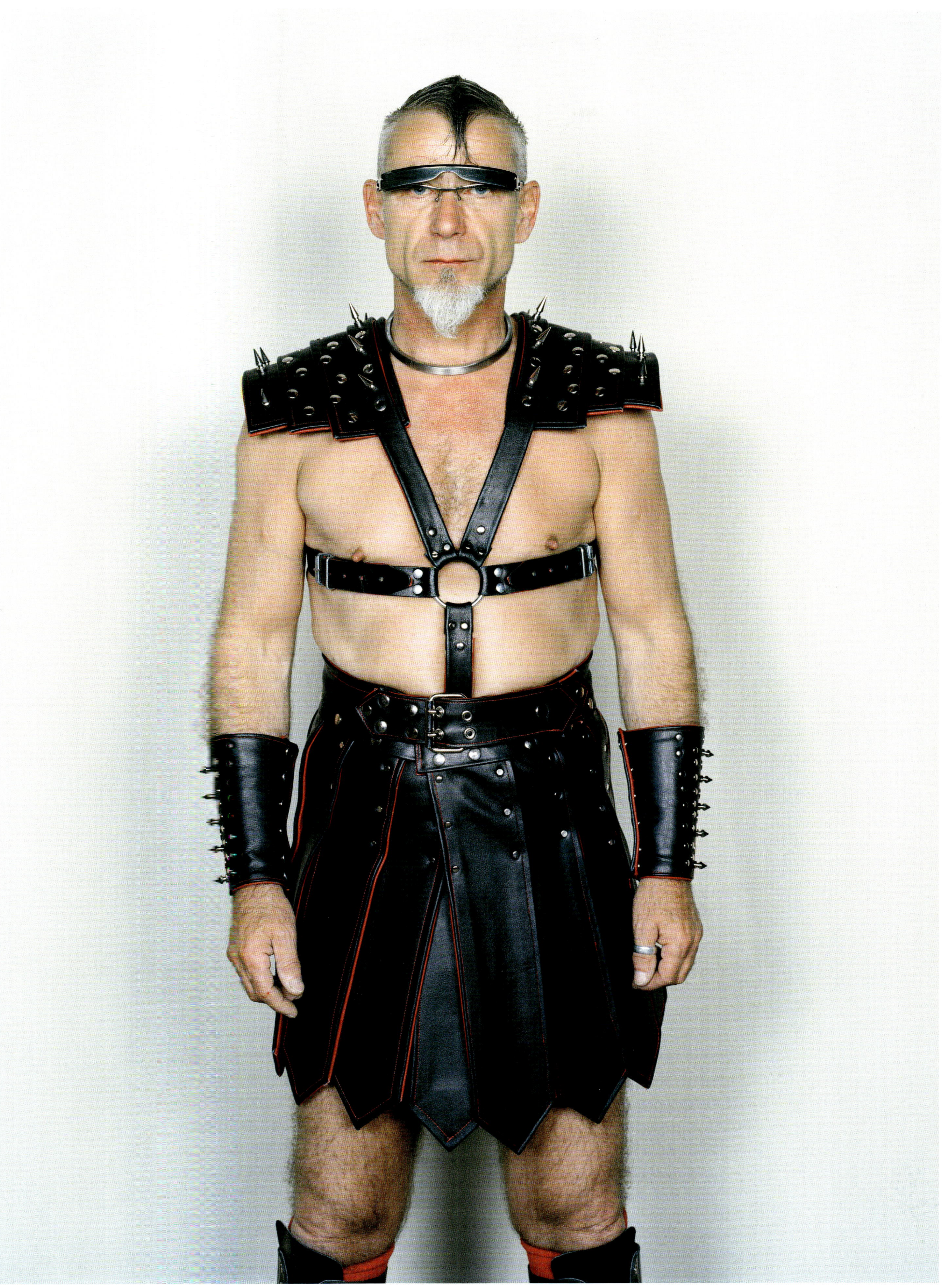

Ringo Berlin

This is my look. I like looking weird. When I was really young I already knew I wanted lots of tattoos and piercings. I had my troll doll out and would draw all over it with a sharpy. People say it's addictive, but I don't really know whether that's true or not, because I always knew I wanted to be heavily modified, and I've kind of built my life around it.

It has an effect on what kind of jobs I can have. And also how people react to me, but I've never cared very much about that. I work in one of the nicer restaurants downtown in Seattle, a wine bar. It's pretty fancy and expensive. People go there before the Symphony, they go in suits and really nice dresses. So it's great to be in a city like Seattle where they don't care that I've got piercings and a bunch of tattoos. They don't like me to wear a large piece in my septum or big hoop earrings, they like me to tone it down a bit. But I've got half-inch stretched ears, my tongue is split, I always wear a nostril ring – and they don't care about any of that, which is really nice.

I like Folsom because I'm an exhibitionist and a voyeur. It's great to walk around the street with my dick out. But apart from that, I'm pretty much out with my everyday freak look. When I first went, it was a sexual thing – I was into the exhibitionism of it. More recently, I've grown to appreciate watching other people, seeing how they let their barriers down. People show sides of themselves that they don't show in their everyday life. People who live a more buttoned-down kind of life really let go, and it creates a beautiful atmosphere. I enjoy seeing so many people embracing their fetish, or whoever they feel they are inside.

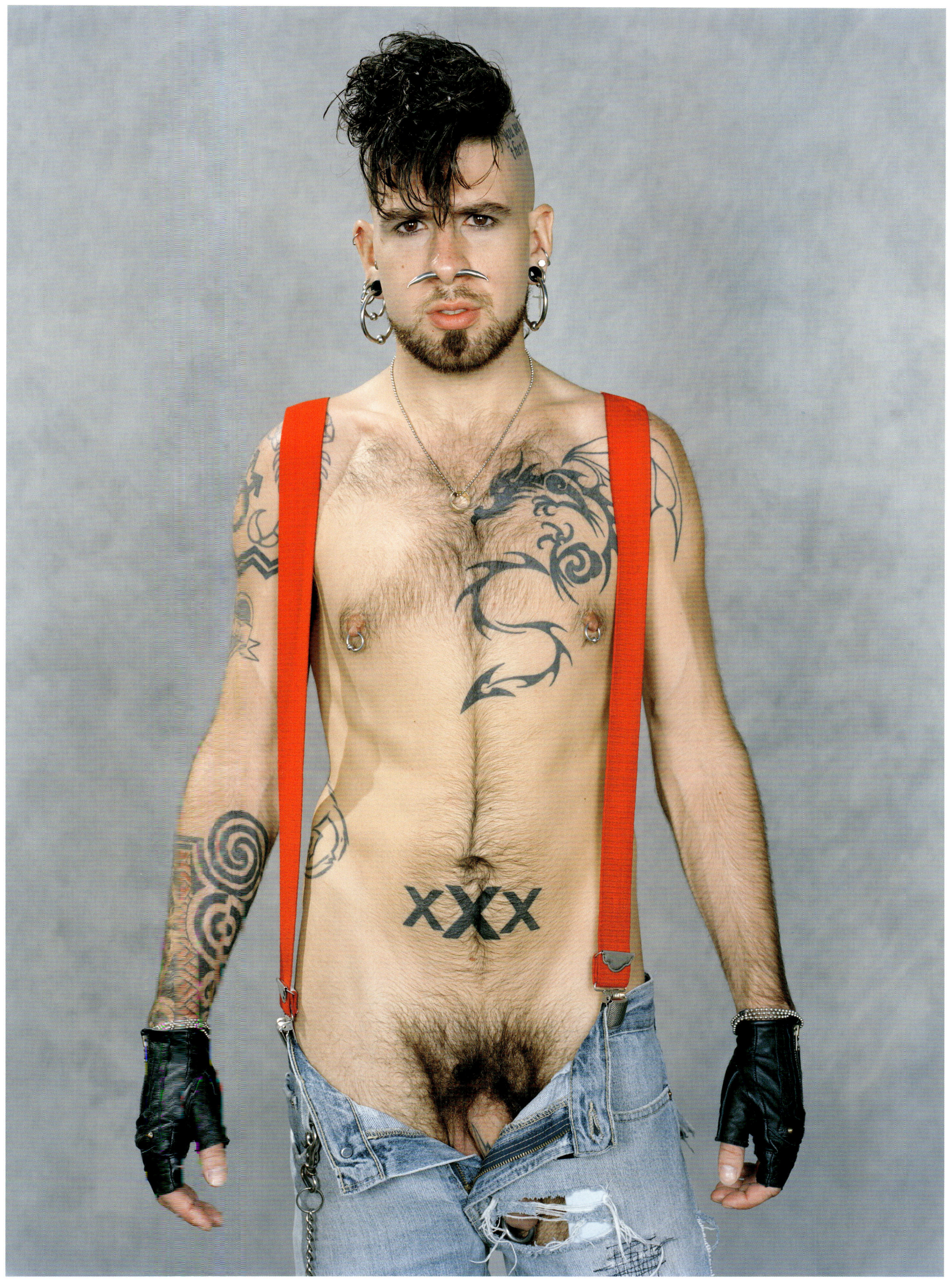

Christopher W L Darling San Francisco

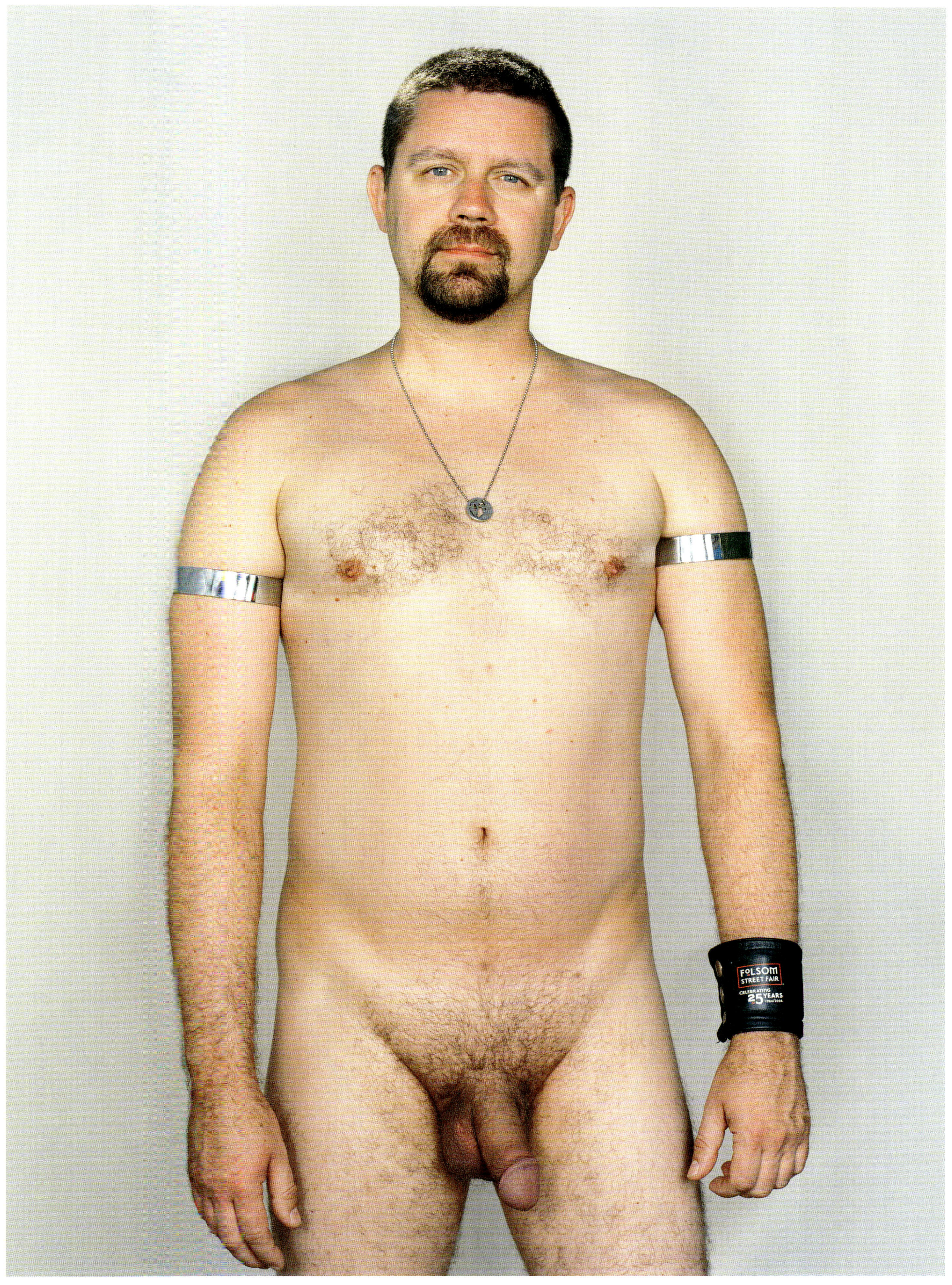

Bob San Francisco

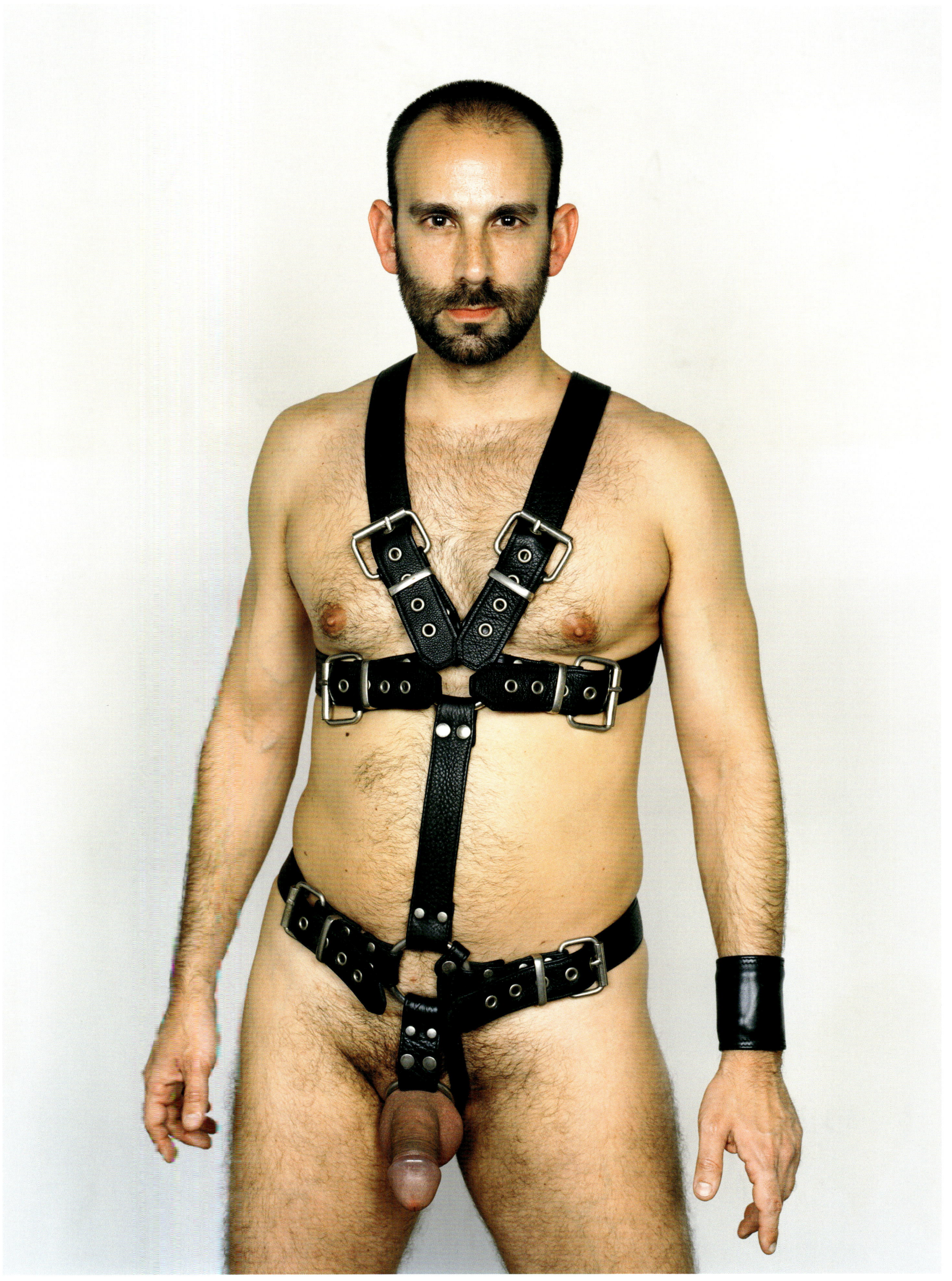

1luvmusclemlt Berlin

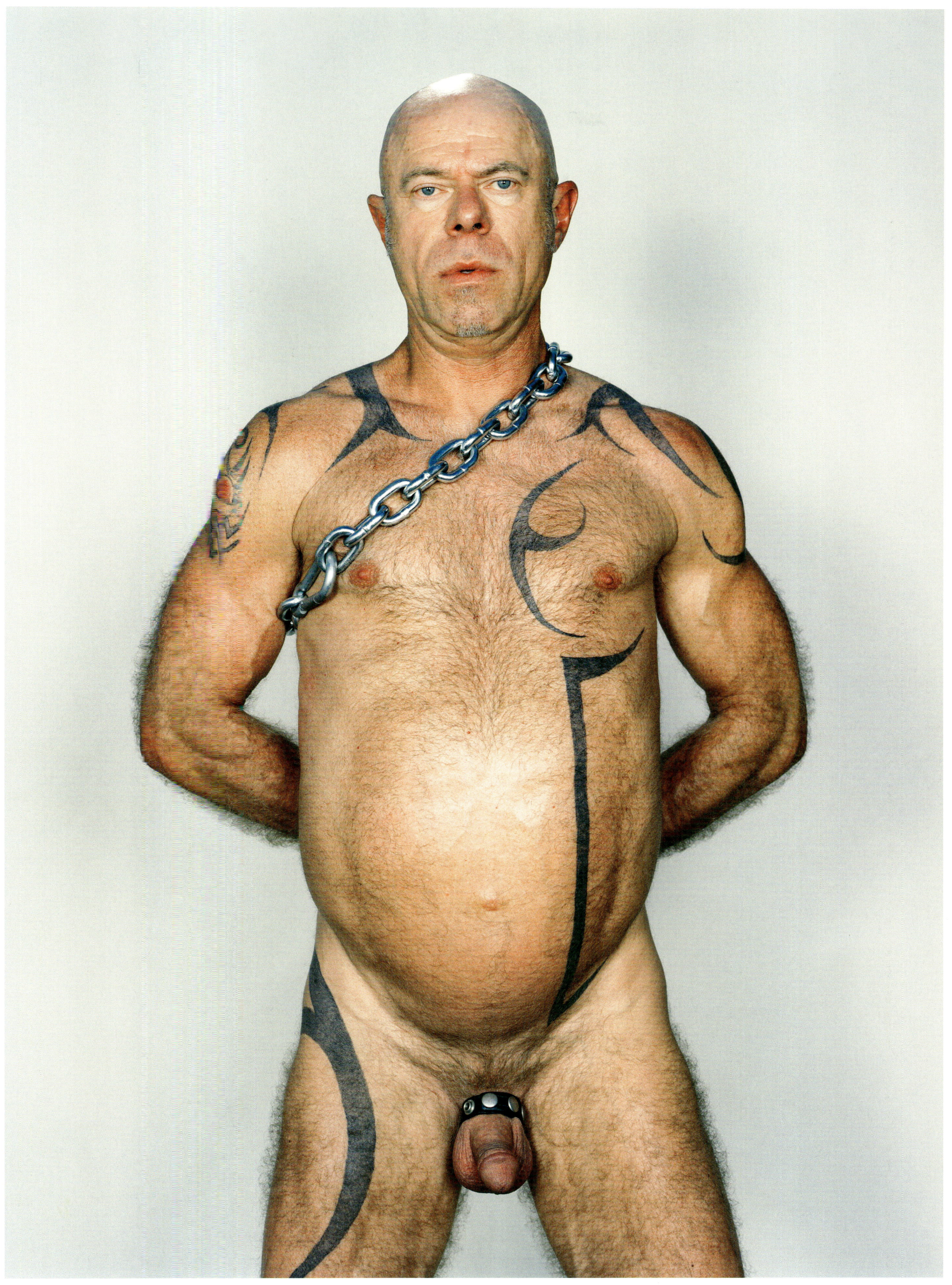

Show Hairy San Francisco

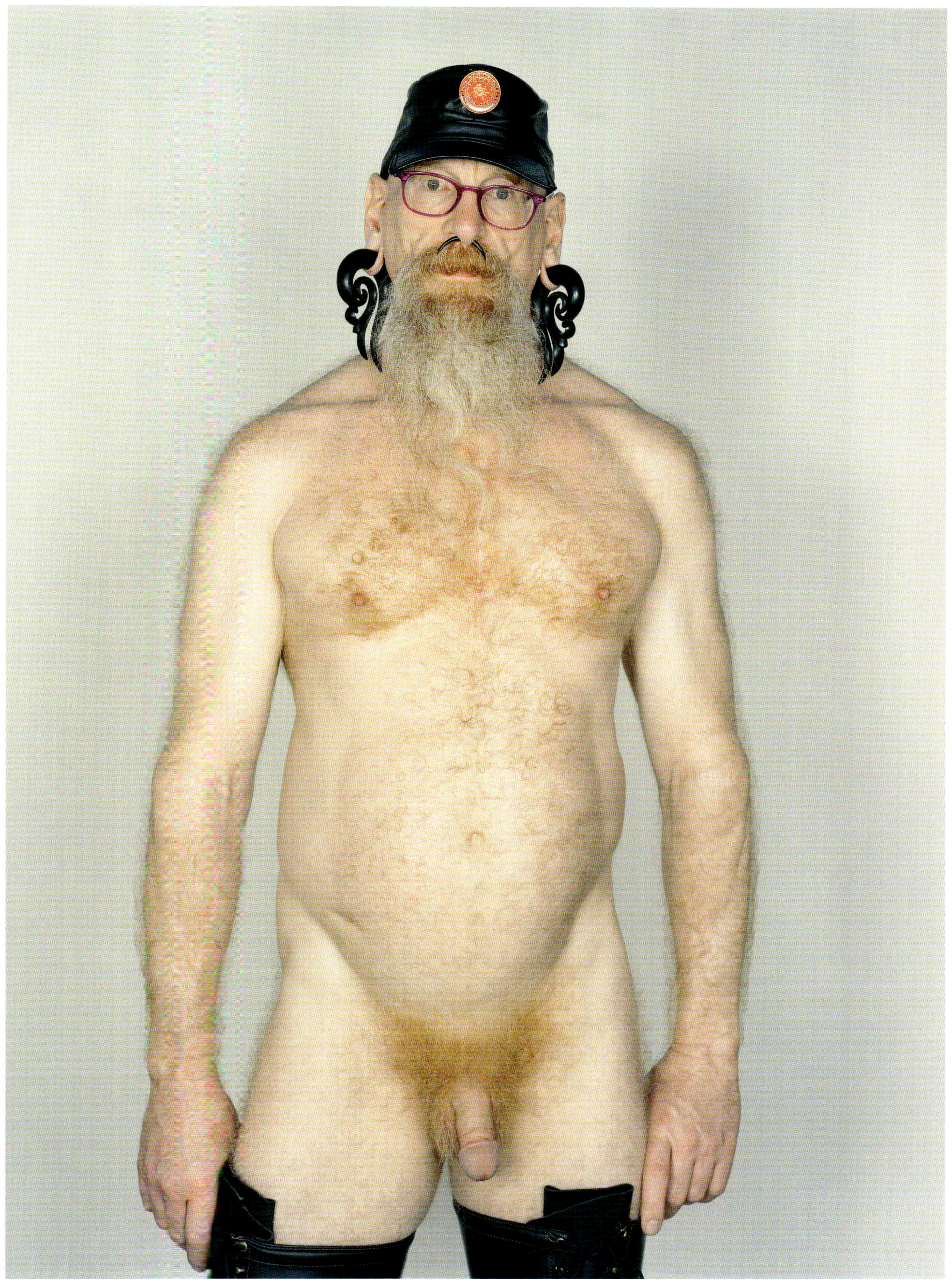

Nude Woody San Francisco

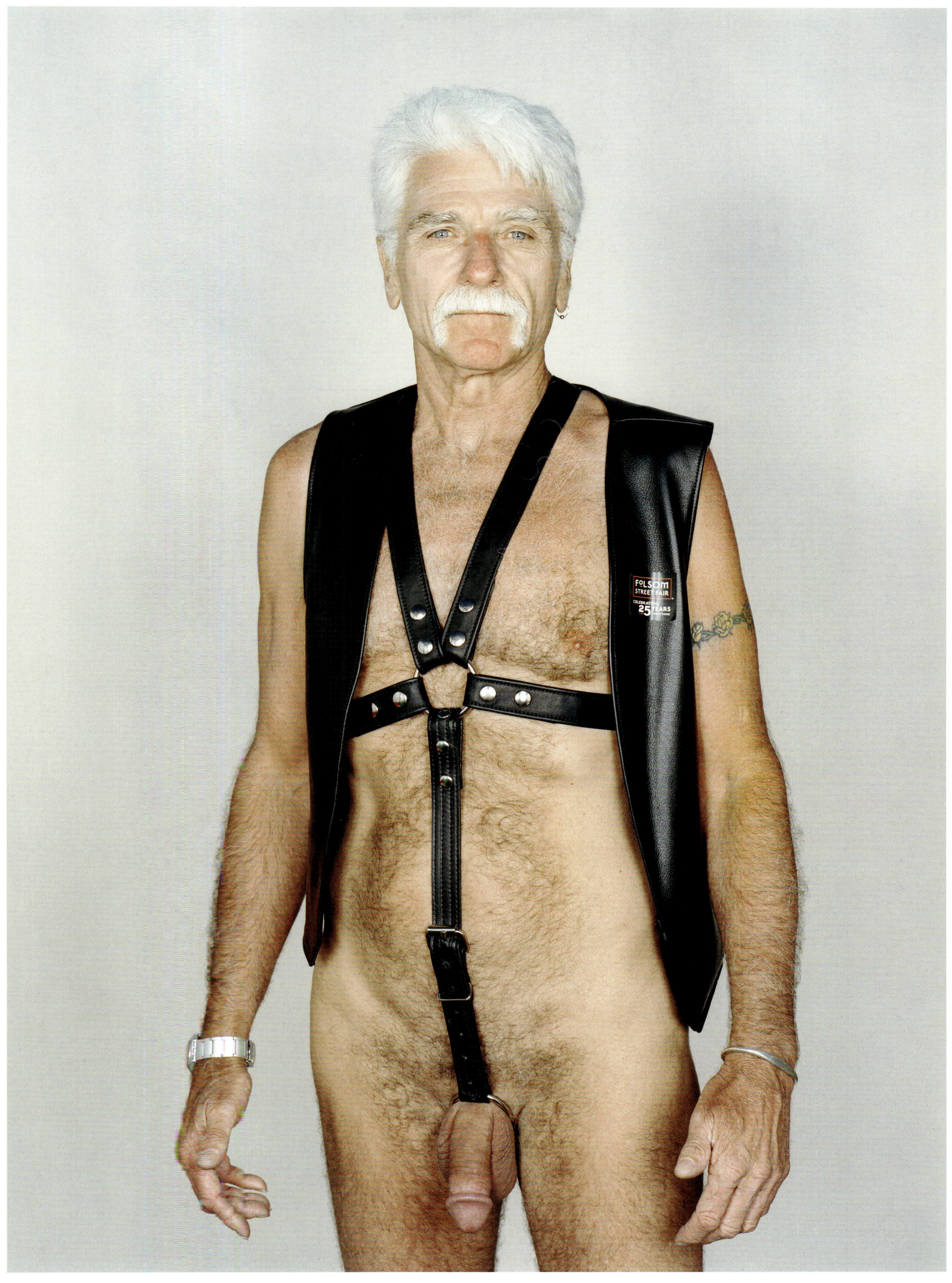

Randy San Francisco

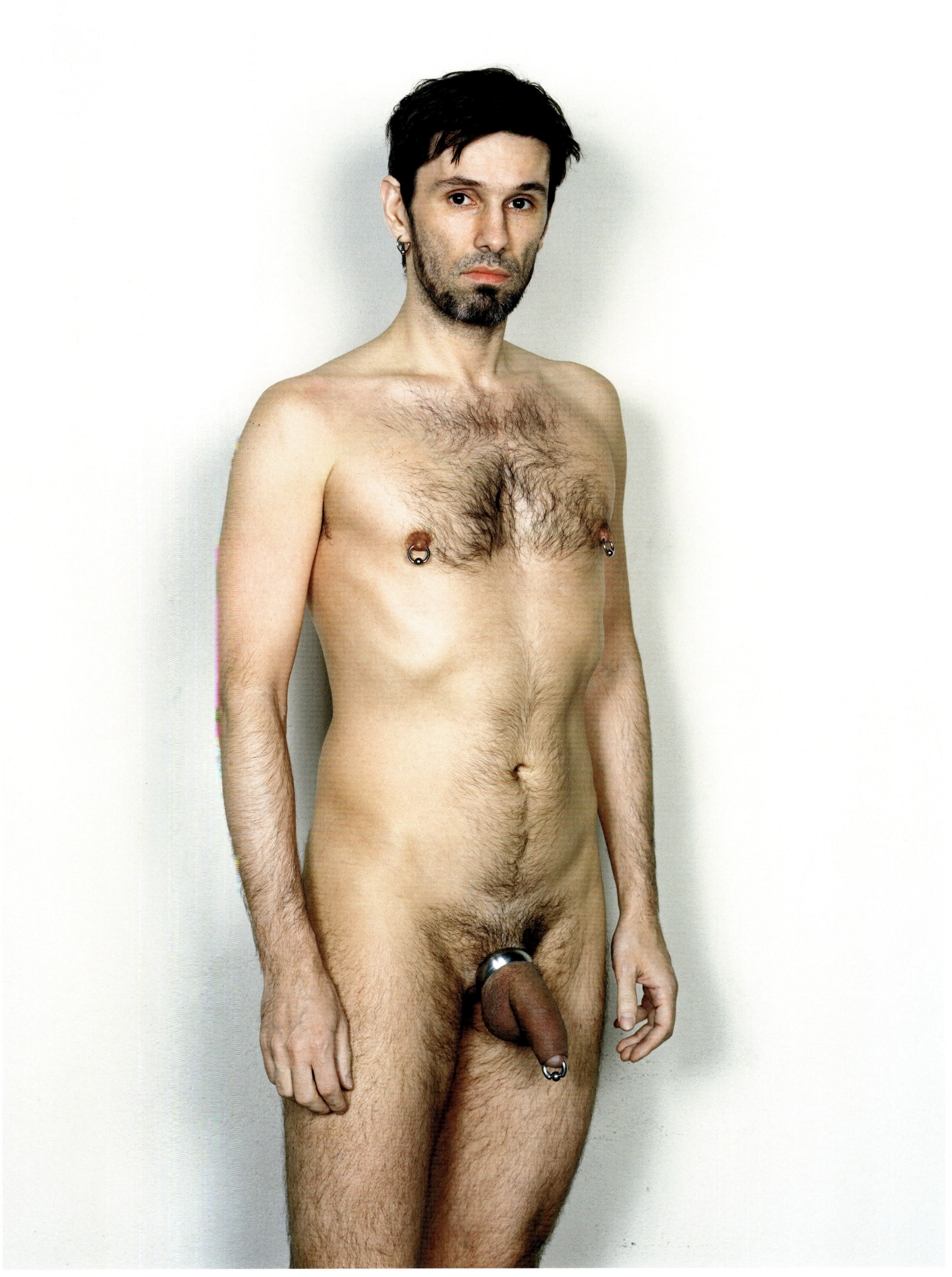

Wolf Berlin

At a nudist beach one time, I saw a guy walking along with something shiny hanging off the end of his penis. I was fascinated by it and I thought, 'I've got to get myself one of those!' Several years went by, and eventually because of the internet I found it was called a 'Prince Albert', and found a local place that would do one for me. People who get tattoos get a little addicted to it, and I guess that's what's happened to me with piercings.

I found out about the Folsom street festival on the internet, which is clear across the continent from Florida where I live. A friend found a good fare to San Francisco, so I went. The weather was nice, and I knew it was okay to walk around naked, so I did. It feels wonderful not having to worry about your clothes. I would live my life naked if I could. I'd go to the shopping mall naked if it were legal.

I got hooked on nudism from going to a nude beach. You really feel at one with nature when you have no clothes on and the sun's warm and the water's warm. I used to really enjoy the sea birds and the big sea turtles. I've now been to maybe half a dozen nudist resorts around the country. You don't have all the trappings of society without your clothes. People meet you face to face, there's nothing to hide, there's nothing that shouts 'I'm a lawyer' or 'I'm a dentist' or 'I drive a truck'. People relate to each other just as people. I feel at home in places like that. Of course being a nudist and an exhibitionist, I enjoy having people around when I'm having sex. I think sex is better when you're in public. What could be more natural than sex, right?

Many gay lads when they're young want to be divas. Then for a while it's all about finding a life partner. And then as you get a little older, it's more like 'Let's try something a little different'. The BDSM community comes along. It's not strictly a gay community – there's a wide range of people involved in it. It's a way to stay on the edge of society and, because it's hidden, you can be part of it and a member of regular society at the same time. It's a lot about discovering yourself. I've discovered many things. I'm not ashamed of it. I like having hot wax dripped over my body and I like getting fucked in public. The big phrase at the time of Woodstock was 'If it feels good, do it'. That's the feeling of Folsom, and that's why it's wonderful. Nobody thinks, 'Oh good Lord, this one's getting tied up!' or 'This one wants to suck dick outside in the street, how horrible!' It's wonderful to see people outside enjoying themselves.

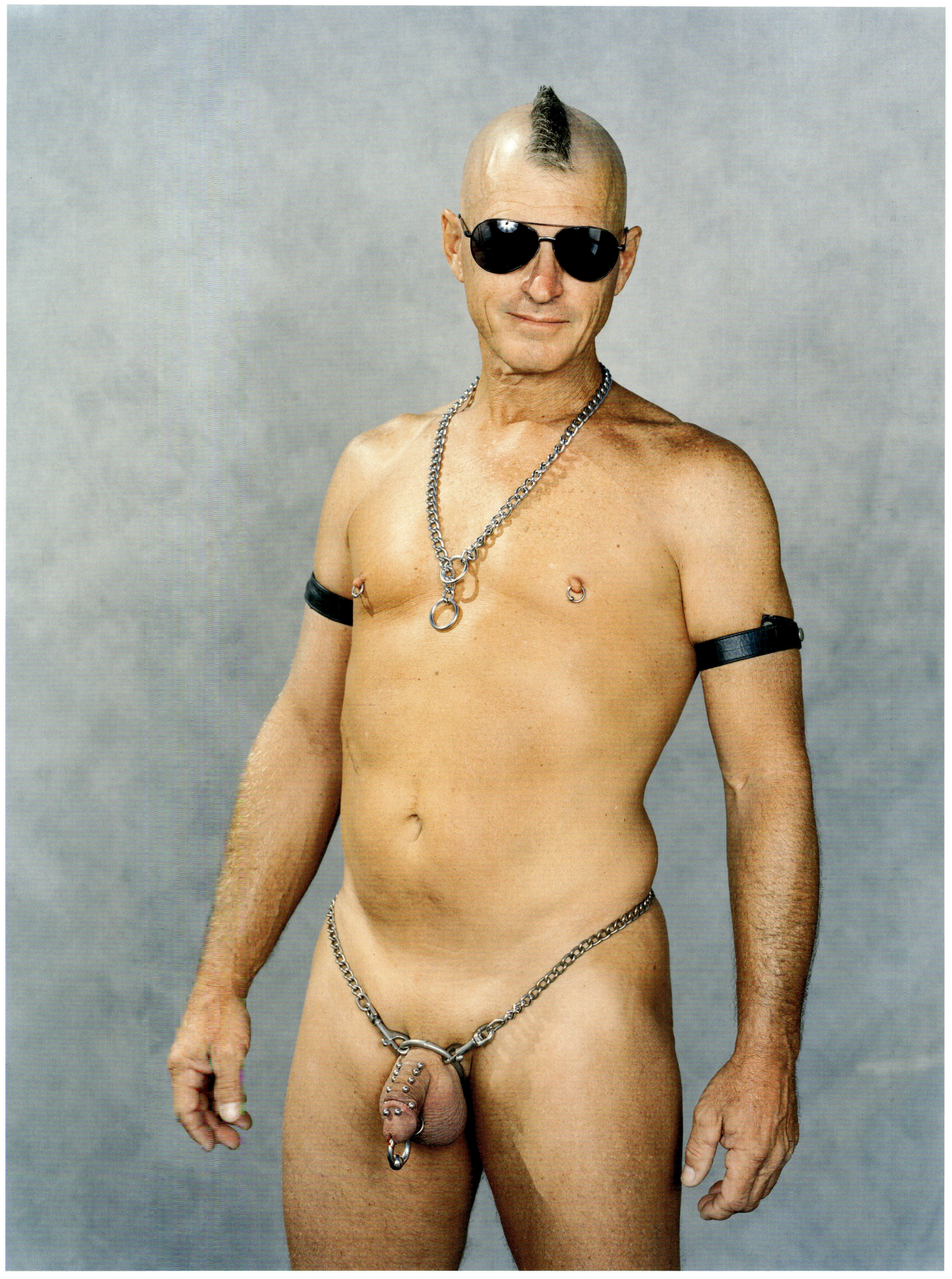

Mars San Francisco

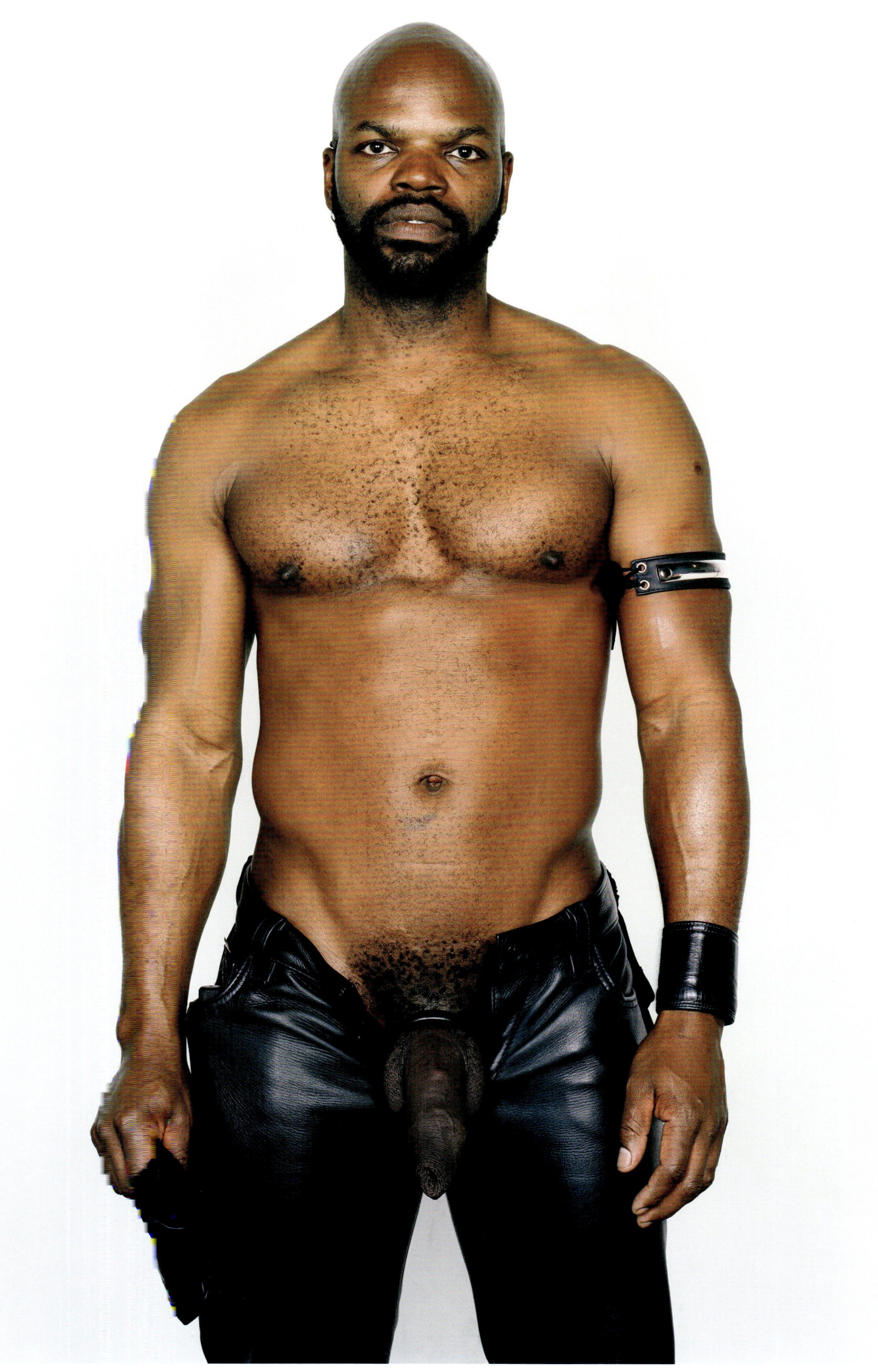

Isiam Berlin

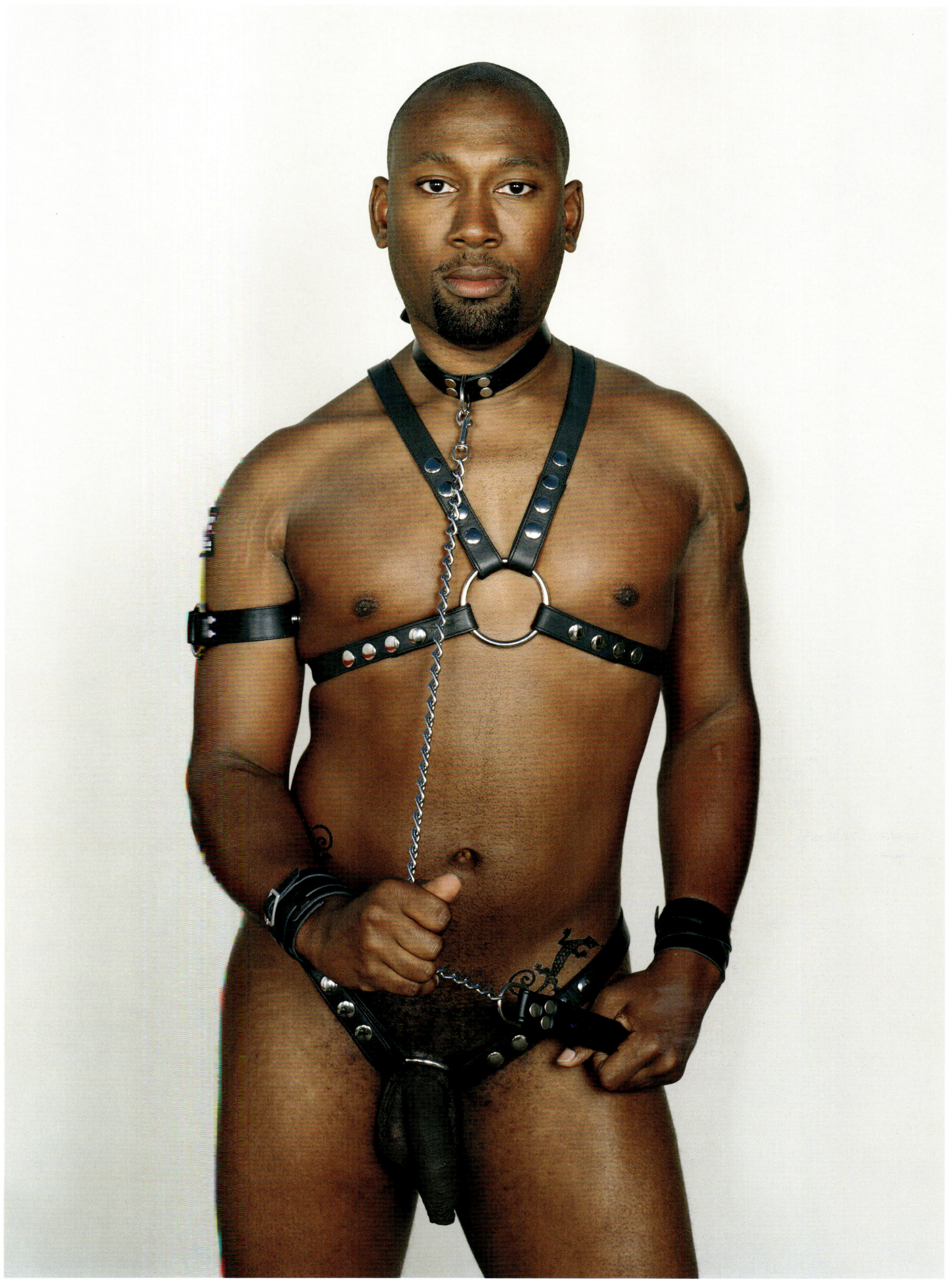

Allen San Francisco

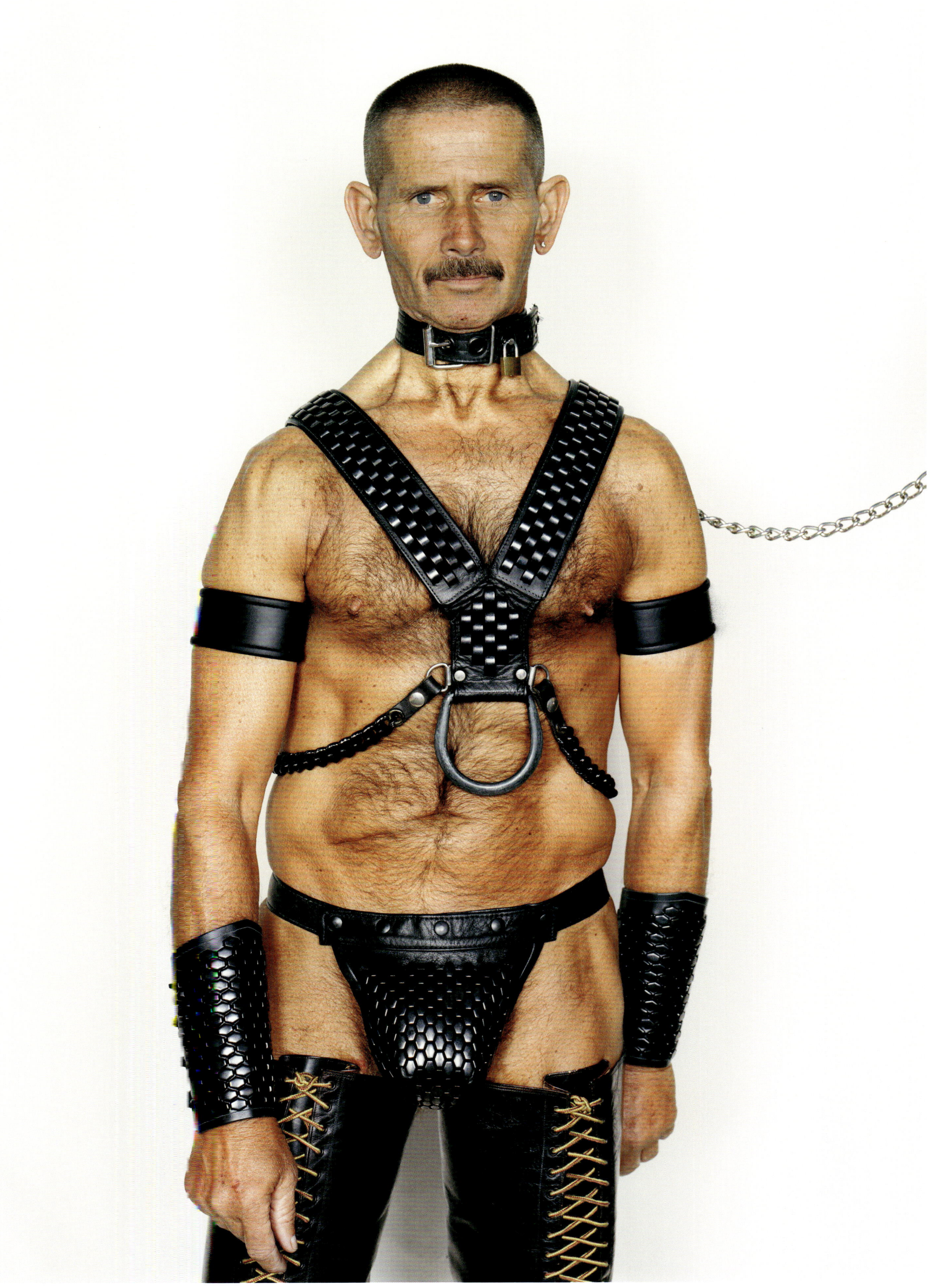

Michael San Francisco

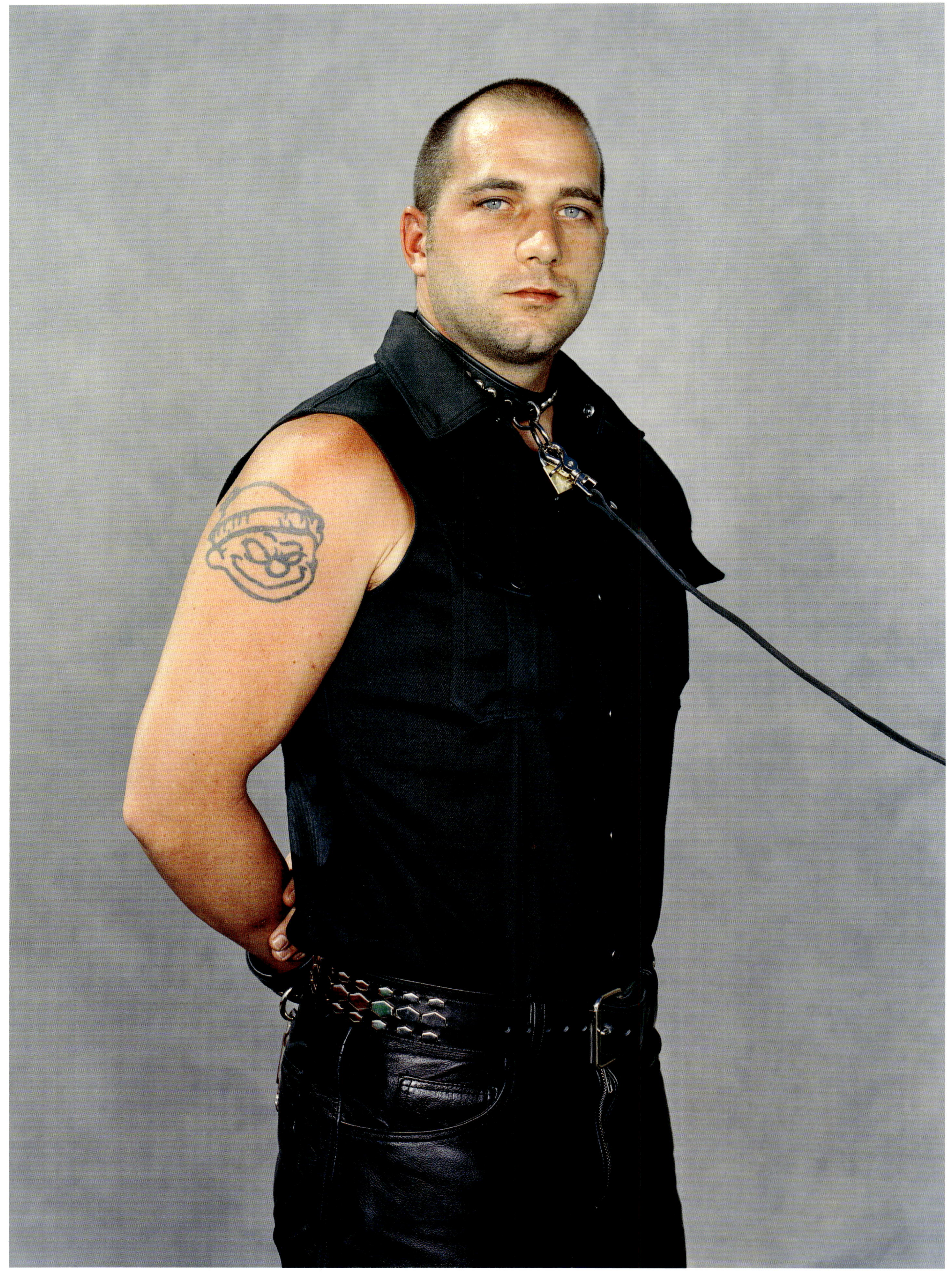

Calvin San Francisco

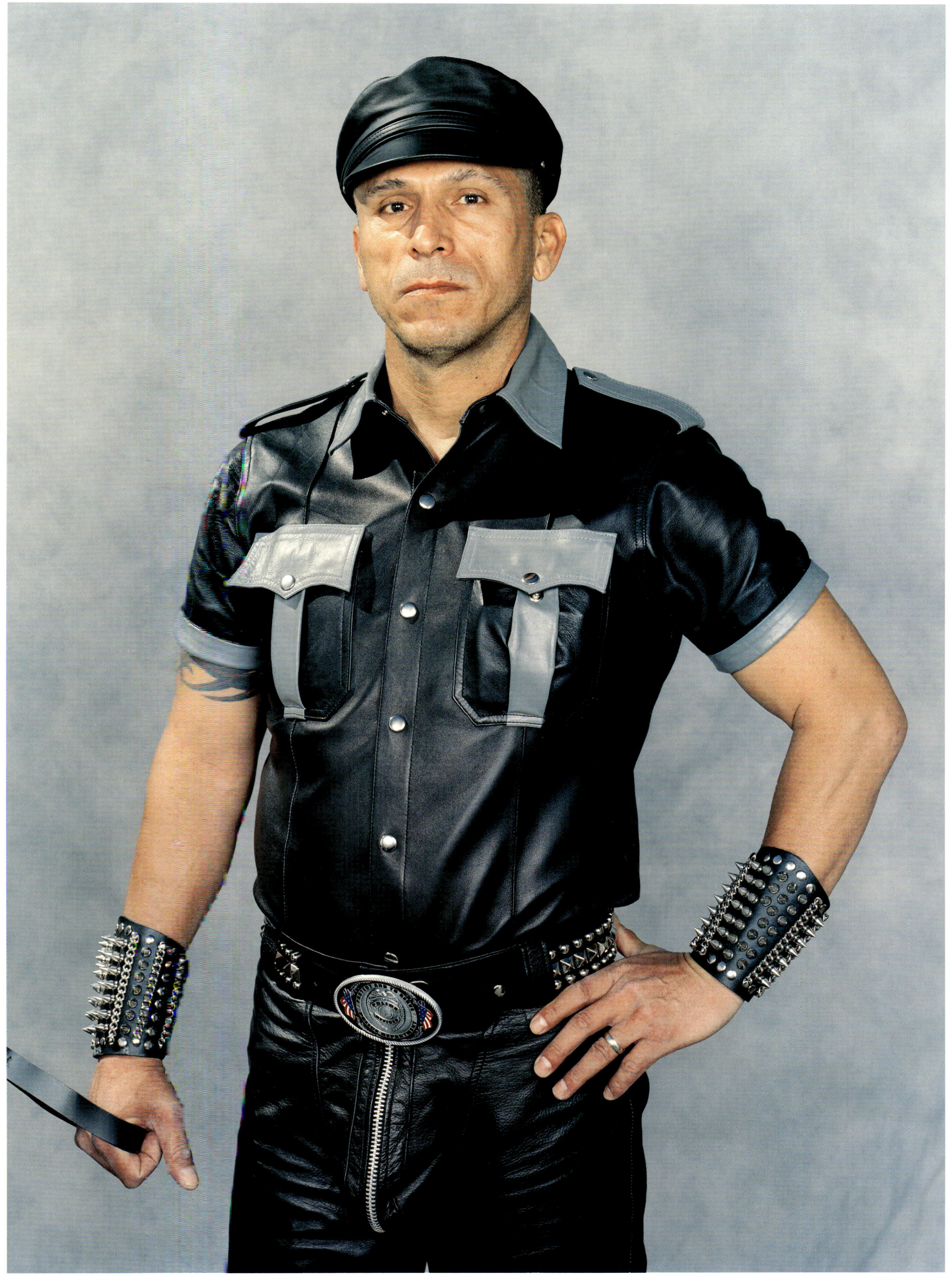

Papi San Francisco

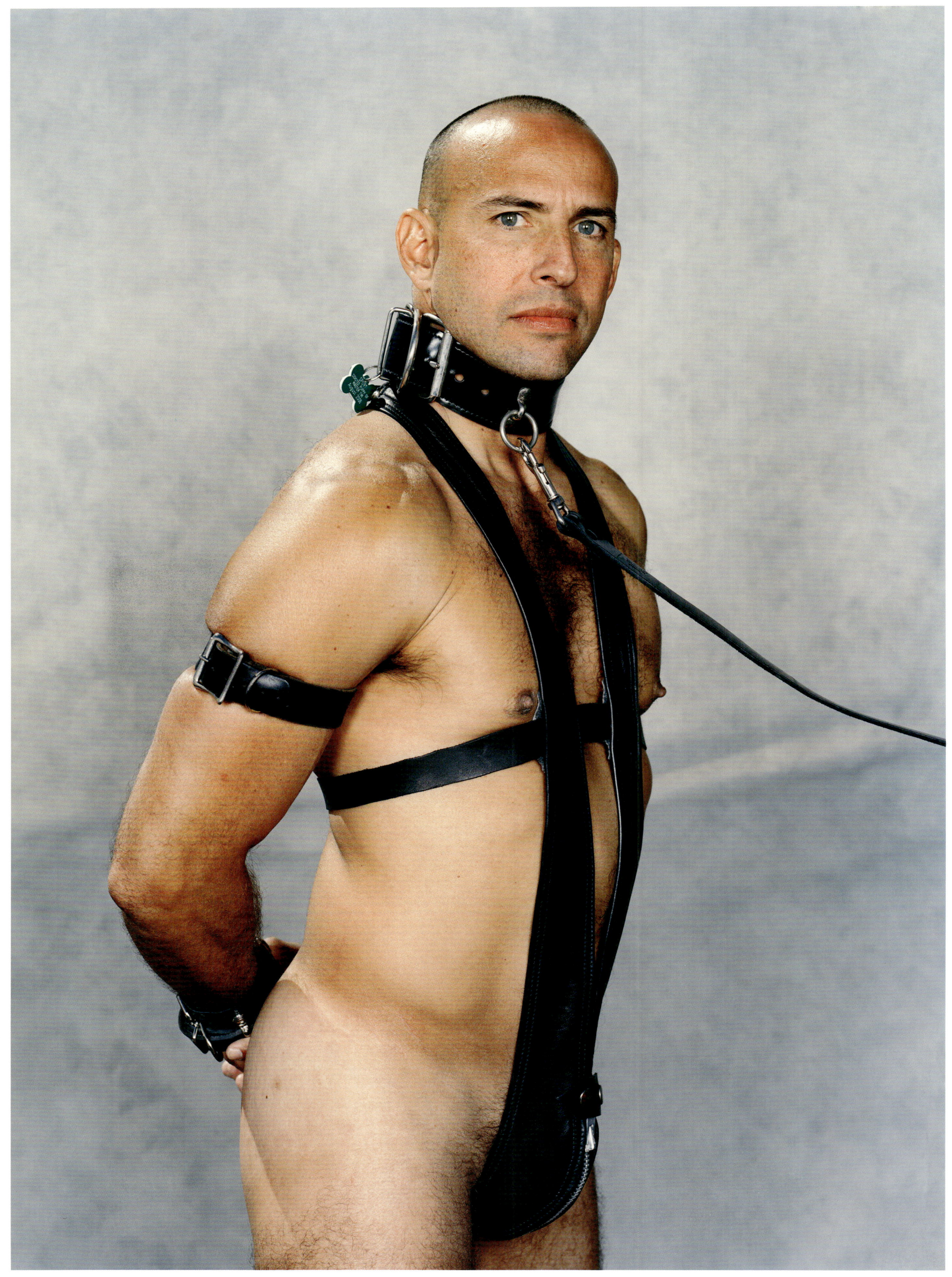

Puppy Sport San Francisco

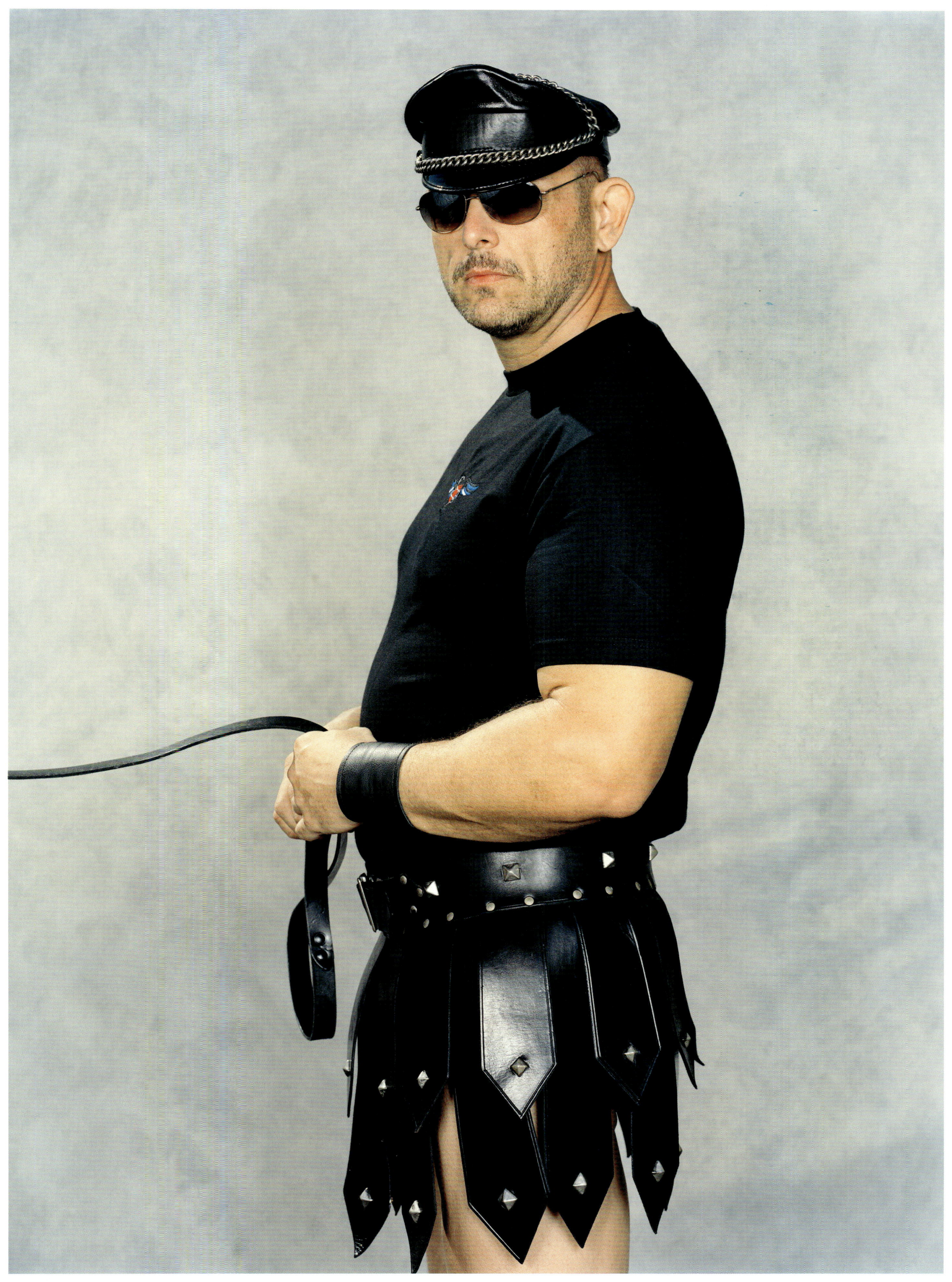

Master Tim San Francisco

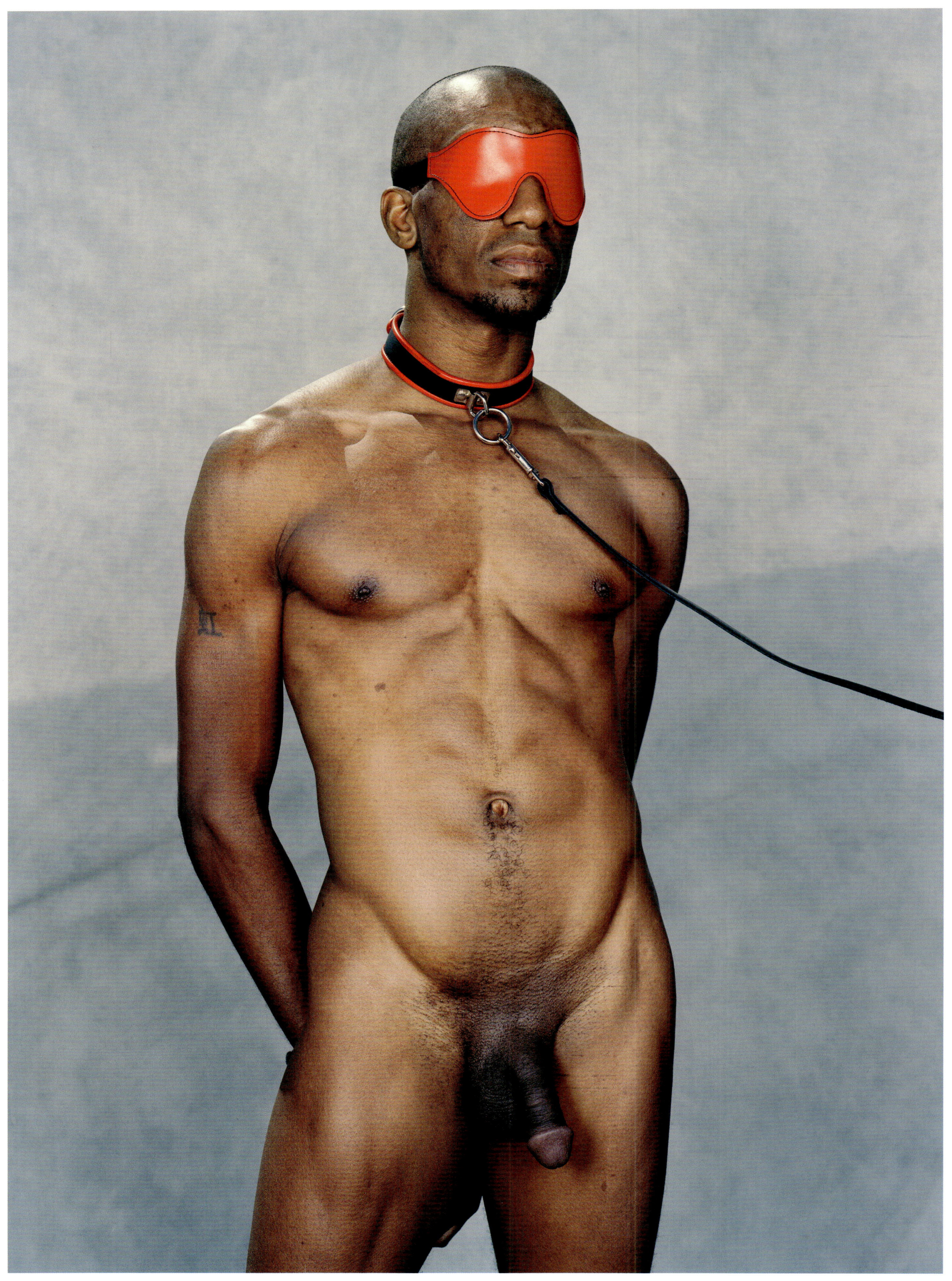

La'la San Francisco

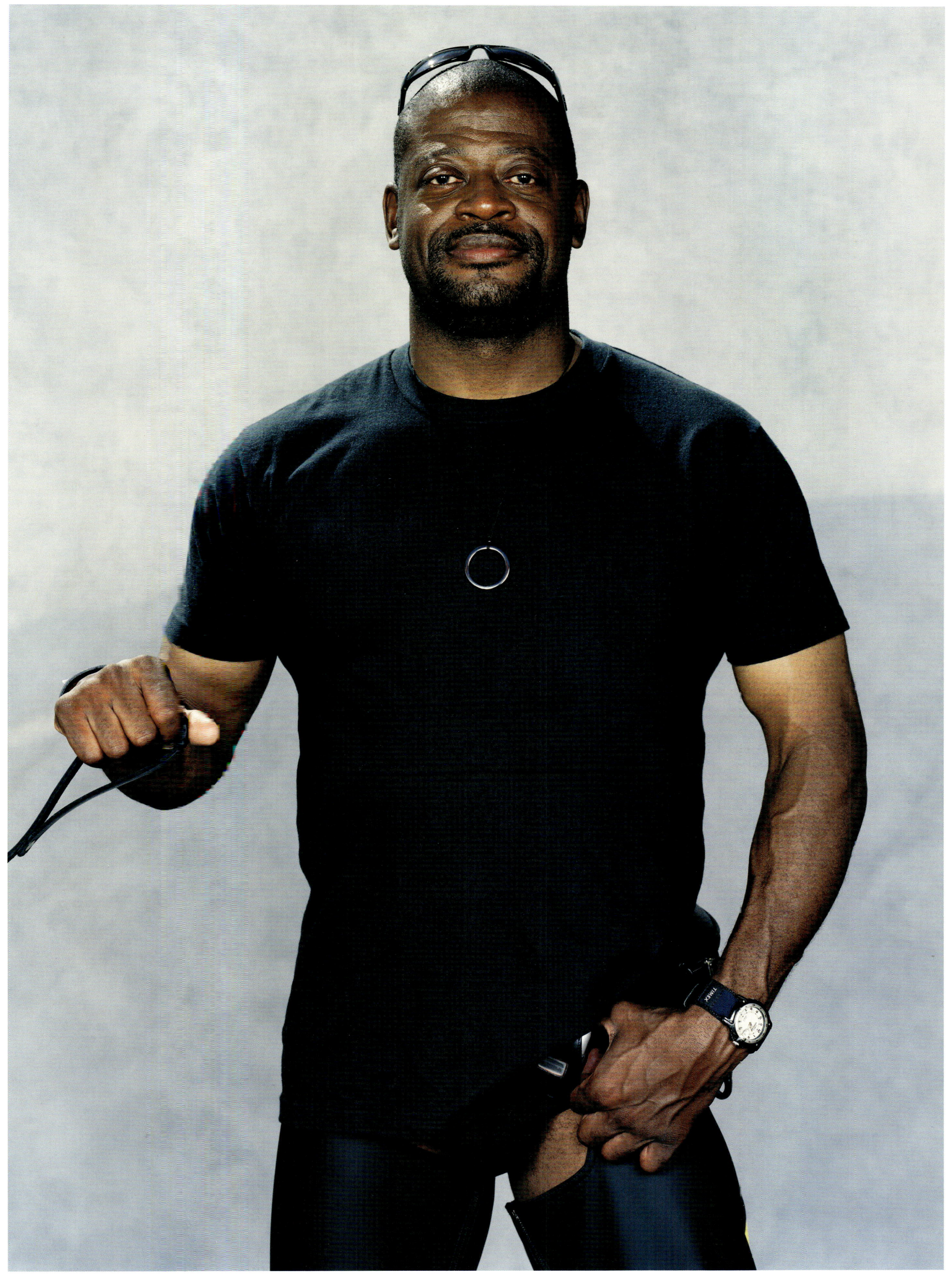

David San Francisco

My name is Phil but everyone calls me Tats, for obvious reasons. I've been involved in the gay leather community for the last fifty years or more. I enjoy the lifestyle, and I've kept up with it even though I'm getting a bit old for it these days.

I'm from the East Coast originally but I've been in San Francisco since 1980. I had seen a lot about the leather scene in a magazine called *Drummer*, and as there was not much of that going on the East Coast where I was, I thought the best thing to do would be to come out here and get involved in the scene. Being as liberal as it is here, I've never had any problems with my tattoos. Admittedly I didn't get my facial tattoos until after I retired, but I had them pretty much all over the rest of my body before that. I had thought about getting my face tattooed before, but by the time that I got to think about it on a serious basis, and not just as a sexual turn-on, I was close to retiring, so I thought I may as well wait.

People here are very accepting. After I had the facial tattoos, I interviewed for a volunteer position with the city's Maritime Museum. It was not a problem. There's no need to hide your identity here.

People have told me I look like Queequeg, in *Moby Dick*. I guess maybe they're right. While I was at the Maritime Museum, it was the 150th anniversary of *Moby Dick*, and the museum asked all the volunteers to come to a big dinner they were having, and to act out the story. Everybody got to pick which part from the book they wanted to play – except for me. I was told I had no choice: I had to be Queequeg. The nice thing was that Patrick Stewart, the actor, was the keynote speaker that evening, and he'd just finished filming the modern version of *Moby Dick*. I met him, and he and I ended up with our picture together, on the front page of the local paper.

I think by the time you get into your sixties, most of the gay community think that you're over the hill. But in the leather community, younger guys seem to appreciate the older men, because of their experience. They see we have quite a bit to teach them about what goes on within the community. We can teach them the respect that is due one another in the community. That's pretty nice for those of us who are my age.

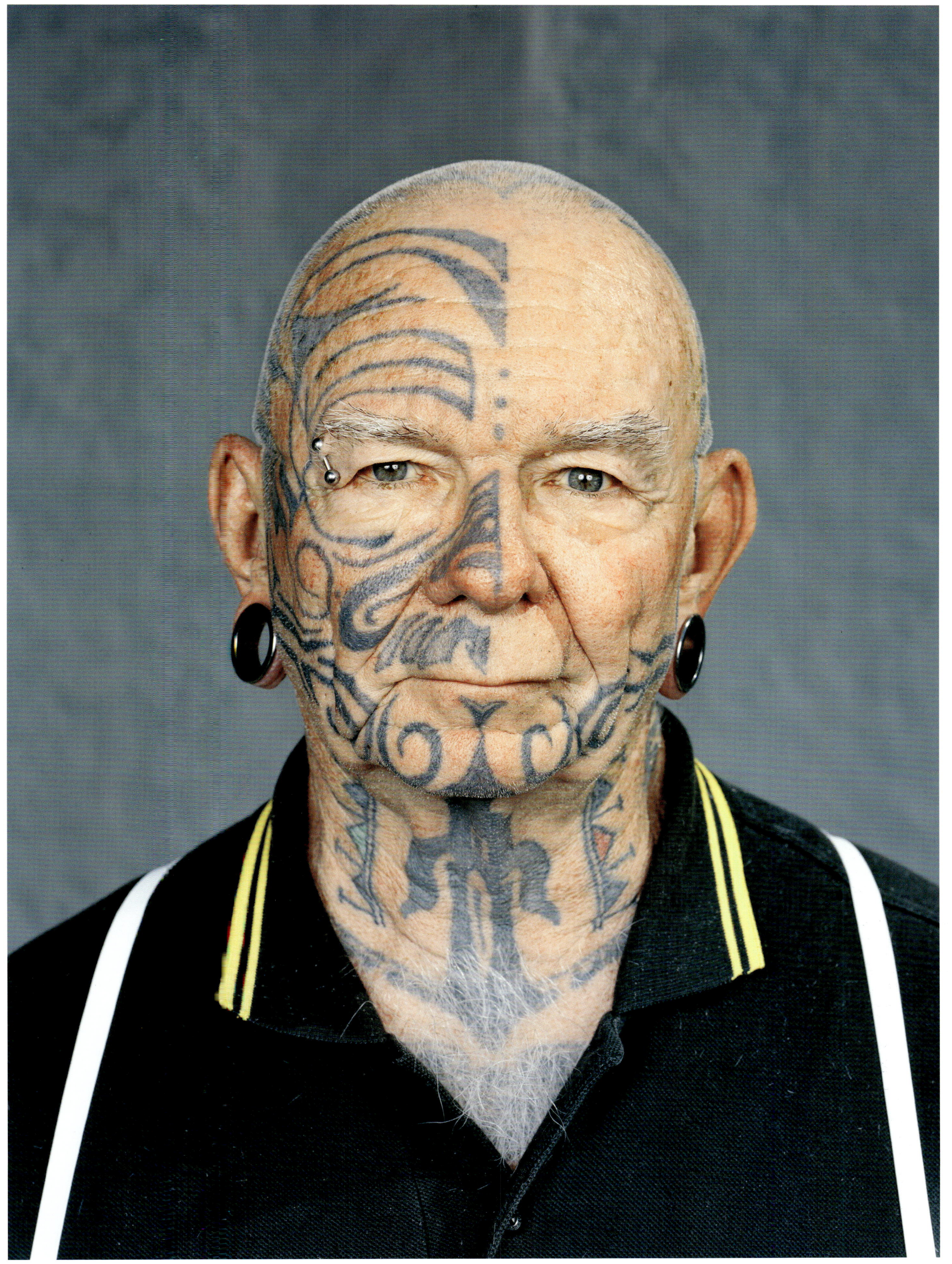

Tats San Francisco

I'm a visual artist and a performance artist. I live in Berlin but travel all over the world to show my work. I'm really into the body art movement. My work is mostly defined on my body, using different techniques, including tattoo and body modification. I do physical live acts, where I cut myself, for instance. All my work in body art involves exploring rituals, especially blood-letting rituals. I'm really obsessed by what ritual is and how it's used in different societies. But I also do performances which are much lighter. I do a burlesque show – striptease and dancing. Everything I do is always politically involved, and really sarcastic, but the burlesque performances are much lighter than the body art. They're easy to watch and have a laugh at. I'm a bondage master too. I do traditional Japanese bondage. I've been working on a self-bondage show where I tie myself up, lift myself into the air, and do some acrobatics. Put me on stage and I'm happy!

I've been living in Berlin for three years now, and for me it is the right place. Before coming here, I was travelling around Europe, living in different cities – southern Spain, Paris, London – but it's here in Berlin that I really feel at home. Artistically, it's really easy to make things. You have lots of opportunities, and people are interested. There's a lot of respect in the city, and lots of education as well, which means lots of freedom. That's really important. Travelling to different places, with most of my body covered by tattoos, I feel people's gaze on me. Sometimes that can be really heavy. But it doesn't happen in Berlin. I think it's the only city where an underground culture survives. Everywhere else, it's died – the mainstream has taken everything. But Berlin still has a big, open underground culture. I say 'open' because it's really welcoming to anyone who wants to join in. It's very gay, but it's not ghetto at all. I used to live in Paris and, well, there's no underground culture there. There's a big gay scene, but it's really ghetto. Here in Berlin, it's not all about being gay or not. There's a lot of freedom in the sex culture, but everyone is welcome.

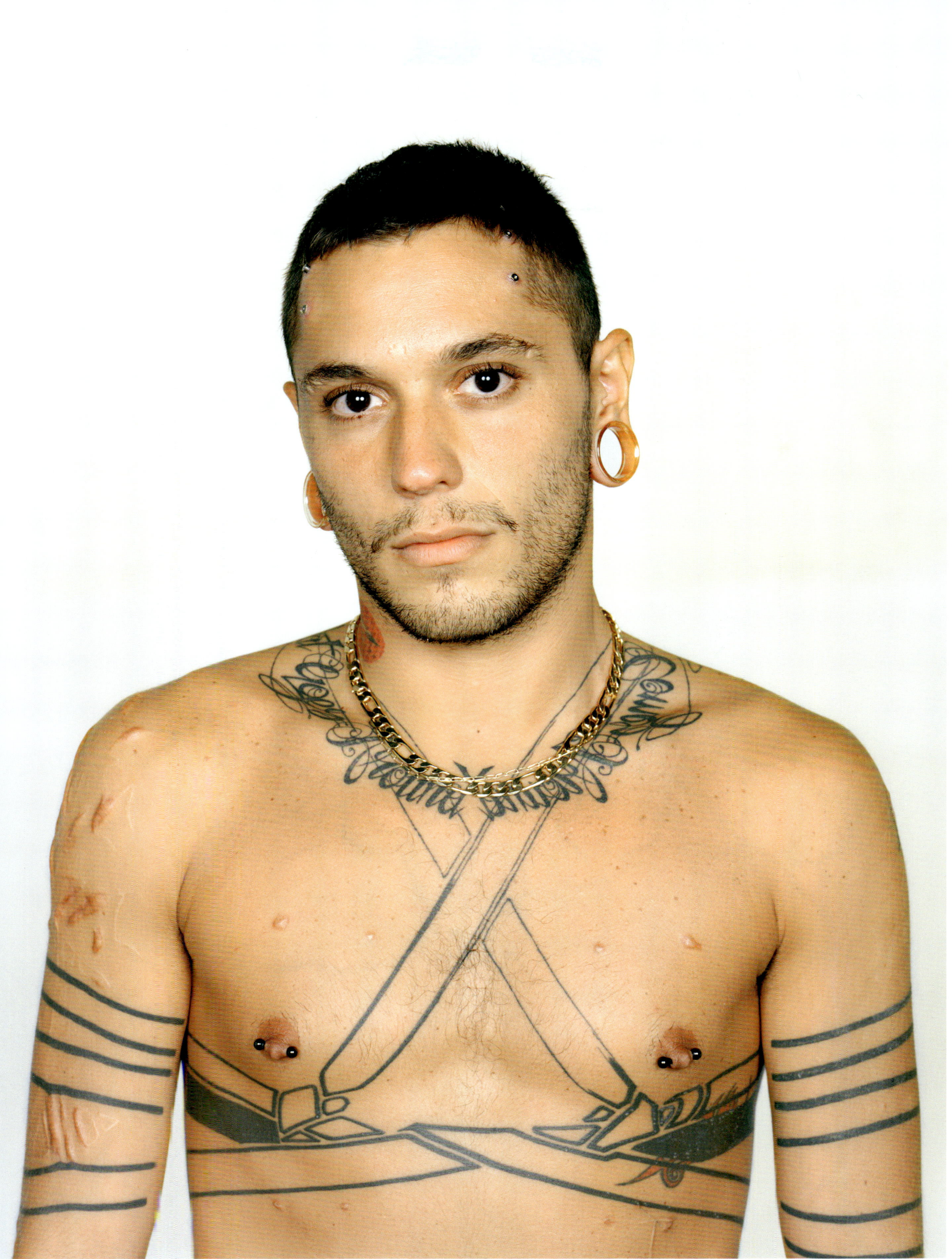

Jon John Berlin

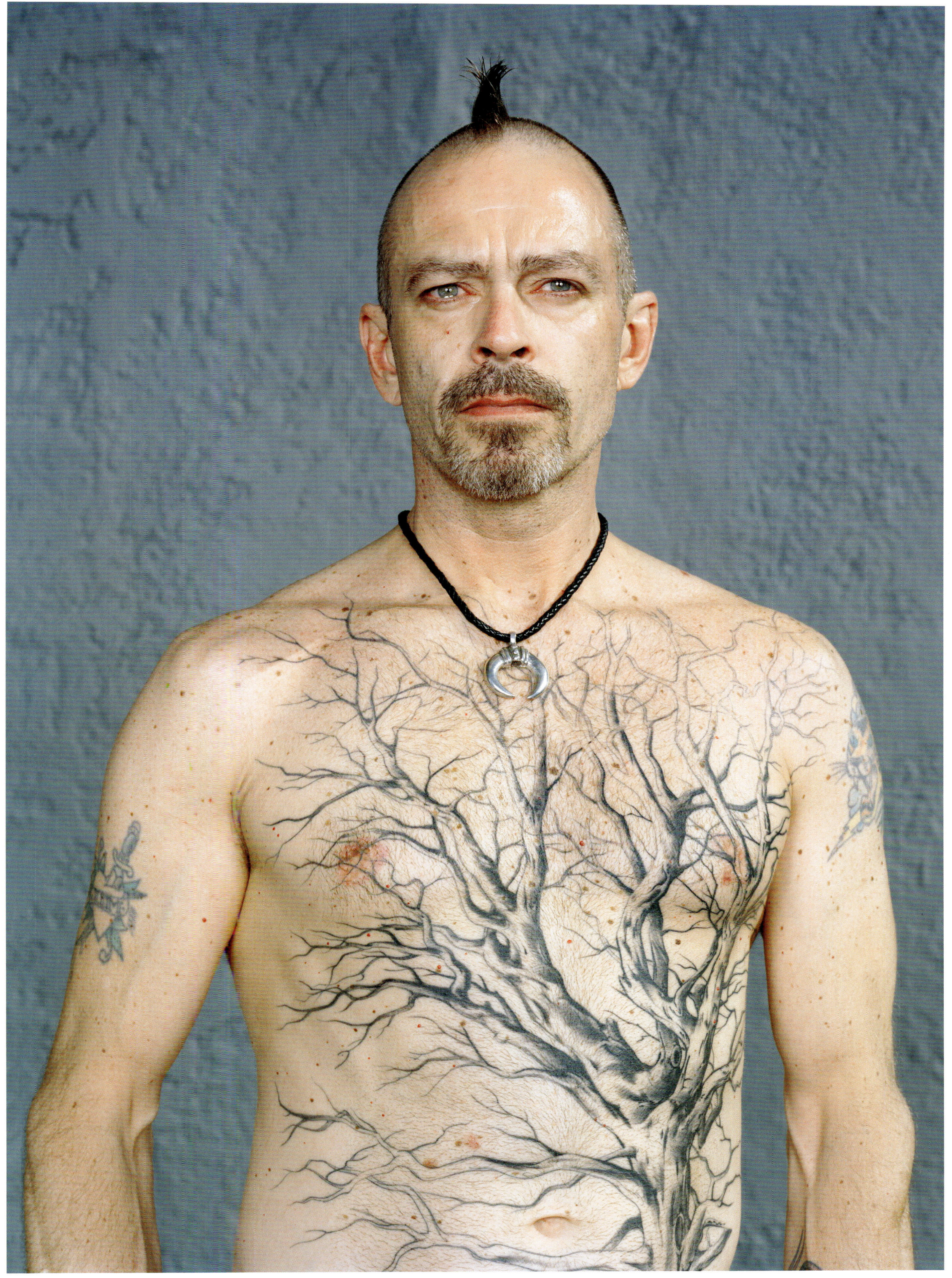

Jim San Francisco

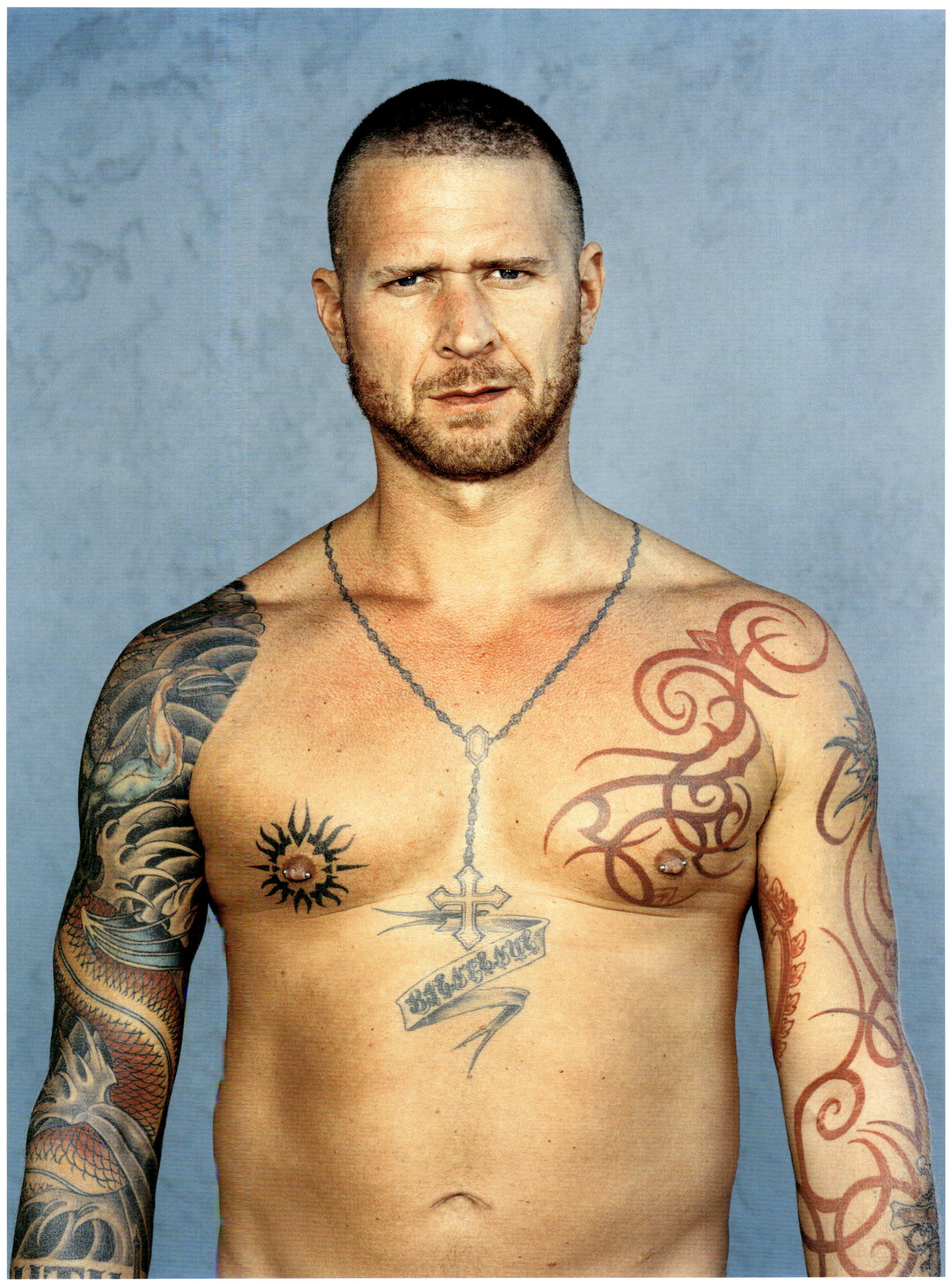

Master D San Francisco

I don't live in Berlin any more and I never want to live there again. It has changed fast over the last few years, in a bad way, especially the gay scene. No party is without drugs. If you don't go to the gym, you're not part of society. When you walk through Schöneberg, you see all the gay guys posing everywhere – when they stand, when they sit… There's nothing natural any longer. To me the Berlin gay scene has lost its soul.

I moved there in 1996, a few years after the wall came down, when it was still interesting. I worked in the New Action bar for five years, a popular sex bar. I saw nearly everything. After a while, I decided I didn't belong in Berlin. I had to leave. My partner and I moved to Leipzig. With a friend, we started to organise a regular party. We called it 'Bärenstolz', which means 'bear glory'. We wanted to make a party for real men: men who are not into cologne or fashion, who are not into glitz. Even though it's a party where nothing happens – just talking and looking and having fun – it's become a very big success. I wouldn't call it a 'bear' scene. It's a 'men' scene.

I guess I'm about 195 cm tall. I don't know exactly. I weigh 120 kilos. I played handball for about ten years, team handball. My body size is genetic – all my family are big. And my father is hairy. When I was young, I couldn't handle it. People would point at me and say, 'Look at him, he's hairy!' But I guess tastes changed and people decided they like hairy men after all. I figured out there was a scene where guys like it, and then a day came when I didn't think about it any longer.

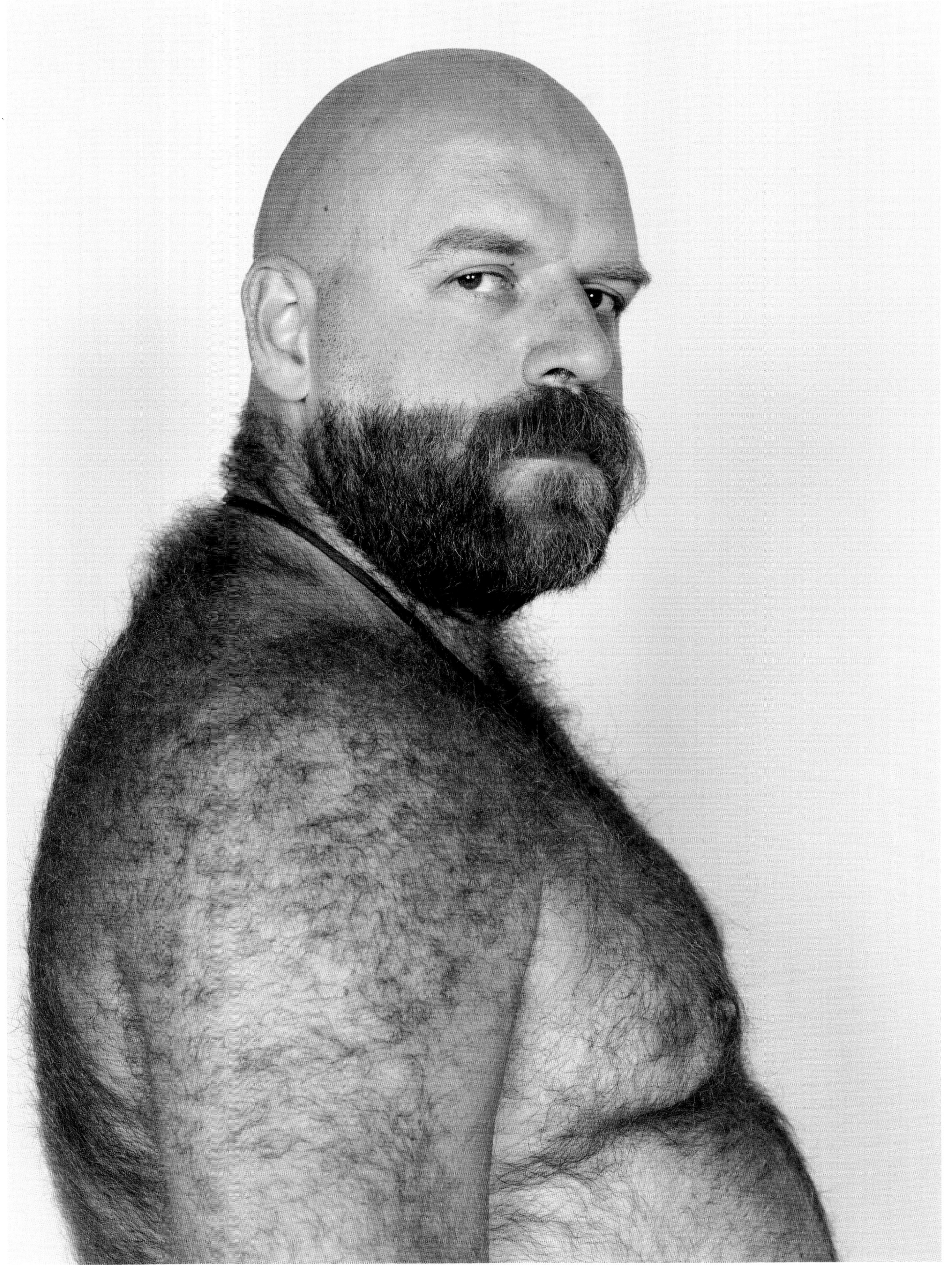

Grizzzlie Berlin

SAN FRANCISCO BERLIN – A CONVERSATION

Stephen Mayes I want to talk about intent – the intent of the participants you photographed, and your intent as authors. Stefan, tell me about your involvement. Was this an exploration of something that you were particularly curious about?

Stefan Ruiz When Chris suggested the subject, I wasn't sure. I thought maybe it might make me uncomfortable. But I thought that was probably a good reason to go ahead with it, to see how it challenged me.

Mayes Did it challenge you?

Ruiz Yes, a little. I got embarrassed a few times, but I guess that's par for the course with me, so perhaps not so much more than anything else I work on.

Mayes As a gay man, Chris is more of an insider, and you're more the observer?

Ruiz Right.

Mayes And yet at the same time, one of the things which I'm curious about is how we're *all* participants. You can look at these pictures as a very specific expression of gay sexuality, but you can also look at them as an expression of sexuality that includes everybody – and we three share that much! Did you find making these pictures in any way a process of self-exploration and self-discovery? Not as a gay man, but in terms of exploring sexuality?

Ruiz One of the reasons I wanted to do it was that I actually wanted to make some male nude portraits. The male nude, especially in a US context, is much more taboo than the female nude. I think that's kind of odd considering nearly half the people in the world are men, and pretty much everyone's seen a naked man. It was one aspect of the topic that I particularly wanted to explore. The pictures seem to make some of the people who see them uncomfortable – more uncomfortable than I felt about making them. And that wasn't to do with the subjects being gay. It's much more to do with people thinking a man displaying himself naked isn't an appropriate topic to photograph. It was funny for me to see how different people react. Some people who I thought would have no problem with the pictures found them problematic, and others who I thought might be shocked had no problem at all.

Mayes Did the men you photographed need any persuasion?

Ruiz No, they wanted to be photographed. We had more people wanting to be photographed than we could manage. And everyone was asked their permission, everyone signed a release.

Chris Boot We chose these two cities during these particular party weekends because they're times when guys dress up, for show. The way they dress and display themselves is a kind of performance for the camera, be that Stefan's camera, or their friends' – or anybody's. Being photographed is part of the point.

Ruiz Yes, in San Francisco especially. We photographed during the Folsom Street Fair, where the idea is that everyone expresses themselves, however they want to, out in the open in broad daylight. And we just set the studio up outside. In Berlin we also photographed in the street, but we photographed inside a couple of clubs, which were in more private spaces, where people wouldn't expect to encounter a photographer.

Boot We were part of the entertainment in the clubs. There was always a bit of a crowd around watching Stefan work, and a line of men waiting to be photographed. Almost everybody we engaged with wanted to be photographed.

Ruiz There were two clubs in Berlin where we photographed. The set-up for one was just outside the doorway, in a courtyard. The other was a big sex party where we were inside the club, in a room off to the side, and where our agreement was that we would *only* photograph there, and only photograph people who agreed to it. We would go out into the club and ask people, or people would just come and find us.

Mayes Chris, what was your motivation and what did you work through in the process?

Boot Stefan and I had talked for a while about wanting to do something together, me as producer and Stefan as photographer. I suggested gay men as a subject. The main motivating factor for me was to do with my history. I was out on the gay scene in London in the late 1970s, which is where I met Tony – who is still my partner – in 1982. We used to go clubbing together most weekends. This was the time when New York was famous for its bath houses and sex on the piers, but London was very conservative and discreet by comparison. Then the tsunami of AIDS/HIV hit the gay world, and Tony's and my response to that was to settle down and leave the scene behind. I used to joke that I wasn't gay any more, I just happened to be with a man. I became convinced that 'gay' was a very particular cultural identity born of resistance to sexual repression, but a label that ceased to be relevant. Then in about 2005, some friends suggested going out to a gay club, and that started a re-engagement with 'gay'. After many years of not being part of it, I was quite shocked – at the prevalence of drugs, at the public sex ... Fetishism, if that is the right word for the 'play gear' and the tattoos and the overt sexual display, was a very minor part of the scene as I remembered it from my youth. That was the period when Robert Mapplethorpe was documenting extreme expressions of gay sexuality, but that was very removed from any reality I knew. And visiting a few clubs and gay social networking sites, it was a surprise to find sexual expression and so-called fetishism had become fashionable, mainstream. Naively, I'd thought that HIV had killed off this wild scene of rampant gay sexuality – but on the contrary, it was back with a vengeance. I thought it would be interesting to explore through the vehicle of a photo project. These mythic gay parties – Berlin at Easter and San Francisco during the Folsom weekend in September – seemed to be the most vivid expressions of the contemporary scene, so I suggested to Stefan that we go and he take photographs, which is what we did.

Something else that fed into this was hearing radical Islamists and right-wing Christians express their hatred of gays, and hearing about gay men being killed, or executed in Iran for instance. And it seemed like there were these two extreme poles, of religious fundamentalists on the one hand, who believed that the way that people behaved – the way that human life was conducted – should be prescribed, and controlled, according to a particular set of religious codes. And on the other, the extreme liberals, if you like, who believe that it's nobody's business to prescribe anything about their lives, and as long as relations are conducted consensually between adults, then anything goes. These seemed like two options for the direction of society as a whole, and I was interested in considering one end of that spectrum.

Mayes So what's the purpose of the book? Do you see this study as being about revelation? Celebration? A question, an exploration? Or do you think it's even necessary to define what the end purpose is?

Boot Well yes, I think you need to define the purpose. I think it's a documentary piece of work about a particular manifestation of male sexuality at a particular moment in time. And it throws up lots of issues that I think are interesting to consider. It's an open text, in the sense that it's not trying to promote a particular viewpoint.

Mayes So who do you think will be reading this?

Boot That I don't know! I don't think this book is *for* gay men. In fact, I tried to interest gay audiences in this work and didn't have much success. For me, this is documentary photography – it's a visual study of something that's going on. It's not for anyone in particular. I kind of think it's for history, if that's not too arrogant a statement. And for me, it provided an excuse to go exploring with a reason.

Ruiz One reason I was interested in doing this was to do with intolerance and tolerance, and wanting to take a stand. I think there's a choice of which side to be on in society: open-minded or closed-minded. I would tend to always want people to be more open-minded and more tolerant and accepting. I want to live in a tolerant society. That is part of my reason for doing this. But in the end, I am not sure that this book will promote tolerance particularly. Like I was saying before, some people like it and some find the pictures uncomfortable. I think if people have a real problem with the pictures then it's more their problem than mine.

Mayes We've already touched on the definition of 'gay', but it seems to me that the word has a political/social rather than sexual definition, and as such, I wondered whether the notion of gayness, as presented by the participants in this book, is a very self-consciously defined social, as much as sexual, expression? A revelling in difference, and revelling in people's reactions to the display?

Boot I think the sexual display is a contribution to being part of a social scene, or a community. I'm not saying that people don't have sex during these weekend gatherings – of course they do. But the street part of it – the gathering of guys from all over, the dressing up – it's all much more social. We always say there isn't a single 'gay community', and there isn't. But these pictures reflect a community that is very real.

Ruiz For me, I felt I was witnessing a community event, albeit different in San Francisco compared to Berlin. People came from all over North America, Europe and the world, to hang out with friends. There was a strong sense of camaraderie.

Mayes When I was looking through the pictures, I would try to guess: was this shot in the US or in Germany? But I couldn't tell. Obviously the photograph is the outcome of a process of filtering and editing. Did you see differences between San Francisco and Berlin?

Ruiz Yes, they felt different. In San Francisco, which is where I'm from, you feel it that the scene's been around a long time. And there's this whole outdoor thing that's going on, involving hundreds of thousands of people. You have the sun, you have this hippy-like element – something left over from the era of the flower children, this idea that everybody should love everybody. Whereas Berlin felt more properly modern, less ideological. Maybe it was just the particular weekends we were there. San Francisco has changed a lot and it's not what it used to be, but it was always known for a sort of open-mindedness, and it still has that sense of being a place where people go to find themselves. I still feel that. The gay community has been established there for a very long time, and the weekend we were there really felt like a celebration of diverse and multifarious sexuality, of being who you are. We were taking pictures outside a bar on one night, and a guy was getting naked in the street, and the police arrived, and paused and looked, and then drove on by. It was like, 'Oh yeah, well it's Folsom'. It's definitely not like that all the time. But in Berlin, you get a sense that anything goes all year round, and people take that tolerance for granted.

Boot In San Francisco I was aware of a very sophisticated sense of mutual responsibility within the community or the communities that gathered for Folsom, which I don't feel was the case in Berlin. I mean, Berlin by comparison feels like a place of freedom without responsibility. You only take responsibility for yourself, and you have no responsibility for anyone else. Which is a type of responsibility, I guess, but it's very stark.

Mayes One of the things I wanted to ask about, which may relate to the different locations, is how much of this work is about performance, and how much of it is about lifestyle? Is there a distinction between presenting yourself as a performance and presenting an expression of who you are?

Ruiz I definitely got the sense that in both places there was a strong element of performance. In the club where we photographed in Berlin, which was in an old factory in an industrial area, people would arrive dressed in their street clothes, with a duffle bag, and there was a changing room. They came in ordinary clothes and emerged from the changing room these transformed characters. So in that sense it seemed like it was all about dressing up, a performance.

Boot I would say this is absolutely about performance. At least some of the guys photographed were participating in a kind of performance art version of sex too, so the performance aspect doesn't necessarily end with the visual appearance. One of the interesting characters we met was Tats with his tattooed face – I mean, in his case it's no longer a performance, it's a lifestyle, in the sense that he can't take his tattoos off. I would say most people in the pictures have a 'normal' life which they return to. Even Tats used to have a 'normal' life. He only got his face tattooed when he retired, when he didn't have to pass for normal any more.

Mayes It strikes me as not so different from drag.

Boot Yes.

Mayes Just as I would define myself as wearing business drag when I go to work ... I'm masquerading as a businessman.

Boot Yes, you're not really a businessman – you just perform as one!

Mayes Exactly! We usually talk about 'drag' when referring to men dressing as women, in a masquerade of femininity. Whereas what we see here is a masquerade of masculinity.

Boot Yes, 'masquerade' is the perfect word actually.

Mayes And in achieving that, in arriving at these destinations and donning the drag, is that an exploration for these people, or is it the full expression of themselves?

Ruiz It's probably both, in different cases. It seemed like with some people they were just beginning to explore things, dressing up for the night or the weekend. It seemed like some people were exploring this whole new community that had opened up to them, and exploring themselves personally.

Boot I thought for some guys, the destination was the look, the visual identity that had been worked on over a period of time, and guys were proud of having got to that point. And those were the guys we were attracted to, for the most part, and who were attracted to being photographed. But clearly a lot of this was about lifestyle. In San Francisco, some of the guys we spoke to were in non-conventional domestic relationships – for instance, a daddy who lived with three boys. Someone explained to me the polyamory movement. Meanwhile, one of the master/slave couples we photographed turned out just to be role playing for the day, for a bit of fun.

Ruiz One thing that struck me at the beginning of this was when we went into one of the gear shops, and how much people were actually buying, and it was really like this consumer thing. People were spending a lot of money and talking about what they were going to wear tomorrow, and things like this. It seemed like the scene was very consumer-oriented, with everyone into the latest gear.

Mayes As an old school activist myself, it's one of the reasons why I abhor the rainbow flag, because to me the rainbow flag is the international symbol of shopping. I really am saddened by the disappearance of the pink triangle, which was a truly political symbol. So I think the consumer aspect of this is huge, and – in my view – very regrettable. But it obviously brings a lot of people satisfaction. What was your take on that, Chris?

Boot Well yes, you're right, but I don't know that consumerism completely dominates. I mean, there were a lot of people in San Francisco who just wanted to get naked, for whom it wasn't about the gear at all.

Ruiz There was also the shopping aspect in Berlin as well. Both these weekend fairs were sponsored by the stores that sell the gear, and they're obviously big weekends for sales. The sex party that we went to in Berlin was put on by one of the gear stores.

Mayes Again from my own experience, part of what I suspect is happening here is that for some people the display is a disguise. The ostensible purpose of dressing flamboyantly or differently, or even *un*dressing flamboyantly or differently, is to reveal yourself, to demonstrate your character, your inner motivations. But very often what it actually does is to distract from your inner character. My experience of dressing unconventionally led me to realise, eventually – and this is the reason why I stopped doing it – that it was a defence. That's to say, it drew attention to me, and I thought therefore I was revealing myself – but the theatrical performance was actually a barrier between myself and society. Do you have any thoughts about that?

Boot We can't really make those judgments about the people that we encountered or the people that we encounter generally, I guess. But yes, I'm sure you're right, that there's a mixture of hiding and disclosing all going on at the same time.

Ruiz We didn't photograph for very long, and we only photographed a very small group of people. But in that time, I would say we got pictures of quite a few different types of people who fit all the different things we've been talking about – people who are hiding, people who are motivated politically, people who dress up for a sense of belonging to a community, and so on.

Mayes Stefan, were you thinking about Mapplethorpe's pictures while you were making your work?

Ruiz Well obviously I'm aware of his photographs, but I didn't want to try to emulate him or better what he did. Maybe I do take portraits that are fairly graphic in a sculptural sense, which he does in some of his work, so there are some similarities. I was just trying to do something very straightforward, unemotional.

Boot You did what it is that you do, which is to look at people. You're sympathetic to them as people but your gaze is detached. You're looking at them as objects almost, there's that element to your scrutinising them. The openness with which you invite them to present themselves allows you to scrutinise them, and it allows the viewer to scrutinise them. You do that with all kinds of people.

Ruiz Yeah, I do other kinds of portraits too. I do environmental portraits, where people are like characters on a set. But here I was doing this other kind of portrait – very straightforward, very clean, very sculptural, focusing on just 'what it is', with the participation of the subject.

I've photographed all types of people in all types of situations, and often I'll be in a situation where there's quite a few people to choose from. And you start almost casting people. That's what we were doing here. We would pick people. Or people would pick us and we'd say, 'Hmm well, yes' or 'no'. We went with people that either Chris or I found interesting or who we thought might make a strong picture.

Boot But quite often that wasn't exuberant visual display.

Ruiz Yes, a lot of times it's the subtlety that makes the picture.

Mayes Is it worth talking about the people you chose not to photograph?

Ruiz There were some people who didn't seem quite real enough, in a certain way, or believable enough. It's not like we're the fashion police or anything, but they were dressed in the wrong way, or they didn't seem serious, authentic.

Mayes We haven't talked about the presence of HIV, and I am wondering if that was present in the clubs – I don't mean the virus itself, but whether awareness of HIV figured in this social structure we've been discussing. Was that something that was ever brought up or referenced? Did you see behaviours that in any way recognised or were responsive to HIV?

Boot We are talking about a scene that is very used to dealing with HIV, and the clubs certainly had safer sex messages and lots of condoms available. Guys didn't talk to us about it, but then it didn't come up in the context in which we met them. I didn't choose to ask people about HIV, in the interviews, except in the case of Christian, who was talking about having sex in the clubs, considering how he's a very young guy and lots of the people in the clubs don't play safe. He turned out to be very sensible about it. I think HIV is reflected in some of the pictures and it's a topic that's in the work, alongside many others. But we haven't chosen to try and force it out.